# Spar

# for

# Construction Workers

*For all builders, developers, general contractors, subcontractors, superintendents, journeymen, laborers, and trade professionals working in construction, as well as all manufacturers, inspectors, and on-site personnel*

by

**William C. Harvey, M.S.**

# TABLE OF CONTENTS

## CHAPTER 3: GRADING AND FOUNDATION

Commands, questions, vocabulary and phrases related to soil, ground layout, compacting, and working with structural concrete, footings, slab, rebar, anchor bolts, block walls, etc.

## CHAPTER 4: STRUCTURAL

Commands, questions, and statements related to structural engineering, working with steel and wood, welding, and the mounting of structural beams, trusses, joists, straps, and sheer walls, etc.

## CHAPTER 5: FRAMING

Commands, questions, and statements related to mounting stud walls, sheathing, plates, or roof rafters, and installing jambs, headers, fire blocks, etc.

## CHAPTER 6: ROOFING

Commands, questions, and statements related to waterproofing, installing flashing, jacks, and hoods, working with sheet metal, building decks, mounting gutters, and laying down shingles, shake, hot mop, etc.

## CHAPTER 7: MECHANICAL

Commands, questions, and statements related to plumbing, electrical work, heating and air conditioning, sewage, exhaust vents, pulling wires and pipes, and the rough installation of phone, cable, and alarms, etc.

## CHAPTER 8: THE EXTERIOR

Commands, questions, and statements related to lathing, wire mesh, scratch coat and brown, as well as finish work such as masonry, siding, trim, exterior paint, etc.

## CHAPTER 9: THE INTERIOR

Commands, questions, and statements related to mounting drywall, texturing, insulating, and painting, as well as the installating of cabinets, fixtures, finished hardware, and floor coverings, etc.

## CHAPTER 10: HARDSCAPE & LANDSCAPE

Commands, questions, and statements related to structures such as patios, walkways, retaining walls, or planters, in addition to landscaping activities such as sprinkler installation, planting, and garden design, etc.

BUSINESS MATTERS
This section leads the reader step-by-step through the employee interview, and includes questions about trade experience, training, and related business matters.

EMERGENCIES AND SAFETY
This section allows English speakers to effectively explain safety procedures in Spanish on the job site, and includes phrases for use in case of sudden medical emergencies.

DEMOLITION AND CLEAN-UP
This section lists key Spanish words and phrases that are used in the demolition of any project. It also lists one-liners that are needed for cleaning up the work area.

CONSTRUCTION COMMANDS
This section contains all the essential commands needed to assign any task in the field of construction.

FORM-A-PHRASE VERB CHART
This section allows learners to build their own sentences in Spanish, using a simple set of verbal expression lists.

PRONUNCIATION GUIDE

## BEFORE YOU BEGIN

A NOTE FROM THE AUTHOR
All across the U.S.A., the scene is pretty much the same. Trucks full of workers, equipment, and tools show up on a construction site, and the job-specific chatter begins as everyone springs into action. What is interesting is that not everyone you hear is speaking English.

I found this out personally a few years ago when my wife and I decided it was time for some remodeling at our home. As the construction project got under way, some of the crew began asking for specific information in their native language – Spanish. All I can say is, I'm sure glad we knew what they were talking about!

SPANISH FOR CONSTRUCTION WORKERS is designed for anyone who works in the field of construction and communicates regularly with those who speak only Spanish. Necessary words and phrases are divided into easy-to-follow chapters, which can be accessed "on-the-job" simply by finding a particular topic. The first two chapters provide fundamental instruction in Spanish, while the remaining chapters focus on specific fields in the world of home building and construction today. The book also includes several "stand-alone" pages which provide the reader with ready-to-use vocabulary and phrases in clear bold print. Pronunciation in English follows every Spanish word, and the most frequently used terminology is strategically placed for quick reference and review. At the end of the book, readers will find a variety of useful support material along with an English to Spanish glossary.

TEACHING SEGMENTS

This book provides readers with the following teaching segments, which are scattered on pages throughout the text:

WORKING WORDS:

This segment includes construction site terminology, questions, descriptions, and commands which relate to the chapter's theme.

THE ONE-LINERS:

This segment lists a specialized group of words and phrases, which can communicate complete messages all by themselves.

GRAMMAR TIME:

This segment presents shortcuts and tips on how to put several Spanish words together using the appropriate verb forms.

CULTURE CLASH:

This segment offers practical insights into the Latino culture, with details related to traditions, beliefs, and general way of life.

JUST A SUGGESTION:

This segment is found throughout the book, and includes additional information, tips, and suggestions about learning Spanish on your own.

TRY SOME:

This segment closes each section with various self-grading practice activities and exercises, so that you won't forget what you're trying to learn.

## HOW TO LEARN SPANISH

If you want to learn Spanish quickly, these are the real keys to your progress and success:

### Keep listening to Spanish!

Listen to fluent speakers of Spanish regularly, and both your grammar and pronunciation will improve! Try listening to Spanish radio stations or music CDs. Find out which TV stations also air in Spanish, and watch Spanish movies on your computer or on DVD. Come up with your own creative way to take in Spanish without having to spend a lot of money!

### Use Spanish words that you already know!

Continue to mutter those words and phrases in Spanish that are familiar to you. Gradually experiment with new vocabulary and verb forms, but don't force yourself to speak more fluently. You must build confidence first before moving ahead, so add to your skills only when you feel ready to do so!

### Learn all you can about the cultural differences between English and Spanish speakers!

In any language, there's a lot more to communication that just the spoken word. Hand and body gestures, along with facial expressions, speak volumes in countries everywhere. Find out about non-verbal messages in Latin America. While you're at it, inquire about certain customs and traditions. Learn more about the Hispanic culture, and your conversational skills in Spanish will drastically improve!

## Relax, and try to have a good time!

Don't overload your circuits! Study and practice Spanish at your own pace. Becoming fluent in a new language takes awhile, so spend lots of time fooling around with it. Try not to panic. Just remember - the Spanish speaker you're talking to is probably having as much trouble as you are. Lighten up, believe in yourself, and everything you learn will somehow begin to make sense!

## Practice, Practice, Practice!

Get together with a fluent Spanish speaker, and try out your new language skills as often as you can. One-on-one practice is best, but remember that it must be in a light, comfortable setting. Obviously, the more you read, write, speak, or listen to Spanish, the more proficient you'll become. Believe it or not, practice does make it **perfecto**!

## MORE SHORTCUTS TO LEARNING SPANISH

- Be friendly, smile, and use all the courteous expressions you know. Spanish has informal forms, too, but this book focuses on the formal ones. By the way, people with pleasant personalities seem to communicate better!

- When you listen to Spanish, try to recognize words that sound like their English equivalents. You should also express comprehension by pointing, moving, or touching things.

- Repeat new words and phrases that you learn several times before trying them out on the job. It's also wise to ask questions during conversations, and not give up when you feel confused.

- If you can't remember a word, try another way to explain yourself. At the same time, let others correct you, since natural mistakes actually help you to learn faster.

- As with every language, Spanish is full of informal idiomatic expressions. Sometimes people on the streets use more "slang" than anything else, so it's always a good idea to ask about words or phrases that you don't understand.

- Remember, too, that Spanish dialects may vary, so don't get discouraged when certain words or sounds seem unfamiliar to you.

# CHAPTER ONE

## BASIC SKILLS
## Las habilidades básicas

PRONUNCIATION

**La pronunciación**

Here's the only thing you need to know about Spanish pronunciation:
ALMOST ALL SPANISH LETTERS HAVE ONLY <u>ONE</u> SOUND.
Start by repeating these five main Spanish sounds, which are called the
vowels:

| | | |
|---|---|---|
| **a** (ah) | like yacht | **cha-cha-cha** |
| **e** (eh) | like met | **excelente** |
| **i** (ee) | like keep | **dividir** |
| **o** (oh) | like open | **loco** |
| **u** (oo) | like spoon | **mula** |

Keep going. These are the consonant sounds you'll need to know. Don't
forget - Spanish sounds are pronounced the way they're written:

<u>Spanish letter</u>                    <u>English sound</u>

**c** (after an **e** or **i**)                    S as in Sam (**cigarro**)

| | |
|---|---|
| **g** (after an **e** or **i**) | h as in Harry (**general**) |
| **h** | silent, like the "k" in knife (**hola**) |
| **j** | h as in hot (**Juan**) |
| **ll** | y as in yes (**llama**) |
| **qu** | k as in kit (**tequila**) |
| **rr** | the rolled "r" sound (**carro**) |
| **v** | b as in blue (**viva**) |
| **z** | s as in sun (**cerveza**) |

The rest of the letters in Spanish are very similar to their equivalents in English, so reviewing them isn't really necessary. To practice these sounds, read the English pronunciation patterns which follow every Spanish word. To review the secrets on how to sound like a native speaker, follow the simple pronunciation tips below:

- Remember that your poor pronunciation won't really hurt communication. Not only are people generally forgiving, but in reality, there aren't that many differences between the two sound systems.

- Just tell yourself: Spanish is pronounced the way it's spelled, and vice-versa. So pronounce each sound the same way every time the corresponding letter appears.

- Spanish sounds are usually made toward the front of the mouth instead of back - with little or no air coming out. And, short, choppy sounds are better than long stretched-out ones.

- Accented (´) parts of words should always be pronounced LOUDER and with more emphasis (**olé**). If there's no accent mark, say the last of the work LOUDER and with more emphasis (**español**). For words ending in a vowel, or in **n** or **s**, the next to the last part of the word is stressed (**importante**). In some cases, the letter **u** doesn't make the "oo" sound (**guitarra, guerra**).

## JUST A SUGGESTION

Go look at yourself in the mirror. Now hold up your right hand and make this pledge:

"I will <u>ruin</u> Spanish."

Did you say it … aloud? Good. Your language skills are limited at best, and your chances of acquiring native-like pronunciation are almost zero. Feel better? So the next time you feel uncomfortable about speaking Spanish – just remember your pledge!

## THE SPANISH ALPHABET
**El abecedario**

Take a few moments to review the alphabet. It can be helpful either when you're on the phone or when you haven't a clue what someone is saying. The key question to ask is:

How do you spell it?  **¿Cómo se deletrea?**

To practice, say each letter aloud, using the pronunciation guide provided:

**a** (ah)

**b** (beh grahn'-deh)

**c** (seh)

**ch** (cheh)*

**d** (deh)

**e** (eh)

**f** (eh'-feh)

**g** (heh)

**h** (ah'-cheh)

**i** (ee)

**j** (hoh'-tah)

**k** (kah)

**l** (eh'-leh)

**ll** (eh'-yeh)*

**m** (eh'-meh)

**n** (eh'-neh)

**ñ** (ehn'-yeh)*

**o** (oh)

**p** (peh)

**q** (koo)

**r** (eh'-reh)

**rr** (eh'-rreh)

**s** (eh'-seh)

**t** (teh)

**u** (oo)

**v** (beh chee'-kah)

**w** (beh doh'-bleh)

**x** (eh'-kees)

**y** (ee-gree-eh'-gah)

**z** (seh'-tah)

\* These letters have been removed from the "official" Spanish alphabet. However, people still refer to them when spelling out a word.

## JUST A SUGGESTION

This next question will also come in handy:

How do you write it? **¿Cómo se escribe?**

> **¿Cómo se escribe su nombre?**
> How do you write your name?

## TRY SOME

Pronounce these common words and then spell them in Spanish. Remember to sound out each letter:

| | |
|---|---|
| **amigo** | **macho** |
| **amor** | **enchilada** |
| **carro** | **pollo** |
| **español** | **chiquita** |

| | |
|---|---|
| excelente | trabajo |
| dinero | nada |
| grande | señor |
| hombre | vino |

## GREETINGS AND EXPRESSIONS

**Los saludos y las expresiones**

Look over these popular exchanges, and highlight the ones you'll need right away. And don't worry about the upside down marks – that's just how they write it in Spanish:

| | |
|---|---|
| Hi! | **¡Hola!** |
| How are you? | **¿Cómo está?** |
| How's it going? | **¡Qué tal!** |
| Real well. | **Muy bien.** |
| And you? | **¿Y usted?** |
| Not bad. | **Más o menos.** |
| What's happening? | **¿Qué pasa?** |
| Nothing much! | **¡Sin novedad!** |
| Good morning | **Buenas días** |
| Good afternoon | **Buenas tardes** |
| Good evening, good night | **Buenas noches** |
| Good-bye | **Adiós** |
| Take it easy | **Cuídese bien** |
| See you tomorrow | **Hasta mañana** |

Here are some more. Remember that the best way to read a greeting or expression is as one long word:

| | |
|---|---|
| I'm sorry | **Lo siento** |
| Come in | **Adelante** |

These groups of words can be used separately:

| | |
|---|---|
| What's your name? | **¿Cómo se llama?** |
| My name is... | **Me llamo...** |
| Nice to meet you! | **¡Mucho gusto!** |
| Same to you | **Igualmente** |
| Please | **Por favor** |
| Thanks a lot | **Muchas gracias** |
| You're welcome | **De nada** |

| | |
|---|---|
| Ready? | **¿Listo?** |
| Any trouble? | **¿Problema?** |
| Finished? | **¿Terminado?** |

| | |
|---|---|
| Wait a moment. | **Espere un momento.** |
| Pay attention. | **Preste atención.** |
| Be careful. | **Tenga cuidado.** |

| | |
|---|---|
| Let's go! | **¡Vamos!** |
| Move it! | **¡Muévese!** |
| Quickly! | **¡Rápido!** |

The following words mean the same thing in English, but are used differently in Spanish. Picture saying them on the job site:

Excuse me! (if you are moving through a crowd)   **¡Con permiso!**

Excuse me! (if you need someone's attention)   **¡Disculpe!**

Excuse me! (if you cough, belch, or sneeze)   **¡Perdón!**

And here are some of my favorites:

| | |
|---|---|
| Do you understand? | **¿Entiende usted?** |
| I don't understand. | **No entiendo.** |
| I don't know. | **No sé.** |
| I speak a little Spanish. | **Hablo poquito español.** |
| I'm learning Spanish. | **Estoy aprendiendo español.** |
| More slowly. | **Más despacio.** |
| Thanks for your patience. | **Gracias por su paciencia.** |
| What does it mean? | **¿Qué significa?** |

And throw in "and" (**y**), "or" (**o**), and "but" (**pero**) as often as possible:

**¡No sé y no entiendo!**

Obviously, you won't find every Spanish expression in this guidebook. However, be on the lookout for segments called THE ONE-LINERS, where you can pick up the perfect phrase for almost any situation.

JUST A SUGGESTION

Start a specialized list of expressions on your own:

| | |
|---|---|
| Bless you! | **¡Salud!** |
| Welcome! | **¡Bienvenidos!** |
| Good luck! | **¡Buena suerte!** |
| | |
| Congratulations! | **¡Felicitaciones!** |
| Merry Christmas! | **¡Feliz navidad!** |
| Happy birthday! | **¡Feliz cumpleaños!** |

## CULTURE CLASH

The word "**tú**" is the informal way of saying "you" in Spanish. This "casual" form is generally exchanged between family and friends. Here are some examples:

You are my friend.

> **Tú eres mi amigo.**

Do you speak Spanish?

> **¿Tú hablas español?**

You don't have a car.

> **Tú no tienes un carro.**

The informal word for "your" is "**tu**", which is the same as "you" but without the accent:

Where's your family?

**¿Dónde está tu familia?**

All "informal" verb forms require changes when you talk in casual settings. We'll learn more about this later. Even Spanish command words take on a slightly different form when you speak "informally". Hopefully, as a Spanish student, you too will be able to make friends and establish "informal" relationships with Spanish-speaking people. And eventually, your new pals will be teaching you more about the "**tú**" form, along with lots of other "inside info." Throughout this guidebook, we'll be learning the formal "**usted**" form, because it's easier to remember and use. You'll find it's perfectly acceptable when speaking with anyone!

TRY SOME

Practice reading these conversations without looking up the translations:

A. **¡Qué tal!**

B. **Muy bien, gracias. ¿Y usted?**

A. **Más o menos.**


A. Ahh-choo! **Perdón.**

B. **¡Salud!**

A. **Muchas gracias.**


A. **¿Cómo se llama?**

B. **Me llamo Felipe. ¿Y usted?**

A. **Me llamo Clayton.**

B. **Mucho gusto.**

A. **Igualmente.**

GRAMMAR TIME

Don't forget that the names for people, places, and things are either masculine or feminine, and have either "**el**" or "**la**" in front. Generally, if the word ends in the letter "**o**" there's an "**el**" in front (i.e., **el carro** , **el niño**). Conversely, if the word ends in an "**a**" there's a "**la**" in front (i.e., **la tortilla**, **la persona**). There are very few exceptions (i.e., **el agua**, **la mano**, **el sofá**).

Words not ending in either an "**o**" or "**a**" need to be memorized (i.e., love, **el amor**; light, **la luz**). In the case of single objects, use "**el**" and "**la**" much like the word "the" in English: The house is big (**La casa es grande**).

Remember too, that "**el**" and "**la**" are used in Spanish to indicate a person's sex. **El supervisor** is a male, while **la supervisora** is a female. Here's how we change words to refer to the female gender:

| | | |
|---|---|---|
| baby | **el bebé** | **la bebé** |
| child | **el niño** | **la niña** |
| teenager | **el muchacho** | **la muchacha** |

To form the plural, words ending in a vowel end in "**-s**", while words ending in a consonant end in "**-es**". Notice how the "**el**" becomes "**los**" and the "**la**" becomes "**las**":

| | | | |
|---|---|---|---|
| man | **el hombre** | woman | **la mujer** |
| men | **los hombres** | women | **las mujeres** |

## PRONOUNS

**Los pronombres**

This group of words is used to identify everyone:

| | |
|---|---|
| I | **Yo** |
| You | **Usted** |
| He | **Él** |
| She | **Ella** |
| They | **Ellos/Ellas** |
| You guys | **Ustedes** |
| We | **Nosotros** |

And these words indicate possession. They replace the "**el**" and "**la**":

| | | |
|---|---|---|
| my | **mi** | **mi amigo** |
| your, his, her, their | **su** | **su casa** |
| our | **nuestro** | **nuestro carro** |

TRY SOME

Practice pronouns by inserting your name and the name of a friend:

**¿Yo? Mi nombre es <u>Roberto</u>.**

**¿Él? Su nombre es <u>Francisco</u>.**

**¿Nosotros? ¡Nuestros nombres son <u>Roberto</u> y <u>Francisco</u>!**

EVERYDAY QUESTIONS

**Las preguntas para todos los días**

One of the first questions you should memorize is the following. It will prevent you from having to repeat yourself in Spanish or English:

Do you have a question? **¿Tiene pregunta?**

Now prepare to response by studying the ten most common question words in Spanish:

| | |
|---|---|
| What? | **¿Qué?** |
| How? | **¿Cómo?** |
| Where? | **¿Dónde?** |
| When? | **¿Cuándo?** |
| Which? | **¿Cuál?** |
| Who? | **¿Quién?** |
| Whose? | **¿De quién?** |
| How much? | **¿Cuánto?** |
| How many? | **¿Cuántos?** |
| Why? | **¿Por qué?** |

Here's how they work in every day conversations:

| | |
|---|---|
| What? | **¿Qué?** |
| What's happening? | **¿Qué pasa?** |
| | |
| How? | **¿Cómo?** |
| How are you? | **¿Cómo está?** |
| | |
| Where? | **¿Dónde?** |
| Where is it? | **¿Dónde está?** |
| | |
| When? | **¿Cuándo?** |
| When is it? | **¿Cuándo es?** |
| | |
| Which? | **¿Cuál?** |
| Which is it? | **¿Cuál es?** |
| | |
| Who? | **¿Quién?** |
| Who is it? | **¿Quién es?** |
| | |
| Whose? | **¿De quién?** |
| Whose is it? | **¿De quién es?** |
| | |
| How much? | **¿Cuánto?** |
| How much does it cost? | **¿Cuánto cuesta?** |
| | |
| How many? | **¿Cuántos?** |

| | |
|---|---|
| How old are you? | **¿Cuántos años tiene?** |

| | |
|---|---|
| Why? | **¿Por qué?** |
| Why not? | **¿Por qué no?** |

By the way, the word "**porque**" means "because", and it sounds a lot like "**¿Por qué?**" ("Why?"):

| | |
|---|---|
| Why doesn't he have a car? | **¿Por qué no tiene carro?** |
| Because he doesn't have a license. | **Porque no tiene licencia.** |

Obviously, not all "question" phrases can be translated literally, so use them as one-liners whenever you can. For example, notice how "you" and "your" are implied, but not included:

| | |
|---|---|
| What's your name? | **¿Cómo se llama?** |
| How old are you? | **¿Cuántos años tiene?** |
| What's your address? | **¿Cuál es su dirección?** |

Here are some of the most common phrases that include question words:

| | |
|---|---|
| How can I help you? | **¿Cómo puedo ayudarle?** |
| What's the matter? | **¿Qué pasó?** |
| Who's calling? | **¿Quién habla?** |

This popular series of questions can be used with the phrase, "**¿Cuál es su...?**":

| What's your…? | ¿Cuál es su…? |
|---|---|
| full name | **nombre completo** |
| address | **dirección** |
| phone number | **número de teléfono** |
| age | **edad** |
| social security number | **número de seguro social** |
| driver's license number | **número de licencia de manejar** |
| | |
| date of birth | **fecha de nacimiento** |
| place of birth | **lugar de nacimiento** |

## JUST A SUGGESTION

To change a question word to refer to more than one thing, simply add "**-es**" to the question word:

| Which one ? | **¿Cuál?** |
|---|---|
| Which ones? | **¿Cuál<u>es</u>?** |

But always be aware of the "**el-la**" business:

| How many men? | **¿Cuán<u>tos</u> hombres?** |
|---|---|
| How many women? | **¿Cuán<u>tas</u> mujeres?** |

# CULTURE CLASH

When referring to others by name, it really helps if you're able to pronounce the names correctly, as it makes people feel much more at ease. Also remember that it's not uncommon for someone in Latin America to have no middle name and two last names. Don't get confused. Here's the order for males:

## José   Antonio   García   Sánchez

First name                              **José Antonio**

**primer nombre**


Father's last name                    **García**

**apellido paterno**


Mother's last name                    **Sánchez**

**apellido materno**


TRY SOME


Answer these questions about yourself aloud:


**¿Cómo se llama?**

**¿Cuál es su dirección?**

**¿Cuántos años tiene?**

**¿Quién es su amigo?**

## ¿Qué pasa?

## PEOPLE AND THINGS
**La gente y las cosas**

Identify folks around you:

## PEOPLE
**La gente**

| | |
|---|---|
| baby | **el bebé/la bebé** |
| child | **el niño/la niña** |
| friend | **el amigo/la amiga** |
| roommate | **el compañero/la compañera** |
| neighbor | **el vecino/la vecina** |
| man | **el hombre** |
| person | **la persona** |
| relative | **el pariente/la pariente** |
| woman | **la mujer** |
| young person | **el muchacho/la muchacha** |
| elderly person | **la persona mayor** |

When referring to others, utilize these new words:

| | |
|---|---|
| Mr. or a man | **Señor (Sr.)** |
| Mrs. or a lady | **Señora (Sra.)** |
| Miss or a young lady | **Señorita (Srta.)** |

Now try naming these common objects if they're somewhere within view:

It's...              Es...

|  |  |
|---------|---------|
| armchair | el sillón |
| book | el libro |
| car | el carro |
| chair | la silla |
| clothing | la ropa |
| couch | el sofá |
| desk | el escritorio |
| door | la puerta |
| equipment | el equipo |
| floor | el piso |
| food | la comida |
| furniture | el mueble |
| house | la casa |
| job | el trabajo |
| lamp | la lámpara |
| light | la luz |
| machine | la máquina |
| money | el dinero |
| paper | el papel |
| pen | el lapicero |
| pencil | el lápiz |
| room | el cuarto |
| table | la mesa |
| telephone | el teléfono |
| tool | la herramienta |
| truck | el camión |
| water | el agua |
| window | la ventana |

## STANDARD COMMANDS

**Los mandatos principales**

Another powerful way to plant Spanish into the memory is through the use of commands. The "command" form of verbs can be practiced all day, since all you're doing is telling others what to do. Be sure to add the word, "please",

**Por favor…**

| | |
|---|---|
| Call! | **¡Llame!** |
| Check! | **¡Revise!** |
| Come! | **¡Venga!** |
| Continue! | **¡Siga!** |
| Drive! | **¡Maneje!** |
| Finish! | **¡Termine!** |
| Go up! | **¡Suba!** |
| Go! | **¡Vaya!** |
| Help! | **¡Ayude!** |
| Listen! | **¡Escuche!** |
| Look! | **¡Mire!** |
| Read! | **¡Lea!** |
| Rest! | **¡Descanse!** |
| Run! | **¡Corra!** |
| Sign! | **¡Firme!** |
| Speak! | **¡Hable!** |
| Start! | **¡Comience!** |
| Walk! | **¡Camine!** |
| Work! | **¡Trabaje!** |
| Write! | **¡Escriba!** |

These commands are expressions and a little harder to pronounce:

| | |
|---|---|
| Hurry up! | **¡Apúrese!** |
| Sit down! | **¡Siéntese!** |
| Stand up! | **¡Levántese!** |
| Stay! | **¡Quédese!** |
| Wait! | **¡Espérese!** |

Most commands can be used with an object. For example, "Bring the wood." is "**Traiga la madera.**" More will be introduced in the chapters just ahead, and there's a longer list in a section called CONSTRUCTION COMMANDS at the back of the book. For now, practice with these:

| | |
|---|---|
| Bring… | **Traiga…** |
| Buy… | **Compre…** |
| Carry… | **Lleve…** |
| Change… | **Cambie…** |
| Clean… | **Limpie…** |
| Close… | **Cierre…** |
| Connect… | **Conecte…** |
| Empty… | **Vacíe…** |
| Fill… | **Llene…** |
| Fix… | **Arregle…** |
| Give... | **Dé...** |
| Load… | **Cargue…** |
| Look for… | **Busque…** |
| Lower… | **Baje…** |
| Move… | **Mueva…** |
| Open… | **Abra…** |
| Park… | **Estacione…** |
| Pick up... | **Recoja...** |
| Put inside… | **Meta…** |
| Put… | **Ponga…** |
| Raise… | **Levante…** |
| Remove… | **Saque…** |
| Set up… | **Prepare…** |
| Take… | **Tome…** |
| Throw out… | **Tire…** |
| Unload… | **Descargue…** |
| Use… | **Use…** |

JUST A SUGGESTION

To give a "command" to more than one person, simply add the letter "**n**" to the singular verb form:

| | |
|---|---|
| **¡Apúre<u>n</u>se!** | Hurry up, you guys! |
| **¡Corra<u>n</u>!** | Run, you guys! |

TRY SOME

Have a native Spanish-speaker command you to touch, look at, or point to things nearby:

| | | | |
|---|---|---|---|
| Touch... | **Toque** | Touch the truck. | **Toque el camión.** |
| Look at... | **Mire** | Look at the car. | **Mire el carro.** |
| Point to... | **Señale** | Point to the house. | **Señale la casa.** |

## COLORS
**Los colores**

The best way to practice these words is to call out the colors of things around you when you're out on the job:

It's...          **Es...**

| | |
|---|---|
| black | **negro** |
| blue | **azul** |
| brown | **café** |
| gray | **gris** |
| green | **verde** |
| orange | **anaranjado** |
| purple | **morado** |
| red | **rojo** |
| white | **blanco** |
| yellow | **amarillo** |
| pink | **rosado** |

In construction, there's a whole range of colors you'll need to know. A more extensive list can be found in *Chapter 8*.

## JUST A SUGGESTION

Two words that simplify things are "light" (**claro**) and "dark" (**oscuro**).

Notice how the word order is "reversed" in Spanish:

| light brown | **café <u>claro</u>** | dark brown | **café <u>oscuro</u>** |
| light blue | **azul <u>claro</u>** | dark blue | **azul <u>oscuro</u>** |
| light green | **verde <u>claro</u>** | dark green | **verde <u>oscuro</u>** |

## GRAMMAR TIME

A "reversal" rule is applied when you give a description in Spanish. The descriptive word generally goes <u>after</u> the word being described. Study these examples:

| The big house | **La casa grande** |
| The green car | **El carro verde** |
| The important man | **El hombre importante** |

To make a description plural, not only do all the nouns and adjectives need to end in "-**s**" or "-**es**", but when they are used together, the genders (the **o**'s and **a**'s) must match as well:

| Two white doors | **Dos puertas blancas** |
|---|---|
| Many red trucks | **Muchos camiones rojos** |
| Three big jobs | **Tres trabajos grandes** |

TRY SOME

Change these sentences to plural:

**el carro rojo**     los _____

**una casa grande** tres _____

**la mesa negra**     las _____

NUMBERS

**Los números**

You can't say much in Spanish without knowing your numbers:

| | |
|---|---|
| 0 **cero** | 14 **catorce** |
| 1 **uno** | 15 **quince** |
| 2 **dos** | 16 **dieciséis** |
| 3 **tres** | 17 **diecisiete** |
| 4 **cuatro** | 18 **dieciocho** |
| 5 **cinco** | 19 **diecinueve** |
| 6 **seis** | 20 **veinte** |
| 7 **siete** | 30 **treinta** |
| 8 **ocho** | 40 **cuarenta** |
| 9 **nueve** | 50 **cincuenta** |
| 10 **diez** | 60 **sesenta** |
| 11 **once** | 70 **setenta** |
| 12 **doce** | 80 **ochenta** |
| 13 **trece** | 90 **noventa** |

For all the numbers in-between, just add **y** (ee), which means "and":

21 **veinte y uno**          34 _____

22 **veinte y dos**          55 _____

23 **veinte y** _____       87 _____

Sooner or later, you'll also need to know how to say the larger numbers in Spanish. They aren't that difficult, so practice aloud:

| 100     | **cien**        |
|---------|-----------------|
| 200     | **doscientos**  |
| 300     | **trescientos** |
| 400     | **cuatrocientos** |
| 500     | **quinientos**  |
| 600     | **seiscientos** |
| 700     | **setecientos** |
| 800     | **ochocientos** |
| 900     | **novecientos** |
| 1000    | **mil**         |
| million | **millón**      |

Everyone on the job needs the "ordinal" numbers, too:

| first | **primero** |
|---|---|
| second | **segundo** |
| third | **tercero** |
| fourth | **cuarto** |
| fifth | **quinto** |
| sixth | **sexto** |
| seventh | **séptimo** |
| eighth | **octavo** |
| ninth | **noveno** |
| tenth | **décimo** |
| eleventh | **undécimo** |
| twelfth | **duodécimo** |

TRY SOME

Change these ordinal numbers to cardinals:

**quinto** _____

**octavo** _____

**primero** _____

Say these numbers aloud in Spanish:

**5,000**     **300**     **67**

## TIME AND PLACE

**El tiempo y el lugar**

To truly communicate with Spanish-speakers, you'll eventually need to include some time-referenced and place-referenced vocabulary. These will do for now:

| | |
|---|---|
| after | **después** |
| always | **siempre** |
| before | **antes** |
| during | **durante** |
| early | **temprano** |
| late | **tarde** |
| later | **luego** |
| never | **nunca** |
| right now | **ahorita** |
| since | **desde** |
| sometimes | **a veces** |
| soon | **pronto** |
| then | **entonces** |
| today | **hoy** |
| tomorrow | **mañana** |
| until | **hasta** |
| while | **mientras** |
| yesterday | **ayer** |
| already | **ya** |

When it comes to locating people or things, always respond as briefly as possible, and don't be afraid to point:

Where is it?          **¿Dónde está?**

| | |
|---|---|
| above | **encima** |
| along | **a lo largo** |
| around | **alrededor** |
| at the bottom | **en el fondo** |
| back | **atrás** |
| behind | **detrás** |
| between | **entre** |
| down | **abajo** |
| far | **lejos** |
| forward | **adelante** |
| here | **aquí** |
| in front | **enfrente** |
| in the middle | **en medio** |
| inside | **adentro** |
| near | **cerca** |
| next to | **al lado** |
| outside | **afuera** |
| over | **sobre** |
| straight ahead | **adelante** |
| there | **allí** |
| to the left | **a la izquierda** |
| to the right | **a la derecha** |
| towards | **hacia** |
| under | **debajo** |
| up | **arriba** |
| way over there | **allá** |

## JUST A SUGGESTION

Collect your own set of "time" and "location" expressions, and use them every day. Once they're mastered, start all over again with a different set:

| | |
|---|---|
| not yet | **todavía no** |
| as soon as | **tan pronto como** |
| two years ago | **hace dos años** |
| | |
| backwards | **al revés** |
| upside down | **boca abajo** |
| the other side | **el otro lado** |

## TRY SOME

Match the opposites:

| | |
|---|---|
| **ayer** | **detrás** |
| **arriba** | **temprano** |
| **siempre** | **abajo** |
| **enfrente** | **nunca** |
| **tarde** | **mañana** |

## TELLING TIME
**Decir la hora**

In Spanish, "Time" in general is "**el tiempo**" . The specific "time" is "**la hora**" . "Time" in reference to an occurrence is "**la vez**".

Here's a common question in any language:

What time is it? **¿Qué hora es?**

To answer in Spanish, simply give the hour, followed by the word **"y"** (and), and the minutes. For example, 6:15 is **"seis y quince"**. To give a specific hour, there is no need for "o'clock":

| It's... | Son las... |
| --- | --- |
| 8:00 | **ocho** |
| 3:40 | **tres y cuarenta** |
| 10:30 | **diez y treinta** |
| 5:00 | **cinco** |
| 12:05 | **doce y cinco** |

To express "at" a certain time, use this phrase:

| At... | A las... |
| --- | --- |
| 2:35 | **dos y treinta y cinco** |
| 11:00 | **once** |
| 7:10 | **siete y diez** |

AM is **"de la mañana"** and PM is **"de la tarde"** or **"de la noche"**:

| It's 6:20 AM | **Son las seis de la mañana.** |
| --- | --- |
| At 9:00 PM | **A las nueve de la tarde.** |

For 1:00 - 1:59, use **"Es la ..."** (instead of **"Son las..."**)

| It's one o'clock. | **Es la una.** |
| It's one-thirty. | **Es la una y treinta.** |

## JUST A SUGGESTION

Learn these other expressions when you find the time:

| a quarter till | **un cuarto para** |
| half past | **y media** |
| midnight | **medianoche** |
| noon | **mediodía** |
| on the dot | **en punto** |

## TRY SOME

Translate into Spanish:

What time is it?

At 8:45 AM.

It's five o'clock.

## DAYS AND MONTHS
**Los días y los meses**

Check out the basic questions and answers related to the date (**la fecha**):

| What's the <u>date</u>? | ¿Cuál es la <u>fecha</u>? |
| On what <u>date</u>? | ¿En qué <u>fecha</u>? |

| Days of the Week | Los días de la semana |

| Monday | lunes |
| Tuesday | martes |
| Wednesday | miércoles |
| Thursday | jueves |
| Friday | viernes |
| Saturday | sábado |
| Sunday | domingo |

| Months of the Year | Los meses del año |

| January | enero |
| February | febrero |
| March | marzo |
| April | abril |
| May | mayo |
| June | junio |
| July | julio |
| August | agosto |
| September | septiembre |
| October | octubre |
| November | noviembre |
| December | diciembre |

To give the date in Spanish, just reverse the word order:

| May 5th | el cinco de mayo |

| June 3<sup>rd</sup> | **el tres de junio** |
| February 15<sup>th</sup> | **el quince de febrero** |

The word "year" is **el año**. Just read it as one large number:

| 2014 | **dos mil catorce** |

The only change in date each month is "the first":

| October 1<sup>st</sup> | **el primero de octubre** |

By the way, on Monday is **"el lunes"**, while On Mondays is **"los lunes"**:

| When? | **¿Cuándo?** | On Tuesday. | **El martes.** |

## JUST A SUGGESTION

Memorize these other "timely" one-liners:

| last night | **anoche** |
| the next day | **el día siguiente** |
| next month | **el próximo mes** |
| last week | **la semana pasada** |
| the weekend | **el fin de semana** |
| the day after tomorrow | **pasado mañana** |
| the day before yesterday | **anteayer** |

TRY SOME

Fill in the blanks with the missing words:

**lunes, _____, miércoles, jueves, _____, sábado, _____**

**_____, febrero, marzo, _____, mayo, _____,**

**julio, agosto, septiembre, _____, _____, diciembre**

## THE WEATHER
**El clima**

In the world of construction, business is often controlled by the weather conditions. Here's the simple question and answer:

How's the weather?        **¿Qué tiempo hace?**

It's going to…        **Va a…**

    rain        **llover**

    snow        **nevar**

It's…        **Hace...**

| | |
|---|---|
| cold | **frío** |
| hot | **calor** |
| nice weather | **buen tiempo** |
| sunny | **sol** |
| windy | **viento** |

| It's... | Está... |
|---------|---------|
| clear | despejado |
| cloudy | nublado |
| drizzling | lloviznando |
| raining | lloviendo |
| snowing | nevando |

| There's... | Hay... |
|------------|--------|
| ice | hielo |
| frost | escarcha |
| fog | neblina |
| a storm | una tormenta |
| a tornado | un tornado |
| a hurricane | un huracán |

## JUST A SUGGESTION

These are great words to use with the time and weather:

| It's... | Es... |
|---------|-------|
| spring | la primavera |
| summer | el verano |
| fall | el otoño |
| winter | el invierno |

## TRY SOME

Translate these phrases about the weather:

It's cold. _____

It's summer. _____

There's a storm. _____

How's the weather? _____

It's hot and windy. _____

## CULTURE CLASH

Not all folks panic when it comes to tardiness - some cultures put less emphasis on "beating the clock" than others. Be direct, and explain the importance of punctuality in certain areas of employment. But be sensitive to those who believe that personal health, family, and friends are valid reasons for being a little late. If you're a stickler for punctuality, inform your crew of the concern:

You have to arrive early.

**Tiene que llegar temprano.**

Don't be late!

**¡No llegue tarde!**

If you're late again, I'll have to let you go.

**Si llega tarde otra vez, tendré que despedirle**.

# DESCRIPTIONS

## Las descripciones

Descriptive words for construction will fill each of the following chapters, but for now, use these words to describe people and things:

| | |
|---|---|
| bad | **malo** |
| big | **grande** |
| good | **bueno** |
| handsome | **guapo** |
| long | **largo** |
| new | **nuevo** |
| old | **viejo** |
| pretty | **bonito** |
| short (in height) | **bajo** |
| short (in length) | **corto** |
| small | **chico** |
| tall | **alto** |
| ugly | **feo** |
| young | **joven** |

Here are more descriptions everyone should know. Simplify the process by breaking them into pairs of "opposites":

| | |
|---|---|
| fat | **gordo** |
| thin | **delgado** |
| | |
| strong | **fuerte** |
| weak | **débil** |
| | |
| dirty | **sucio** |
| clean | **limpio** |
| | |
| slow | **lento** |
| fast | **rápido** |
| | |
| easy | **fácil** |
| difficult | **difícil** |
| | |
| cold | **frío** |
| hot | **caliente** |
| | |
| rich | **rico** |
| poor | **pobre** |
| | |
| inexpensive | **barato** |
| expensive | **caro** |

## JUST A SUGGESTION

Add these words to elaborate:

| | |
|---|---|
| **más grande** | bigger |
| **lo más grande** | biggest |
| **tan grande como** | as big as |
| **un poco grande** | a little big |
| **muy grande** | very big |

| | |
|---|---|
| **demasiado grande** | too big |
| **tan grande** | so big |

## TRY SOME

Match these opposites:

| | |
|---|---|
| **viejo** | **fácil** |
| **limpio** | **chico** |
| **malo** | **sucio** |
| **gordo** | **joven** |
| **difícil** | **pobre** |
| **rico** | **delgado** |
| **grande** | **bueno** |

## GRAMMAR TIME

To say "a" or "an" in Spanish, use "**un**" for masculine words or "**una**" for feminine words:

| | |
|---|---|
| A truck | **Un camión** |
| A big truck | **Un camión grande** |

| | |
|---|---|
| A machine | **Una máquina** |
| A red machine | **Una máquina roja** |

And to say "some", use "**unos**" or "**unas**", and don't forget the rule about plurals:

| | |
|---|---|
| Some floors | **Unos pisos** |
| Some dirty floors | **Unos pisos sucios** |
| | |
| Some tables | **Unas mesas** |
| Some new tables | **Unas mesas nuevas** |

TO BE

**Estar & Ser**

There are two ways to say "to be" in Spanish: **ESTAR** and **SER**. **ESTAR** is used to indicate the location or condition of someone or something, while **SER** is used for everything else. Here are the eight basic forms:

| TO BE | ESTAR | SER |
|---|---|---|
| I'm | estoy | soy |
| You're; He's, She's, It's | está | es |
| You're (plural), They're | están | son |
| We're | estamos | somos |

Notice how both "**está**" and "**es**" mean "is" in Spanish, but are used differently. The word "**está**" expresses a temporary state, condition, or location, while "**es**" expresses an inherent characteristic or quality, including origin and ownership:

| | |
|---|---|
| The man is fine. | **El hombre está bien.** |
| The man is in the room. | **El hombre está en el cuarto.** |

| | |
|---|---|
| The man is big. | **El hombre es grande.** |
| The man is American. | **El hombre es americana.** |

Now, to talk about more that one person, place, or thing, replace "**está**" with "**están**", and "**es**" with "**son**". Don't forget that all words must "agree" when you change to plurals:

| | |
|---|---|
| The paper is on the table. | **El papel está en la mesa.** |
| The papers are on the table. | **Los papeles están en la mesa.** |

| | |
|---|---|
| It's a neighbor. | **Es un vecino.** |
| They are neighbors. | **Son vecinos.** |

Check out these other examples and read them aloud as you focus on their structure and meaning:

| | |
|---|---|
| Are the doors black? | **¿Son negras las puertas?** |
| The tools are in the house. | **Las herramientas están en la casa.** |
| They are not important. | **No son importantes.** |

| Are they clean? | ¿Están limpios? |

To say "I am" and "we are" in Spanish, you must also learn the different forms. As with "**está**" and "**están**", the words "**estoy**" and "**estamos**" refer to the location or condition of a person, place, or thing. And, just like "**es**" and "**son**", the words "**soy**" and "**somos**" are used with everything else:

| I am fine. | **Estoy bien.** |
| We are in the truck. | **Estamos en el camión.** |
| I am Lupe. | **Soy Lupe.** |
| We are Cuban. | **Somos cubanos.** |

Two other words, "**estás**" and "**eres**" (from the informal "**tú**" form), may also be used to mean "you are" among friends, family and small children:

How are you, Mary?  You are very pretty.

**¿Cómo estás, María? Tú eres muy bonita.**

JUST A SUGGESTION

As you've probably learned, sometimes it's OK to drop the subject pronoun since it's usually understood who is involved:

| I am fine. | **(Yo) Estoy bien.** |
| They are not at home. | **(Ellos) No están en casa.** |

TRY SOME

Fill in the blanks with correct form of "**estar**":

Yo _____ bien.

Ella no _____ en su casa.

Ellas _____ en la mesa.

Fill in the blanks with correct form of "**ser**":

Nosotros _____ americanos.

Yo _____ hombre.

Juan _____ doctor.

TO HAVE

**Tener**

"**Tener**" (to have) is another common verb in construction Spanish. Take just a moment to practice:

| TO HAVE | Tener |
|---|---|
| I have | **tengo** |
| You have, he has, she has, it has | **tiene** |
| They have, you (plural) have | **tienen** |
| We have | **tenemos** |

Read these sample sentences aloud:

| | |
|---|---|
| I have a problem. | **Tengo un problema.** |
| He has a white car. | **Tiene un carro blanco.** |
| They have four children. | **Tienen cuatro niños.** |
| We have a big house. | **Tenemos una casa grande.** |

Even though "**tener**" literally means "to have," sometimes it's used instead to mean "to be" in order to express the following:

| | |
|---|---|
| (I am) afraid | **(tengo) miedo** |
| (we are) at fault | **(tenemos) la culpa** |
| (they are) cold | **(tienen) frío** |
| (she is) 15 years old | **(tiene) quince años** |
| (I am) hot | **(tengo) calor** |
| (they are) hungry | **(tienen) hambre** |
| (he is) sleepy | **(tiene) sueño** |
| (we are) thristy | **(tenemos) sed** |
| (you are) right | **(tienes) razón** |
| (I am) lucky | **(tengo) suerte** |
| (you guys are) careful | **(tienen) cuidado** |

JUST A SUGGESTION

Again, don't use the informal form for "you have" until you're with family or friends:

| You have (informal) | **tienes** |
|---|---|
| Do you have a phone? | **¿Tienes teléfono?** |

## TRY SOME

Use "**tengo**" (I have) to answer these questions:

**¿Tiene usted un carro blanco?**

**¿Cuántos amigos tiene usted?**

**¿Tienes mucha hambre?**

## THERE IS and THERE ARE
**Hay**

"There is" and "there are" are very common expressions in Spanish. In both cases, use the little word, "**hay**":

| There's one bathroom. | **Hay un baño.** |
|---|---|
| There are two bathrooms. | **Hay dos baños.** |

## JUST A SUGGESTION

To express the negative in Spanish, put the word "**no**" in front of the verb.

| There are no more. | **No hay más.** |
|---|---|
| José is not my friend. | **José no es mi amigo.** |
| I do not have the job. | **No tengo el trabajo.** |

Spanish also uses a "double negative", so when you respond, say "**no**" twice in your sentences. To ask a question, simply raise your voice at the end:

**¿Hay problemas?**          **No, no hay problemas.**

TRY SOME

Translate these:

**Hay dos hombres en la casa.**

**No hay agua.**

**¿Hay problema?**

# CHAPTER TWO

## MORE VOCABULARY
### Más vocabulario

## GENERAL HEALTH
### La salud en general

Begin this chapter on Spanish vocabulary with one-word replies about your health:

| How are you? | ¿Cómo está? |
| --- | --- |
| I'm… | Estoy… |

| | |
| --- | --- |
| angry | **enojado** |
| bored | **aburrido** |
| fine | **bien** |
| happy | **feliz** |
| not bad | **así - así** |
| not well | **mal** |
| OK | **regular** |
| sad | **triste** |
| sick | **enfermo** |
| tired | **cansado** |
| worried | **preocupado** |

## JUST A SUGGESTION

For females, simply change the final letter "**o**" to "**a**":

| Ella is... | Ella está... |
|---|---|
| anxious | **ansiosa** |
| calm | **calmada** |
| comfortable | **cómoda** |
| confused | **confundida** |
| excited | **emocionada** |
| interested | **interesada** |
| relaxed | **relajada** |
| scared | **asustada** |
| surprised | **sorprendida** |

## THE BODY

**El cuerpo**

Here's an overview of body parts in Spanish, in addition to a command phrase, so that you can practice while you follow along:

| Point to (the)... | **Señale...** |
|---|---|

| | |
|---|---|
| ankle | **el tobillo** |
| arm | **el brazo** |
| back | **la espalda** |
| chest | **el pecho** |
| ear | **la oreja** |
| elbow | **el codo** |
| eye | **el ojo** |
| face | **la cara** |
| finger | **el dedo** |
| foot | **el pie** |
| hair | **el pelo** |
| hand | **la mano** |
| head | **la cabeza** |
| hip | **la cadera** |
| knee | **la rodilla** |
| leg | **la pierna** |
| mouth | **la boca** |
| neck | **el cuello** |
| nose | **la nariz** |
| rib | **la costilla** |
| shoulder | **el hombro** |
| stomach | **el estómago** |
| throat | **la garganta** |
| toe | **el dedo del pie** |
| tooth | **el diente** |
| wrist | **la muñeca** |

Sometimes there is pain involved, so try these:

My_____ hurts.  **Me duele _____.**   **Me duele el cuello.**

My_____hurt.  **Me duelen _____.**   **Me duelen los hombros.**

## JUST A SUGGESTION

You never know if someone's got physical problems. For more emergency Spanish, check out the EMERGENCY AND SAFETY section at the end of the book:

Do you have trouble with (your)...?     **¿Tiene problemas con...?**

| | |
|---|---|
| blood | **la sangre** |
| bone | **el hueso** |
| gallbladder | **la vesícula** |
| heart | **el corazón** |
| kidney | **el riñon** |
| liver | **el hígado** |
| lung | **el pulmón** |
| muscle | **el músculo** |
| nerve | **el nervio** |
| skin | **la piel** |

## TRY SOME

Delete the word that doesn't belong with the others:

**la nariz, el ojo, la boca, el codo**

**bien, preocupado, triste, enfermo**

**el corazón, el pie, el riñon, el hígado**

## FAMILY
**La familia**

Here are the basic family members in Spanish:

| | |
|---|---|
| brother | **el hermano** |
| daughter | **la hija** |
| father | **el padre** |
| husband | **el esposo** |
| mother | **la madre** |
| sister | **la hija** |
| son | **el hijo** |
| wife | **la esposa** |

**"La familia"** is a big deal in Spanish-speaking countries, so go as far as you can with this list below:

Where's (the)…?       **¿Dónde está …?**

| | |
|---|---|
| aunt | **la tía** |
| brother-in-law | **el cuñado** |
| cousin | **el primo** |
| daughter-in-law | **la nuera** |
| father-in-law | **el suegro** |
| granddaughter | **la nieta** |
| grandfather | **el abuelo** |
| grandmother | **la abuela** |
| grandson | **el nieto** |
| mother-in-law | **la suegra** |
| nephew | **el sobrino** |
| niece | **la sobrina** |
| sister-in-law | **la cuñada** |
| son-in-law | **el yerno** |
| uncle | **el tío** |

Culturally, many Hispanics prefer to live or work with a relative. It's also common in Spanish to add "**ito**" or "**ita**" endings when you'd like to indicate smallness or affection:

**Es su hermanito.**

It's his little brother.

**Mi abuelita está en su casita.**

My grandma is in her little house.

OCCUPATIONS

**Las profesiones**

Do you know what your job title is "**en español**"? These common professions in construction refer to males (**el**), while for females (**la**), the "**o**" endings simply change to "**a**":

I'm (the)…          **Soy…**

| | |
|---|---|
| architect | **el arquitecto** |
| builder | **el constructor** |
| carpenter | **el carpintero** |
| contractor | **el contratista** |
| designer | **el diseñador** |
| dry waller | **el yesero** |
| electrician | **el electricista** |
| engineer | **el ingeniero** |
| inspector | **el inspector** |
| installer | **el instalador** |
| laborer | **el obrero** |
| landscaper | **el jardinero** |
| painter | **el pintero** |
| plumber | **el plomero** |
| stonemason | **el albañil** |
| sub-contractor | **el subcontratista** |
| truck driver | **el camionero** |

He's (the)…          **Es…**

| | |
|---|---|
| apprentice | **el aprendiz** |
| boss | **el jefe** |
| client | **el cliente** |
| employee | **el empleado** |
| employer | **el empresario** |
| foreman | **el capataz** |
| general | **el contratista principal** |
| helper | **el ayudante** |
| lead man | **el líder** |
| manager | **el gerente** |
| owner | **el dueño** |
| sub | **el menor** |
| supervisor | **el supervisor** |

## JUST A SUGGESTION

Don't get confused when Spanish-speakers mention these other common professions:

| | |
|---|---|
| cashier | **el cajero** |
| clerk | **el dependiente** |
| cook | **el cocinero** |
| dentist | **el dentista** |
| doctor | **el doctor** |
| driver | **el chofer** |
| firefighter | **el bombero** |
| lawyer | **el abogado** |
| machinist | **el operario de máquina** |
| mail carrier | **el cartero** |
| mechanic | **el mecánico** |
| nurse | **el enfermero** |
| police officer | **el policía** |
| salesman | **el vendedor** |
| secretary | **el secretario** |
| teacher | **el maestro** |
| waiter | **el mesero** |

## GRAMMAR TIME

Jot down the forms of this popular verb. It's ideal for work-related chit-chat:

| TO NEED | necesitar |
|---------|-----------|
| I need | **Necesito** |
| | **Necesito un carro.** |
| You need; He, She, It needs | **Necesita** |
| | **No necesita el plomero.** |
| You(plural), They need | **Necesitan** |
| | **¿Necesitan usar el baño?** |
| We need | **Necesitamos** |
| | **Necesitamos más trabajo.** |

TRY SOME

Translate these:

**Mi hermano es carpintero.**

**Mi tío es contratista.**

**Mis primas son pinteras.**

FOOD and DRINK

**La comida y las bebidas**

Listen for these Spanish words around mealtime.

I need…             **Necesito…**

| breakfast | **el desayuno** |
| lunch | **el almuerzo** |
| dinner | **la cena** |

The phrase **Me gusta** or **Me gustan** (plural) means "I like" :

| I like… | **Me gusta(n)…** |

## FOOD La comida

| | |
|---|---|
| bread | el pan |
| meat | la carne |
| cheese | el queso |
| fish | el pescado |
| chicken | el pollo |
| steak | el bistec |
| soup | la sopa |
| salad | la ensalada |
| ham | el jamón |
| butter | la mantequilla |
| egg | el huevo |
| turkey | el pavo |
| rice | el arroz |
| pork | el cerdo |
| roast beef | el rosbif |
| seafood | el marisco |
| roll | el panecillo |

## FRUITS and VEGETABLES Las frutas y los vegetales

| | |
|---|---|
| beans | los frijoles |
| carrot | la zanahoria |
| corn | el maíz |
| lettuce | la lechuga |
| garlic | el ajo |
| onion | la cebolla |
| peas | las arvejitas |
| potato | la papa |
| sweet potato | el camote |
| tomato | el tomate |
| apple | la manzana |
| banana | el plátano |
| grape | la uva |
| lemon | el limón |
| orange | la naranja |
| peach | el melocotón |
| pear | la pera |
| pineapple | la piña |
| plum | la ciruela |
| raisin | la pasita |
| strawberry | la fresa |

## SNACKS and DESSERTS Las meriendas y los postres

| | |
|---|---|
| cake | la torta |
| candy | el dulce |
| chips | las papitas |
| chewing gum | el chicle |
| cookie | la galleta |
| cracker | la galleta salada |
| ice cream | el helado |
| pie | el pastel |

## DRINKS Las bebidas

| | |
|---|---|
| beer | la cerveza |
| coffee | el café |
| decaffeinated coffee | el café descafeinado |
| diet soda | la soda de dieta |
| hot chocolate | el chocolate caliente |
| iced tea | el té helado |
| juice | el jugo |
| lemonade | la limonada |
| milk | la leche |
| shake | el batido |
| soft drink | el refresco |
| tea | el té |
| water | el agua |

# JUST A SUGGESTION

If you're picking up lunch for everyone or simply joining the crew for a meal, you'll have to talk about other foods. Notice the question:

Do you like (the)…?     **¿Le gusta(n)…?**

hamburger        **la hamburguesa**

hot dog          **el perro caliente**

french fries     **las papas fritas**

You'll be in big trouble if you can't figure out what these mean:

**el sandwich**

**la pizza**

**el ketchup**

Here's another easy pattern:

_____ soft drink     **el refresco_____**

small            **chico**

medium           **mediano**

large            **grande**

CLOTHING

**La ropa**

To identify people or things around the job site, you may need the names for clothing:

Where is/are…?    **¿Dónde esta(n)…?**

CLOTHING  **La ropa**

| belt | **el cinturón** |
|------|----------------|
| boots | **las botas** |
| cap | **la gorra** |
| dress | **el vestido** |
| gloves | **los guantes** |
| jacket | **la chaqueta** |
| hat | **el sombrero** |
| overcoat | **el abrigo** |
| pants | **los pantalones** |
| raincoat | **el impermeable** |
| sandals | **las sandalias** |
| shirt | **la camisa** |
| shoes | **los zapatos** |
| shorts | **los calzoncillos** |
| socks | **los calcetines** |
| sweater | **el suéter** |
| sweatsuit | **la sudadera** |
| T-shirt | **la camiseta** |
| tennis shoes | **los tenis** |

| You need (the)… | Necesita… |
|---|---|
| buckle | **la hebilla** |
| button | **el botón** |
| pocket | **el bolsillo** |
| sleeve | **la manga** |
| strap | **la correa** |
| zipper | **el cierre** |

| Use (the)… | Use… |
|---|---|
| gloves | **los guantes** |
| helmet | **el casco** |
| uniform | **el uniforme** |

For the names of additional safety items, check out the EMERGENCY AND SAFETY section at the end of the book.

JUST A SUGGESTION

One effective technique to remember the names for things is to write the name of an object in Spanish on a removable sticker, and place it on whatever you're trying to learn. Start with a few personal items:

| | |
|---|---|
| cell phone | **el teléfono celular** |
| cigarettes | **los cigarillos** |
| envelopes | **los sobres** |
| magazines | **las revistas** |
| matches | **los fósforos** |
| newspapers | **los periódicos** |
| toilet paper | **el papel higiénico** |
| stamps | **las estampillas** |
| comb | **el peine** |
| hairbrush | **el cepillo** |
| sunglasses | **los lentes del sol** |
| umbrella | **el paraguas** |
| handkerchief | **el pañuelo** |
| ring | **el anillo** |
| watch | **el reloj de pulsera** |

TRY SOME

Write three Spanish words under each category:

FOOD          DRINK          CLOTHING

_____     _____     _____

_____     _____     _____

_____     _____     _____

## TRANSPORTATION

**El transporte**

There are vehicles all over the job site. Although more will be mentioned ahead, try these phrases with the common transportation words below:

| We need (the)… | Necesitamos… |
|---|---|
| car | **el carro** |
| truck | **el camión** |
| pick up | **la camioneta** |
| semitrailer | **el semi-remolque** |
| tractor trailor | **el camión tractor** |
| dump truck | **el camión volquete** |
| flatbed truck | **el camión de plataforma** |
| van | **la vagoneta** |
|  |  |
| Move (the)… | **Mueva…** |
|  |  |
| bulldozer | **la oruga** |
| loader | **la cargadora** |
| forklift | **la carretilla elevadora** |

Now name all the vehicles on the street:

| delivery truck | **el camión de reparto** |
|---|---|
| garbage truck | **el camión de recogida de basura** |
| street sweeper | **el vehículo de barredor** |
| tank truck | **el camión cisterna** |
| tow truck | **la grúa** |

These words are used in conversations about vehicles:

| It needs… | Necesita… |
|-----------|-----------|
| gas | **la gasolina** |
| oil | **el aceite** |
| fluid | **el fluido** |
| | |
| diesel | **diésel** |
| regular | **regular** |
| unleaded | **sin plomo** |

| Go to (the)… | Vaya a… |
|--------------|---------|
| loading zone | **la zona de carga** |
| unloading zone | **la zona de descarga** |
| parking area | **el estacionamiento** |
| | |
| lot | **el lote** |
| site | **el sitio** |
| road | **el camino** |

## JUST A SUGGESTION

Many motor vehicles are identified by their names in English:

**el jeep**

**el RV**

**el SUV**

CULTURE CLASH

"Car" in Spanish can be "**carro**", "**coche**" or "**automóvil**", depending upon where a person is from. Many folks are accustomed to walking which is "**a pie**" in Spanish. Listen closely to these other means of transport:

| It's (the)… | **Es…** |
|---|---|
| bus | **el autobús** |
| train | **el tren** |
| subway | **el metro** |
| bike | **la bicicleta** |
| motorcycle | **la motocicleta** |
| plane | **el avión** |
| helicopter | **el helicóptero** |
| boat | **el barco** |

THE CITY

**La ciudad**

If your job is in town, make sure you know as many "city words" as possible. Use the question, **¿Qué lugar?** (What place?), to find out where everything is located:

| Where's (the)... | ¿Dónde está...? |
|---|---|
| airport | **el aeropuerto** |
| bank | **el banco** |
| bus station | **la estación de autobús** |
| church | **la iglesia** |
| college | **el colegio** |
| factory | **la fábrica** |
| fire department | **el departamento de bomberos** |
| gas station | **la gasolinera** |
| hospital | **el hospital** |
| library | **la biblioteca** |
| supermarket | **el supermercado** |
| movie theater | **el cine** |
| park | **el parque** |
| police station | **la estación de policía** |
| post office | **el correo** |
| school | **la escuela** |
| store | **la tienda** |
| shopping center | **el centro comercial** |
| city hall | **el municipio** |
| warehouse | **el almacén** |

Now give directions:

| It's near (the) ... | **Está cerca de ...** |
|---|---|
| building | **el edificio** |
| city block | **la cuadra** |
| corner | **la esquina** |
| highway | **la carretera** |
| sidewalk | **la acera** |
| street | **la calle** |
| traffic light | **el semáforo** |

| Go to (the)… | Vaya a… |
|---|---|
| neighborhood | **el vecindario** |
| outskirts | **las afueras** |
| downtown | **el centro** |

These are the four basic directions:

| east | **el este** |
|---|---|
| north | **el norte** |
| south | **el sur** |
| west | **el oeste** |

Call out everything as you pass by:

| alley | **el callejón** |
|---|---|
| billboard | **el letrero** |
| bridge | **el puente** |
| bus stop | **la parada de autobús** |
| fountain | **la fuente** |
| mailbox | **el buzón** |
| railroad track | **la vía del ferrocarril** |
| skyscraper | **el rascacielos** |
| stop sign | **el señal de parada** |
| telephone pole | **el poste de teléfono** |
| toll booth | **la caseta de peaje** |
| tower | **el torre** |
| tunnel | **el túnel** |

JUST A SUGGESTION

Here are more simple patterns:

It's a _____ zone.            **Es una zona _____**

residencial                       **residencial**
commercial                        **comercial**

It's _____ property.              **Es propiedad _____.**

private                           **privada**
public                            **pública**

TRY SOME

Join the occupation with its usual place of employment:

**el maestro**          **la gasolinera**

**el doctor**           **el restaurante**

**el mecánico**         **la escuela**

**el cocinero**         **el hospital**

**el contratista**      **el edificio**

# THE OUTDOORS

## Las afueras

Construction jobs often include some work outdoors. Check out these words that describe the land around us:

Look at (the)…          **Mire…**

| | |
|---|---|
| land | **el terreno** |
| beach | **la playa** |
| desert | **el desierto** |
| field | **el campo** |
| forest | **el bosque** |
| gulch | **la barranca** |
| hill | **el cerro** |
| lagoon | **la laguna** |
| lake | **el lago** |
| mountain | **la montaña** |
| sea | **el mar** |
| pond | **la charca** |
| river | **el río** |
| sea | **el mar** |
| stream | **el arroyo** |
| swamp | **el pantano** |
| valley | **el valle** |

Now identify everything you see in the area:

| Look at (the)… | Mire… |
|---|---|

| | |
|---|---|
| dirt | **la tierra** |
| dust | **el polvo** |
| gravel | **la grava** |
| mud | **el lodo** |
| rock | **la piedra** |
| sand | **la arena** |

| | |
|---|---|
| bush | **el arbusto** |
| grass | **el pasto** |
| plant | **la planta** |
| tree | **el árbol** |
| weed | **la hierba mala** |

## JUST A SUGGESTION

These should be learned by all construction workers. Focus on the base word:

| | |
|---|---|
| sewerage | **la alcantarillado** |
| storm drain | **la alcantarilla** |
| manhole cover | **la boca de la alcantarilla** |

## TRY SOME

Fill in the blanks with Spanish words you know:

**El mar tiene una _____ .**

**El pasto tiene mucha _____ .**

**El bosque tiene muchos _____ .**

TOOLS and MATERIALS

**Las herramientas y los materiales**

Build up your skills with some basic tools and equipment. Pound away at these items using a few command words:

| Unload (the)... | **Descargue...** |
| Bring (the)... | **Traiga...** |
| Use (the)... | **Use...** |

| | |
|---|---|
| compressor | **el compresor de aire** |
| generator | **el generador** |
| sawhorse | **el caballete** |
| scaffold | **el andamio** |
| toolbox | **la caja de herramientas** |
| trashcan | **el cesto de basura** |
| work table | **el tablero de trabajo** |
| wheelbarrow | **la carretilla** |

## TOOLS **Las herramientas**

| | |
|---|---|
| ax | **el hacha** |
| caulking gun | **la pistola de sellador** |
| chain | **la cadena** |
| chisel | **el cincel** |
| circular saw | **la serrucha circular** |
| clamp | **la prensa de sujetar** |
| cordless drill | **el taladro inalámbrico** |
| extension cord | **el cordón eléctrico** |
| glue | **el pegamento/la cola** |
| hacksaw | **la sierra para cortar metal** |
| hammer | **el martillo** |
| hose | **la manguera** |
| ladder | **la escalera** |
| level | **el nivel** |
| measuring tape | **la cinta métrica** |
| nail gun | **la pistola clavadora** |
| nail | **el clavo** |
| paint brush | **la brocha de pintar** |
| paint | **la pintura** |
| Phillips head | **el desarmador cruz** |
| pliers | **el alicates** |
| rope | **la soga** |
| sandpaper | **el papel de lija** |
| saw | **el serrucho/la sierra** |
| scraper | **el raspador** |
| screw | **el tornillo** |
| screwdriver | **el desarmador** |
| shovel | **la pala** |
| staple | **la grapa** |
| tape | **la cinta** |
| utility knife | **la cuchilla** |
| vice | **el torno de banco** |
| wire | **el alambre** |
| wrench | **la llave inglesa** |

## MATERIALS Los materiales

| | |
|---|---|
| alloy | **la aleación** |
| aluminum | **el aluminio** |
| bronze | **el bronce** |
| cardboard | **el cartón** |
| copper | **el cobre** |
| fabric | **la tela** |
| fiberglass | **la fibra de vidrio** |
| foam | **la espuma** |
| glass | **el vidrio** |
| iron | **el hierro** |
| liquid | **el líquido** |
| lumber | **el madero** |
| mesh | **la malla** |
| metal | **el metal** |
| plaster | **el yeso** |
| plastic | **el plástico** |
| plywood | **la madera contrachapada** |
| powder | **el polvo** |
| rubber | **la goma** |
| steel | **el acero** |
| stone | **la piedra** |
| wall tile | **el azulejo** |
| floor tile | **la baldosa** |
| roof tile | **la teja** |
| tin | **el estaño** |
| wood | **la madera** |

You messed up the place, so don't forget your cleaning tools:

I need (the)…                **Necesito…**

| | |
|---|---|
| broom | **la escoba** |
| brush | **el cepillo** |
| bucket | **el balde** |
| dustpan | **la pala de recoger basura** |
| mop | **el trapeador** |
| rag | **el trapo** |
| sponge | **la esponja** |
| towel | **la toalla** |
| trashbag | **la bolsa para basura** |

Be clear on how much or how many you need. These words work well with your numbers:

Carry (the)...          **Lleve...**

| | |
|---|---|
| bag | **la bolsa** |
| barrel | **el barril** |
| basket | **la canasta** |
| bottle | **la botella** |
| box | **la caja** |
| bucket | **el balde** |
| bundle | **el lío** |
| can | **la lata** |
| canister | **el bote** |
| crate | **la caja para transporte** |
| dozen | **la docena** |
| ton | **la tonelada** |
| group | **el grupo** |
| handful | **el puñado** |
| jar | **la jarra** |
| package | **el paquete** |
| packet | **el bolsillo** |
| pair | **el par** |
| piece | **el pedazo** |
| pile | **el montón** |
| row | **la hilera** |
| set | **el juego** |
| sheet | **la hoja** |
| stack | **la pila** |
| tank | **el tanque** |
| truckload | **la camionada** |
| tub | **la tina** |
| tube | **el tubo** |

TRY SOME

Connect the words that go together:

| | |
|---|---|
| el tornillo | la caja |
| el clavo | el hierro |
| la tina | la tuerca |
| el paquete | el serrucho |
| la sierra | el martillo |
| el acero | el balde |

Translate:

| | |
|---|---|
| el acrílico | _____ |
| el ácido | _____ |
| el asbesto | _____ |
| el asfalto | _____ |
| el aditivo | _____ |

## CULTURE CLASH

"**Spanglish**" is a universal trend to blend Spanish words with English words. All across America, millions of immigrants have come to realize that it's easier to communicate in "**Spanglish**" than in "Spanish". Notice the trend:

| English | Spanglish | Spanish |
|---|---|---|
| carpet | **la carpeta** | **la alfombra** |
| lunch | **el lonche** | **el almuerzo** |
| muffler | **el mofle** | **el silenciador** |
| caulking | **el cáquin** | **la masilla** |

| truck | **la troca** | **el camión** |
|---|---|---|

## AT WORK
### En el trabajo

This group of construction words relates to your paperwork:

| Look at (the)… | **Mire…** |
|---|---|

| | |
|---|---|
| blueprint | **el cianotipo** |
| calendar | **el calendario** |
| contract | **el contrato** |
| design | **el diseño** |
| drawing | **el dibujo** |
| form | **el formulario** |
| illustration | **la ilustración** |
| invoice | **la factura** |
| layout | **el trazado** |
| map | **el mapa** |
| paperwork | **el papeleo** |
| photo | **la foto** |
| plans | **los planos** |
| schedule | **el horario** |
| specifications | **las especificaciones** |

Continue to chatter about the job:

| We need more… | **Necesitamos más…** |
|---|---|

| | |
|---|---|
| materials | **materiales** |
| machines | **máquinas** |

| | |
|---|---|
| workers | **obreros** |

| | |
|---|---|
| Pick up (the)… | **Recoja…** |

| | |
|---|---|
| debris | **los escombros** |
| spillage | **el derrame** |
| trash | **la basura** |

| | |
|---|---|
| It doesn't have (the)… | **No tiene…** |

| | |
|---|---|
| air | **el aire** |
| fuel | **el combustible** |
| gas | **el gas** |
| light | **la luz** |
| power | **el poder eléctrico** |
| water | **el agua** |

| | |
|---|---|
| Where's (the)…? | **¿Dónde está…?** |

| | |
|---|---|
| dumpster | **el basurero grande** |
| fence | **la cerca** |
| office | **la oficina** |
| porta-potty | **el retrete** |
| shack | **la chabola** |
| shed | **el cobertizo** |

## JUST A SUGGESTION

Interject this question to get more detail about the project:

| What_____? | ¿Qué_____? |
|---|---|
| kind | **clase** |
| type | **tipo** |
| brand | **marca** |

## GRAMMAR TIME

Work commands can be strings of words, also. Notice how the word "**me**" (me) can be added to the end of a simple command to create a complete phrase:

| | |
|---|---|
| Listen to me | **Escúcheme** |
| Explain to me | **Explíqueme** |
| Tell me | **Dígame** |
| Call me | **Llámeme** |
| Give me | **Deme** |
| Send me | **Mándeme** |
| Answer me | **Contésteme** |
| Bring me | **Traígame** |

## MEASUREMENTS
**Las medidas**

All workers require this selection of Spanish vocabulary. Focus on the questions first:

| How much? | **¿Cuánto?** |
|---|---|
| How many? | **¿Cuántos?** |

| | |
|---|---|
| What's it measure? | **¿Cuánto mide?** |
| What's it weigh? | **¿Cuánto pesa?** |

| | |
|---|---|
| How…? | **¿Cuánto mide de…?** |
| long | **largo** |
| high | **alto** |
| deep | **profundo** |

When you respond, remember to drop the "**el**" or "**la**" if you add a number:

| inch | **la pulgada** | > | two inches | **dos pulgadas** |
|---|---|---|---|---|

| | |
|---|---|
| cent | **el centavo** |
| cup | **la taza** |
| dollar | **el dólar** |
| feet | **el pie** |
| gallon | **el galón** |
| inch | **la pulgada** |
| mile | **la milla** |
| ounce | **la onza** |
| pint | **la pinta** |
| pound | **la libra** |
| quart | **el cuarto** |
| ton | **la tonelada** |
| yard | **la yarda** |

| | |
|---|---|
| What's (the)…? | **¿Cuál es…?** |

| | |
|---|---|
| amount | **la cantidad** |
| count | **la cuenta** |
| depth | **la profundidad** |
| distance | **la distance** |
| height | **la altura** |
| length | **el largo** |
| size | **el tamaño** |
| speed | **la velocidad** |
| temperature | **la temperature** |
| width | **el ancho** |

## JUST A SUGGESTION

The word "**pies**" is used all the time in construction:

| | |
|---|---|
| linear feet | **pies lineares** |
| square feet | **pies cuadrados** |
| cubic feet | **pies cúbicos** |

## TRY SOME

Go ahead and translate:

| | |
|---|---|
| **dos galones** | _____ |
| **cinco dólares** | _____ |
| **tres toneladas** | _____ |

| | |
|---|---|
| eight ounces | _____ |
| twelve feet | _____ |
| fifty cents | _____ |

SPANISH VERBS

**Los verbos en español**

Although the Spanish verbs **"estar"**, **"ser"**, and **"tener"** are extremely useful, they do not express action. Learning how to use Spanish verbs will allow you to talk about anything. Spend a few moments memorizing this brief list of helpful beginning verbs. Notice that Spanish action words end in the letters **ar**, **er**, or **ir**, and they aren't to be confused with the command forms you learned earlier:

**AR** verbs

| | |
|---|---|
| to answer | **contestar** |
| to arrive | **llegar** |
| to ask | **preguntar** |
| to begin | **empezar** |
| to buy | **comprar** |
| to call | **llamar** |
| to carry | **llevar** |
| to change | **cambiar** |
| to clean | **limpiar** |
| to close | **cerrar** |
| to drive | **manejar** |
| to end | **terminar** |
| to give | **dar** |
| to help | **ayudar** |

| | |
|---|---|
| to lift | **levantar** |
| to listen | **escuchar** |
| to load | **cargar** |
| to look | **mirar** |
| to pay | **pagar** |
| to rest | **descansar** |
| to speak | **hablar** |
| to stop | **parar** |
| to take | **tomar** |
| to throw away | **tirar** |
| to turn off | **apagar** |
| to unload | **descargar** |
| to use | **usar** |
| to walk | **caminar** |
| to wash | **lavar** |
| to work | **trabajar** |

## ER verbs

| | |
|---|---|
| to bring | **traer** |
| to do | **hacer** |
| to drink | **beber** |
| to eat | **comer** |
| to learn | **aprender** |
| to move | **mover** |
| to put | **poner** |
| to read | **leer** |

| | |
|---|---|
| to return | **volver** |
| to run | **correr** |
| to see | **ver** |
| to sell | **vender** |
| to turn on | **prender** |
| to understand | **entender** |

**IR** verbs

| | |
|---|---|
| to allow | **permitir** |
| to come | **venir** |
| to go | **ir** |
| to leave | **salir** |
| to live | **vivir** |
| to measure | **medir** |
| to open | **abrir** |
| to receive | **recibir** |
| to say | **decir** |
| to sleep | **dormir** |
| to write | **escribir** |

As you might have guessed, many Spanish verbs resemble their English equivalent:

| | |
|---|---|
| to connect | **conectar** |
| to control | **controlar** |
| to install | **instalar** |

| to organize | **organizar** |
|---|---|
| to refer | **referir** |

Careful! False look-alikes are everywhere!

| **contestar** | = | to answer, not to "contest" |
|---|---|---|
| **embarazar** | = | to impregnate, not to "embarrass" |
| **asistir** | = | to attend, not to "assist" |

You can never learn enough action words in Spanish. Over five hundred verbs are listed on pages throughout this book, and they can also be found at the end in the glossary. So, don't forget -- whenever you hear a verb you don't know, it's always wise to look up its base form and meaning.

## JUST A SUGGESTION

Some Spanish verb infinitives have "**se**" attached. Learn to practice them separately:

| to stand up | **levantarse** |
|---|---|
| to sit down | **sentarse** |
| to lie down | **acostarse** |

## GRAMMAR TIME

One of the most effective ways to put your verbs into action is to combine them with simple phrases that create complete commands. For example, look what happens when you add these verb infinitives to "**Favor de...**", which implies, "Would you please...":

Would you please...  **Favor de...**

write the number  **escribir el número**

drive the truck  **manejar el camión**

speak more slowly  **hablar más despacio**

Be sure to check out other key words that precede Spanish verbs. There's a complete list on the FORM-A-PHRASE page at the back of the book.

TRY SOME

Write a Spanish verb with an opposite meaning:

**escuchar**    _____

**venir**    _____

**sentarse**    _____

**correr**    _____

**vender**    _____

THE ONE-LINERS

As a beginning Spanish student involved in training, you should try to acquire as much vocabulary as you can. Without a doubt, you are going to need a variety of practical one-word responses to communicate with people who work for you. Scan this list, and choose those that suit you best.

| | |
|---|---|
| alone | **solo** |
| also | **también** |
| anyone | **cualquier persona** |
| anything | **cualquier cosa** |
| anywhere | **en cualquier sitio** |
| enough | **bastante** |
| everybody | **todos** |
| everything | **todo** |
| everywhere | **por todas partes** |
| no one | **nadie** |
| no where | **en ningún sitio** |
| none | **ninguno** |
| nothing | **nada** |
| only | **solamente** |
| same | **mismo** |
| someone | **alguien** |
| something | **algo** |
| somewhere | **en algún sitio** |
| too much | **demasiado** |
| most | **la mayor parte** |
| the rest | **los demás** |

TRY SOME

Practice these short questions and answers aloud:

| | |
|---|---|
| **¿Quién?** | **Nadie.** |
| **¿Cuántos?** | **Ninguno.** |
| **¿Dónde?** | **Por todas partes.** |

## CULTURE CLASH

Trust is very important in the Hispanic culture, especially in working relationships. Throughout the day, feel free to open up about yourself, your family, and what you do in your spare time. Since language is a barrier, build rapport by showing Spanish speakers that you're trying to learn their language. Don't be shy, always be honest, and make everyone feel that they're part of the team.

# INTRODUCTION TO CHAPTERS THREE TO TEN

Chapters Three to Ten address seven different trades in the field of construction. Please take note of the following tips as you read through the entire text:

1. Several words are repeated in each chapter, because not all vocabulary or activities in construction are entirely trade-specific.

2. You may find more than one Spanish translation for an English word, since the meaning of one word may change slightly when used in a different setting or context. The same holds true for some of the Spanish words.

3. Simply for convenience, everything presented in this book is in the masculine form. Changes must be made when referring to a female.

4. Commands, questions, and statements are primarily addressed to an individual. Changes must be made when addressing more than one person.

5. Although each chapter is filled with the names for items in Spanish, many Spanish-speaking construction workers will attempt to use English or a mixture of the two languages (*Spanglish*) in order to communicate. In fact, if the item you are looking for is not mentioned in the book, there's a good chance it is generally referred to in English.

# CHAPTER THREE

## GRADING AND FOUNDATION
### La nivelación y los cimientos

WORKING WORDS: GRADING AND FOUNDATION

Everyone involved in this phase of the project should know the following vocabulary words:

| | |
|---|---|
| ground | **el suelo** |
| soil | **la tierra** |
| trench | **la zanja** |
| | |
| concrete | **el concreto** |
| slab | **la losa** |
| form | **el molde** |
| | |
| footing | **la zapata** |
| rebar | **la varilla** |
| brace | **la riostra** |

Now create a few simple phrases:

Look at (the)…          **Mire…**

| | |
|---|---|
| boundary | **el límite** |
| land | **el terreno** |
| layout | **el diseño** |
| lot | **el lote** |
| plot | **la parcela** |
| property | **la propiedad** |
| surface | **la superficie** |

Where's the…?          **¿Dónde está…?**

| | |
|---|---|
| area | **la área** |
| line | **la linea** |
| place | **el lugar** |
| site | **el sitio** |
| space | **el espacio** |
| spot | **el punto** |
| zone | **la zona** |

Now tell the crew what kind of "ground" it is:


It has (the)…          **Tiene…**

| | |
|---|---|
| bedrock | **la roca** |
| clay | **el barro** |
| dirt | **la tierra** |
| gravel | **la grava** |
| landfill | **el terreno suelto** |
| limestone | **la piedra caliza** |
| mud | **el lodo** |
| rock | **la piedra** |
| rubble | **la rocalla** |
| sand | **la arena** |
| sandstone | **la arenisca** |
| sediment | **el sedimento** |

## JUST A SUGGESTION

Most words in English are easy to pronounce in Spanish. Notice the two patterns:

| | |
|---|---|
| absorption | **la absorsión** |
| condition | **la condición** |
| connection | **la conexión** |
| installation | **la instalación** |
| separation | **la separación** |
| specification | **la especificación** |

| | |
|---|---|
| compression | **la compresión** |
| corrosion | **la corrosión** |
| erosion | **la erosión** |
| extension | **la extensión** |
| suspension | **la suspensión** |
| tension | **la tensión** |

TRY SOME

Translate these important sentences into Spanish:

Where is the place?  _____

Look at the surface.  _____

It has rocks.  _____

## WORKING WORDS: GRADING EQUIPMENT

Open up with common hand tools:

Give me (the)…          **Deme…**

| | |
|---|---|
| pick | **el pico** |
| shovel | **la pala** |
| wheelbarrow | **la carretilla** |

This time, point out a few important vehicles. Remember that the word for

truck is "**el camión**":

Where's (the)…?  **¿Dónde está…?**

| | |
|---|---|
| cement truck | **el camión hormigonera** |
| crane truck | **el camión grúa** |
| dump truck | **el camión volquete** |
| flatbed truck | **el camión plataforma** |
| pick-up truck | **la camioneta** |
| water tank truck | **el camión cisterna** |

Now identify some heavy equipment. Notice how many words that refer to machinery end in the letters "**-adora**":

Bring (the)...          **Traiga...**

| | |
|---|---|
| loader | **la cargadora** |
| grader | **la niveladora** |
| roller | **la aplanadora** |
| scraper | **la rastreadora** |
| trencher | **la excavadora** |
| compactor | **la compactadora** |
| driller | **la perforadora** |
| backhoe | **la retroexcavadora** |

The actual word for bulldozer is "**el bulldozer**" or "**el tractor oruga**", but sometimes workers simply refer to machines in English by their make, brand, or function:

**el Bobcat**

**el Caterpillar**

**el Deere**

**el Padfoot**

**el SuperPac**

**el DynaPac**


**los earthmovers**

**los skiploaders**

**los eighteen-wheelers**


Keep talking about your grading equipment:


Move (the)…                 **Mueva…**


| | |
|---|---|
| jackhammer | **el martillo neumático** |
| electric trowel | **la paleta eléctrica** |
| power shovel | **la pala motorizada** |
| hand compactor | **la compactadora manual** |
| hydraulic pile driver | **el vibrador hidráulico** |


And, be specific when it comes to equipment parts:


Fix (the)…   **Arregle…**

| | |
|---|---|
| bit | **la broca** |
| blade | **la hoja** |
| bucket | **el cucharón** |
| cab | **la cabina** |
| cable | **el cable** |
| drum | **el rulo** |
| engine | **el motor** |
| gear | **el engranaje** |
| handle | **el mango** |
| hose | **la manguera** |
| lever | **la palanca** |
| lid | **la tapa** |
| nossle | **la boquilla** |
| panel | **el panel** |
| screen | **el mosquitero** |
| shaft | **el eje** |
| valve | **la válvula** |
| wheel | **la rueda** |

Here's a common pattern in construction tools:

| The pneumatic … | … **neumático/a** |
|---|---|
| drill | **el taladro** |
| hammer | **el martillo** |
| nailer | **la clavadora** |
| screwdriver | **el desarmador** |
| wrench | **la llave** |

## JUST A SUGGESTION

You may be sending crew members to the truck to get something, so these words will be needed, too:

It's in, on, or at (the)…    **Está en…**

dashboard            **el tablero**

glove compartment    **la guantera**

steering wheel       **el timón**

seat                 **el asiento**

visor                **la visera**

truckbed             **el trasero**


Now, put words together to give detail:

front seat           **el asiento delantero**

passenger side       **el lado del pasajero**

rear seat            **el asiento trasero**


TRY SOME


Name three pieces of grading equipment that end with the letters "**-adora**".

_____

_____

_____


Draw a picture of the following:

**la manguera**

**la rueda**

**el timón**

## WORKING WORDS: LAYING THE FOUNDATION

Begin this section by mentioning what is being built:

It's (the)…  **Es…**

| | |
|---|---|
| basement | **el sótano** |
| building | **el edificio** |
| garage | **el garaje** |
| house | **la casa** |
| room | **el cuarto** |

Now try words that you may not know:

| | |
|---|---|
| add-on | **la adición** |
| apartment | **el apartamento** |
| cabin | **la cabaña** |
| complex | **el complejo** |
| condominium | **el condominio** |
| farm house | **la granja** |
| high-rise | **el edificio de muchos pisos** |
| town house | **la casa lujosa** |

Now mention other features that require cement work:

Work on (the)…         **Trabaje en…**

| | |
|---|---|
| curb | **el bordillo** |
| deck | **la terraza** |
| driveway | **el camino de entrada** |
| fence | **la cerca** |
| floor | **el piso** |
| ground floor | **el primer piso** |
| patio | **el patio** |
| porch | **el pórtico** |
| sidewalk | **la acera** |
| stairs | **las escaleras** |
| steps | **los escalones** |
| stoop | **el umbral** |
| subfloor | **el subpiso** |
| wall | **el muro/la pared** |

Foundation work has begun, so make your statements clear:

(The) _____ goes here.          _____ **va aquí.**

| | |
|---|---|
| base | **la base** |
| form | **el molde** |
| joint | **la junta** |
| pad | **la plataforma** |
| slab | **la losa** |
| template | **la plancha** |

It needs (the)...          **Necesita...**

| | |
|---|---|
| anchor | **el anclaje** |
| bar | **la barra** |
| barrier | **la barrera** |
| block | **el bloque** |
| brace | **la riostra** |
| brick | **el ladrillo** |
| buttress | **la contrafrente** |
| caisson | **el cilindro** |
| chicken wire | **el alambre de gallinera** |
| drainpipe | **el tubo de drenaje** |
| fitting | **el acoplamiento** |
| footing | **la zapata/el cimiento** |
| girder | **la viga** |
| hook | **el gancho** |
| insulation | **el aislamiento** |
| pilaster | **la pilastra** |
| pilon | **la columna** |
| rebar | **la varilla** |
| retaining wall | **el muro de apoyo** |
| sandbag | **el saco de arena** |
| shoring | **el apuntamiento** |
| sill plate | **la placa de solera** |
| stud | **el barrote** |
| tie | **el amarre** |
| weep hole | **el hueco para drenaje** |
| wire mesh | **la malla de alambre** |

When working on the foundation, use the appropriate equipment and materials:

Unload (the)…        **Descargue…**

| | |
|---|---|
| chipper | **la melladera** |
| crusher | **la aplastadora** |
| cutter | **la cortadora** |
| driller | **la perforadora** |
| grinder | **la moledora** |
| spreader | **la esparcidora** |

Carry (the)…        **Lleve …**

| | |
|---|---|
| cement | **el cemento** |
| mixture | **la mezcla** |
| mortar | **la argamasa** |
| sand | **la arena** |
| water | **el agua** |

Do you have (the)…?     **¿Tiene…?**

| | |
|---|---|
| mallet | **el mazo** |
| mixer | **la mezcladora** |
| pick | **el pico** |
| pump | **la bomba** |
| rake | **el rastrillo** |
| shovel | **la pala** |
| sledge | **la almádena** |
| wheelbarrow | **la carretilla** |

Give me (the)…        **Deme…**

| | |
|---|---|
| brick cutting saw | **la sierra para cortar ladrillos** |
| bush hammer | **el martillo para texturizar** |
| cement saw | **la sierra para cortar cemento** |
| chisel | **el cincel** |
| darby | **la paleta de madera** |
| edger | **la llana para bordes** |
| finishing broom | **el cepillo de acabado** |
| finishing trowel | **la llana para acabado** |
| groover | **la ranuradora** |
| hawk | **el esparavel** |
| joint compound | **la pasta para las uniones** |
| jointer | **el marcador de juntas** |
| mason's trowel | **la llana de madera** |
| masonry hammer | **la maceta** |
| steel trowel | **la paleta de acero** |
| stretcher | **el tensor** |
| tamper | **el pisón** |
| tie | **el sujetador** |
| tongs | **las tenazas** |

I have (the)…               **Tengo…**


_____ float             **la llana _____**


    rubber                 **de goma**

    magnesium              **metálica**

    bull                   **mecánica**


It has a _____ finish.    **Tiene acabado de _____.**


    trowel                         **la paleta**

    broom                          **la escoba**

|          |           |
|----------|-----------|
| salt     | **la sal** |

Be sure to ask about the names for minerals and chemicals:

| Use…     | **Use…**        |
|----------|-----------------|
| alkaline | **el alcalino** |
| gypsum   | **el yeso**     |
| lime     | **la cal**      |
| salt     | **la sal**      |
| sulfate  | **el sulfato**  |

## JUST A SUGGESTION

As always, listen for words that are similar to English:

| concrete | **el concreto**  |
|----------|------------------|
| pavement | **el pavimiento** |
| cement   | **el cemento**   |

| It's _____ cement. | **Es el cemento _____.** |
|----------------------|----------------------------|

| structural         | **estructural**           |
|--------------------|---------------------------|
| reinforced         | **reforzado**             |
| sulphate resistant | **resistente al sulfato** |

And here's some Spanglish:

**el gypcrete**

**el gunite**

**el shotcrete**


TRY SOME


Circle the one word that doesn't belong with the others:


**el cincel, el martillo, el sótano**

**la taladra, la argamasa, el cemento**

**el piso, el pico, la pared**


Now translate these new words into English:


**el experto**

**el especialista**

**el profesional**


**el condominio**

**la mansión**

**el dúplex**


WORKING WORDS: ON THE JOB SITE

As you break ground, identify everyone who's been working on the project.
Begin with those words you already know:

He's (the)…          **Es…**

| | |
|---|---|
| builder | **el constructor** |
| contractor | **el contratista** |
| inspector | **el inspector** |
| laborer | **el obrero** |
| general | **el contratista principal** |
| owner | **el dueño** |
| project manager | **el gerente** |
| sub-contractor | **el subcontratista** |
| supervisor | **el supervisor** |

Now name the land, grading or foundation experts:

Talk to (the)…       **Hable con…**

| | |
|---|---|
| architect | **el arquitecto** |
| designer | **el diseñador** |
| electrician | **el electricista** |
| engineer | **el ingeniero** |
| geologist | **el geólogo** |
| plumber | **el fontanero/el plomero** |
| surveyor | **el agrimensor** |
| technician | **el técnico** |

You'll need plenty of words as the grading project gets under way. Some were presented earlier:

The _____ goes there.        _____ va allí.

| | |
|---|---|
| canal | **el canal** |
| drainage | **el drenaje** |
| hole | **el hoyo** |
| load | **la carga** |
| marker | **el marcador** |
| post | **el poste** |
| slope | **la cuesta** |
| stake | **la estaca** |
| string | **la cuerda** |
| trench | **la zanja** |
| walk board | **la tabla para caminar** |

Where's the…        **¿Dónde está…?**

| | |
|---|---|
| gas line | **la línea de gas** |
| power cable | **la electricidad** |
| sewage system | **la alcantarilla** |
| street main | **la conexión urbana** |
| water pipe | **la tubería** |

The word "**nivel**" (level) is also used a lot in grading and foundation work:

| | |
|---|---|
| sea level | **a nivel del mar** |
| on grade | **a nivel** |
| water table | **el nivel de agua** |

And if problems with the project arise, keep it short:

There's trouble with (the)…     **Hay problemas con…**

| | |
|---|---|
| age | **la edad** |
| condition | **la condición** |
| movement | **el movimiento** |
| shape | **la forma** |
| strength | **la resistencia** |
| support | **el apoyo** |

There are…     **Hay…**

| | |
|---|---|
| bubbles | **burbujas** |
| bumps | **bultos** |
| cracks | **grietas** |
| holes | **huecos** |
| leaks | **agujeros** |

It's…     **Está…**

| | |
|---|---|
| bent | **doblado** |
| broken | **quebrado** |
| cracked | **agrietado** |
| damaged | **dañado** |
| defective | **defectuoso** |
| eroded | **erosionado** |
| ruined | **destruído** |
| stained | **manchado** |

Pick up (the)…     **Recoja…**

| | |
|---|---|
| chips | **la gravilla** |
| pieces | **los pedacitos** |
| chunks | **las tajadas** |

JUST A SUGGESTION

When you're hauling or towing, remember the word, "**remolque**":

| | |
|---|---|
| towing | **el remolque** |
| tow hook | **el gancho de remolque** |
| tow line | **la cuerda de remolque** |

TRY SOME

Translate these sentences into English:

**La zanja va allí.**

**Hable con la dueña.**

**¿Dónde está el arquitecto?**

Connect the words that go together best:

| | |
|---|---|
| **húmedo** | **agujero** |
| **sal** | **quebrado** |
| **hueco** | **mojado** |
| **dañado** | **piedra** |
| **roca** | **sulfato** |

# WORKING WORDS: DESCRIBING THE JOB

Look! It'll be easier if you learn descriptions as opposites:

| | | | | | | | | | |
|---|---|---|---|---|---|---|---|---|---|
| hard | **duro** | light | **ligero** | open | **abierto** | | | | |
| soft | **blando** | dark | **oscuro** | closed | **cerrado** | | | | |
| thick | **grueso** | straight | **recto** | better | **mejor** | | | | |
| narrow | **estrecho** | crooked | **torcido** | worse | **peor** | | | | |
| deep | **profundo** | wet | **mojado** | dull | **romo** | | | | |
| shallow | **bajo** | dry | **seco** | sharp | **afilado** | | | | |
| empty | **vacío** | rough | **áspero** | tight | **apretado** | | | | |
| full | **lleno** | smooth | **liso** | loose | **flojo** | | | | |
| wide | **ancho** | heavy | **pesado** | clear | **claro** | | | | |
| narrow | **estrecho** | light | **ligero** | dark | **oscuro** | | | | |
| real | **verdadero** | loud | **ruidoso** | sloppy | **chapucero** | | | | |
| fake | **falso** | quiet | **quieto** | neat | **pulcro** | | | | |

Some descriptive words tell "where":

| | |
|---|---|
| high | **alto** |
| low | **bajo** |
| above | **encima** |
| under | **debajo** |
| up | **arriba** |
| down | **abajo** |

| | | | |
|---|---|---|---|
| backwards | **hacia atrás** | | |
| forward | **adelante** | | |

| | | | |
|---|---|---|---|
| near | **cerca** | | |
| far | **lejos** | | |

Grading and foundation projects will also need specialized descriptions:

| | | | |
|---|---|---|---|
| level | **nivel** | partial | **parcial** |
| sloped | **inclinado** | complete | **completo** |
| | | | |
| solid | **sólido** | even | **igual** |
| hollow | **hueco** | uneven | **desigual** |
| | | | |
| flat | **llano** | temporary | **provisional** |
| steep | **empinado** | permanent | **permanente** |

Keep looking for patterns. For example, the prefixes "**in**" and "**des**" in Spanish imply "not":

| | |
|---|---|
| correct | **correcto** |
| incorrect | **incorrecto** |
| | |
| stable | **estable** |
| unstable | **instable** |

| | |
|---|---|
| comfortable | **cómodo** |
| uncomfortable | **incómodo** |
| | |
| covered | **tapado** |
| uncovered | **destapado** |
| | |
| stuck | **pegado** |
| unstuck | **despegado** |
| | |
| loaded | **cargado** |
| unloaded | **descargado** |

Now be a bit more detailed as you describe everything:

| It's… | **Es…/Está…** |
|---|---|

| | |
|---|---|
| adjustable | **ajustable** |
| continuous | **contínuo** |
| embedded | **incrustado** |
| enclosed | **encerrado** |
| expansive | **expandido** |
| exposed | **expuesto** |
| muddy | **lodoso** |
| organized | **organizado** |
| perforated | **perforado** |
| prefabricated | **prefabricado** |
| protected | **protegido** |
| removable | **desmontable** |
| rocky | **rocoso** |
| symmetrical | **simétrico** |
| underground | **subterráneo** |

If water is a concern, use these descriptive words:

Is it…?                          **¿Es/Está…?**

| | |
|---|---|
| frozen | **congelado** |
| moist | **húmedo** |
| rustproof | **inoxidable** |
| soaked | **empapado** |
| waterproof | **impermeable** |
| watertight | **hermético** |
| wet | **mojado** |

## JUST A SUGGESTION

Practice putting descriptive words AFTER the objects, instead of before:

| fine | **fino** | > | <u>fine</u> material | **material <u>fino</u>** |
|---|---|---|---|---|
| used | **usado** | > | <u>used</u> car | **carro <u>usado</u>** |
| lost | **perdido** | > | <u>lost</u> money | **dinero <u>perdido</u>** |

## TRY SOME

What's the opposite?

**ancho**          _____

**correcto**       _____

**ruidoso** _____

**seco** _____

**alto** _____

**vacío** _____

Now translate these descriptions without any help:

**natural**        **regular**        **interior**

**artificial**       **irregular**      **exterior**

| | |
|---|---|
| **simple** | **geológico** |
| **exacto** | **normal** |
| **original** | **rural** |
| **necesario** | **profesional** |
| **terrible** | **total** |
| **magnífico** | **diligente** |
| **correcto** | **fantástico** |
| **probable** | **remodelado** |
| **posible** | **imaginativo** |
| **preliminar** | **lateral** |

## WORKING WORDS: TECHNICAL DETAIL

Here are some technical words that are needed during grading or foundation work. Some you learned earlier:

| What's (the)...? | ¿Cuál es...? |
|---|---|
| measurement | **la medida** |
| height | **la altura** |
| depth | **la profundidad** |
| length | **el largo** |
| distance | **la distancia** |
| width | **el ancho** |
| temperature | **la temperatura** |
| size | **el tamaño** |
| grade | **el grado** |
| angle | **el ángulo** |
| volume | **el volumen** |
| percent | **el porcentaje** |
| load | **la carga** |
| flow | **el flujo** |
| force | **la fuerza** |
| pressure | **la presión** |
| thickness | **el grueso** |
| amount | **la cantidad** |
| count | **la cuenta** |
| ratio | **la proporción** |
| speed | **la velocidad** |
| circumference | **la circunferencia** |
| time | **la hora** |

Add short phrases to explain everything:

| It's... | **Está...** |
|---|---|
| U-form | **en la forma de la "U"** |
| L-shape | **en la forma de la "L"** |
| parallel | **paralelo** |

| | |
|---|---|
| round | **redondo** |
| square | **cuadrado** |

| | |
|---|---|
| It's (the)… | **Es…** |

| | |
|---|---|
| circle | **el círculo** |
| cone | **el cono** |
| curve | **la curva** |
| cylinder | **el cilindro** |
| oval | **el óvalo** |

These words are spelled the same in English:

| | |
|---|---|
| diagonal | **diagonal** |
| horizontal | **horizontal** |
| vertical | **vertical** |

Look how many words are similar in the two languages:

| | |
|---|---|
| triangle | **el triángulo** |
| rectangle | **el rectángulo** |
| | |
| diameter | **el diámetro** |
| perimeter | **el perímetro** |
| | |
| cubic | **cúbico** |
| metric | **métrico** |

Use these examples to create your own set of measurements:

| | |
|---|---|
| 2 inches above | **dos pulgadas por encima** |
| 2 inches below | **dos pulgadas por debajo** |
| 2 inches thick | **dos pulgadas de gruesa** |
| 2 inches high | **dos pulgadas de alto** |
| 2 inches by 4 inches | **dos por cuatro pulgadas** |

| | |
|---|---|
| twice | **dos veces** |
| one at a time | **una a la vez** |
| once again | **una vez más** |

| | |
|---|---|
| a half | **una mitad** |
| a quarter | **un cuarto** |
| a third | **un tercero** |

How technical do you want to get?

| | |
|---|---|
| HP | **caballos de fuerza** |
| PSI | **libras por pulgadas cuadradas** |
| MPH | **millas por hora** |

JUST A SUGGESTION

Don't forget the metric system:

| | | |
|---|---|---|
| 5/8 mi. | = | **el kilómetro** |
| 2.2 lbs. | = | **el kilógramo** |
| 33° F | = | **0° C** |

TRY SOME

Write these out in Spanish:

ht. _____

½ _____

lb. _____

psi _____

2 X 6 _____

What are these shapes called in Spanish?

Δ _____

□ _____

○ _____

<u>WORKING WORDS:</u> ON-SITE ACTIONS

The following are Spanish "verbs" which help to put all of this vocabulary into "action". To practice, use this expression:

We're going… **Vamos a…**

| | |
|---|---|
| to build | **construir** |
| to bury | **enterrar** |
| to channel | **canalizar** |
| to compact | **compactar** |
| to cover | **cubrir** |
| to crush | **demoler** |
| to cut | **cortar** |
| to dig | **excavar** |
| to dump | **descargar** |
| to filter | **filtrar** |
| to float | **flotar** |
| to grade | **nivelar** |
| to grind | **moler** |
| to haul | **transportar** |
| to hold | **sostener** |
| to join | **juntar** |
| to lay foundation | **cimentar** |
| to level | **nivelar** |
| to mark | **marcar** |
| to measure | **medir** |
| to mix | **mezclar** |
| to mount | **amontar** |
| to pour | **echar** |
| to prep | **hacer todo listo** |
| to pump | **bombear** |
| to reinforce | **reforzar** |
| to screed | **enrasar** |
| to set up | **eregir** |
| to shore up | **apuntalar** |
| to smooth out | **alisar** |
| to soak | **empapar** |
| to spread | **esparcir** |
| to sprinkle | **rociar** |
| to stamp | **hollar** |
| to step | **pisar** |
| to support | **apoyar** |
| to surround | **rodear** |
| to survey | **medir** |
| to tape | **encintar** |
| to tie | **atar** |
| to trench | **poner zanjas** |
| to trowel | **paletear** |
| to ventilate | **ventilar** |
| to vibrate | **vibrar** |
| to water down | **regar** |
| to waterproof | **impermeabilizar** |
| to wrap | **forar** |

Work on those other actions that you'll need right away:

| I want… | **Quiero…** |
|---------|-------------|
| to calculate | **calcular** |
| to design | **diseñar** |
| to draw | **dibujar** |
| to examine | **examinar** |
| to guess | **adivinar** |
| to plan | **planear** |
| to test | **probar** |

A few verbs are a little different, because they have "**se**" at the end:

| It's going… | **Va a…** |
|-------------|-----------|
| to crack | **agrietarse** |
| to overlap | **superponerse** |
| to settle | **depositarse** |
| to shift | **moverse** |
| to sink | **hundirse** |

Notice the English in these:

| | |
|---|---|
| to absorb | **absorber** |
| to adjust | **ajustar** |
| to indicate | **indicar** |
| to insist | **insistir** |
| to inspect | **inspeccionar** |
| to install | **instalar** |
| to permit | **permitir** |
| to prohibit | **prohibir** |
| to recommend | **recomendar** |
| to reduce | **reducir** |

Add your own words to this model:

It needs …          **Necesita…**

to withstand        **aguantar**

to harden           **endurecer**

to flow             **fluir**

And keep memorizing words in pairs with opposite meanings:

| | |
|---|---|
| to break | **romper** |
| to repair | **reparar** |
| | |
| to take out | **sacar** |
| to put in | **meter** |
| | |
| to begin | **comenzar** |
| to finish | **acabar** |
| | |
| to add | **añadir** |
| to remove | **quitar** |
| | |
| to fill | **llenar** |
| to empty | **vaciar** |

## JUST A SUGGESTION

Look how many words have the same basic form or "root":

| | |
|---|---|
| to erode | **erosionar** |
| eroded | **erosionada** |
| erosion | **la erosión** |

And here's another pattern in Spanish verbs:

| | |
|---|---|
| to cover | **tapar** |
| to uncover | **destapar** |
| | |
| to fold | **doblar** |

| | |
|---|---|
| to unfold | **desdoblar** |
| to plug in | **enchufar** |
| to unplug | **desenchufar** |
| to hook | **enganchar** |
| to unhook | **desenganchar** |

## TRY SOME

Fill in a Spanish verb with an opposite meaning:

| | |
|---|---|
| **enterrar** | _____ |
| **reducir** | _____ |
| **permitir** | _____ |
| **desdoblar** | _____ |
| **comenzar** | _____ |

What do you think these mean?

**dividir**

**separar**

**conectar**

**formular**

**calibrar**

## GRAMMAR TIME

In order to express your thoughts in Spanish, you'll need to learn as many "verb tenses" as possible. We'll start with the "present progressive" tense because it refers to what's happening <u>right now</u>.  The present progressive is similar to our "-ing" form in English. Simply change the base verb ending slightly, and then combine the new form with the four forms of the verb "**estar**" (**estoy, está, están, estamos**). The "**ar**" verbs change to "**ando**", while the "**er**" and "**ir**" verbs become "**iendo**".   Study these examples:

| | |
|---|---|
| to walk | **camin<u>ar</u>** |
| walking | **camin<u>ando</u>** |
| We're walking to work. | **Estamos caminando al trabajo.** |

| | |
|---|---|
| to eat | **com<u>er</u>** |
| eating | **com<u>iendo</u>** |
| The boss is eating. | **El jefe está comiendo.** |

| | |
|---|---|
| to write | **escrib<u>ir</u>** |
| writing | **escrib<u>iendo</u>** |
| I'm writing the number. | **Estoy escribiendo el número.** |

JUST A SUGGESTION

Learn the differences between the <u>affirmative</u>, <u>negative</u>, and <u>interrogative</u> (question) forms in Spanish. Notice the words order in each one:

<u>AFFIRMATIVE</u>

| | |
|---|---|
| The boss is eating. | **El jefe está comiendo.** |

## NEGATIVE

| | |
|---|---|
| The boss isn't eating. | **El jefe no está comiendo.** |

## INTERROGATIVE

| | |
|---|---|
| Is the boss eating? | **¿Está comiendo el jefe?** |

## TRY SOME

Now change these base verbs to the "present progressive" tense:

| | |
|---|---|
| **caminar** | **caminando** |
| **manejar** | _____ |
| **vender** | _____ |
| **recibir** | _____ |
| **seguir** | _____ |

## THE ONE-LINERS

If you usually get lost when someone is speaking Spanish to you, just try to relax and do the best you can with the phrases below. They really help!

| | |
|---|---|
| Do you understand? | **¿Entiende usted?** |
| I don't understand. | **No entiendo.** |
| I comprehend. | **Yo comprendo.** |
| I don't know. | **No sé.** |
| I speak a little Spanish. | **Hablo poquito español.** |
| I'm learning Spanish. | **Estoy aprendiendo español.** |
| More slowly. | **Más despacio.** |
| Thanks for your patience | **Gracias por su paciencia.** |
| What does it mean? | **¿Qué significa?** |
| Again, please. | **Otra vez, por favor** |
| Any questions? | **¿Tiene pregunta?** |
| Is everything OK? | **¿Está bien todo?** |
| Say it in English. | **Dígalo en inglés.** |

| | |
|---|---|
| Letter by letter. | **Letra por letra.** |
| Number by number. | **Número por número.** |
| Word for word. | **Palabra por palabra.** |

CULTURE CLASH

As with every language, Spanish is full of informal idiomatic expressions. Sometimes people on the streets use more "slang" than anything else, so it's always a good idea to ask about words or phrases that you don't understand.

You'll also hear the word "**chingadera**" used a lot on construction sites throughout the Southwest. It is basically equivalent to "whatchamacallit". The difference is that "**chingadera**" is a derivative of a dirty word. Foul language exists in every country, so make it clear that none of it will be allowed as long as you're around. Use this line in Spanish:

Please don't use foul language.

**Por favor, no diga groserías.**

# CHAPTER FOUR

## STRUCTURAL

**El esqueleto estructural**

WORKING WORDS: STRUCTURAL WORK

Interject these words related to structural projects whenever you can:

| | |
|---|---|
| framework | **el entramado** |
| flooring | **la instalación de los suelos** |
| roofing | **la instalación de los tejados** |
| | |
| carpentry | **la carpentería** |
| welding | **la soldadura** |
| masonry | **la mampostería** |
| | |
| mounting | **el montaje** |
| reinforcement | **el refuerzo** |
| support | **el soporte** |

Now be a bit more specific:

Look at (the)…                                  **Mira…**

| | |
|---|---|
| anchor | **el anclaje** |
| backing | **el respaldo** |
| barrier | **la barrera** |
| base | **la base** |
| blocking | **el bloque** |
| brace | **la riostra** |
| buttress | **la contrafrente** |
| cap | **la corona** |
| clip | **la sujetadora** |
| column | **la columna** |
| connector | **la conexión** |
| collar beam | **el travesaño** |
| fascia | **la fachada** |
| footing | **la zapata** |
| girder | **la viga** |
| hanger | **el gancho** |
| header | **la cabecera** |
| hold down | **el soporte** |
| iron fitting | **el herraje** |
| joint | **la unión** |
| joist | **la vigueta** |
| lining | **el encofrado** |
| main beam | **la viga maestra** |
| partition | **el tabique** |
| pillar | **el pilar** |
| pipe | **el tubo** |
| plate | **la placa** |
| post | **el poste** |
| rail | **el riel** |
| rebar | **la varilla** |
| retaining wall | **el muro de contensión** |
| rim joist | **el anillo** |
| saddle | **el asiento** |
| sheer panel | **la cabria** |
| shim | **el calzo** |
| sill | **el antepecho** |
| stirrup | **el estribo** |
| strap | **la cubrejunta** |
| strong wall | **el muro fuerte** |
| strut | **el puntal** |
| stud | **el barrote** |
| tie | **la traviesa** |
| truss | **el armazón** |
| wedge | **la cuña** |
| wrapping | **el forro** |

The words "**la viga**" or "**la vigueta**" can refer to beams, girders, rafters, or joists, depending upon where the speaker is from. Like all technical vocabulary, they're often used with other words to provide more descriptive detail:

| | |
|---|---|
| load-bearing girder | **la viga de carga** |
| reinforcement beam | **la vigueta de refuerzo** |
| temporary support joist | **la viga de soporte provisional** |

## JUST A SUGGESTION

Don't forget those words that were used to lay the foundation:

| | |
|---|---|
| foundation | **el cimiento** |
| slab | **la losa** |
| reinforced concrete | **el hormigón armado** |

## TRY SOME

Draw a picture of the following:

**el tubo**

**la columna**

**el muro**

# WORKING WORDS: MORE STRUCTURAL MATERIALS

Keep referring to any material that you'll need to complete the job. As always, open with a simple command word:

Move (the)…              **Mueva…**

| | |
|---|---|
| raw lumber | **la madera cruda** |
| iron rebar | **la varilla de hierro** |
| steel mesh | **la malla de acero** |
| cement block | **el bloque de hormigón** |
| sheet metal | **la plancha de metal** |

Structural work often includes the use of steel or "**el acero**":

| | |
|---|---|
| corrugated steel | **el acero corrugado** |
| steel beams | **las vigas de acero** |
| steel plates | **las planchas de acero** |
| steel tubes | **los tubos de acero** |
| structural steel | **el acero estructural** |

Describe the shape of each steel beam required:

| | |
|---|---|
| angles | **los angulares** |
| channels | **los canales** |
| I-beams | **los de la forma de la "I"** |
| round beams | **los redondos** |
| square beams | **los cuadrados** |
| T-beams | **los de la forma de la "T"** |

As always, use English to name specialized materials. Note the word order:

| | |
|---|---|
| ABS stabilizers | **Los soportes ABS** |
| Glue-lam beams | **Las vigas Glue-lam** |
| Hardy walls | **Los muros Hardy** |
| OSB boards | **Las tablas OSB** |
| PSL beams | **Las vigas PSL** |
| SDS screws | **Los tornillos SDS** |
| Simpson strong walls | **Los muros Simpson** |
| ST straps | **Las cubrejuntas ST** |
| UBC caps | **Las coronas UBC** |

And memorize these words that refer to things in general:

| | |
|---|---|
| I have (the)… | **Tengo…** |

| | |
|---|---|
| bar | **la barra** |
| bundle | **el bulto** |
| coil | **el rollo** |
| course | **la hilera** |
| panel | **el panel** |
| piece | **la pieza** |
| section | **la sección** |
| sheeting | **la lámina** |
| strip | **la tira** |

JUST A SUGGESTION

There's a good chance these other metals will be needed, too:

| alloy | **la aleación** |
| aluminum | **el aluminio** |
| brass | **el latón** |
| bronze | **el bronce** |
| copper | **el cobre** |
| manganese | **el mangonese** |
| nickel | **el níquel** |
| tin | **el estaño** |
| zinc | **el zinc** |

TRY SOME

Name three different types of metal in Spanish.

What is the difference between "**una barra**" and "**una lámina**"?

Name two different types of steel beams in Spanish.

## WORKING WORDS: MORE EQUIPMENT

Get busy unloading everything you need for the structural project:

We need (the)…    **Necesitamos…**

| | |
|---|---|
| bar bender | la dobladora |
| boom | el aguilón |
| conveyor | la cinta transportadora |
| crane | la grúa |
| cutter | la cortadora |
| driller | la taladra |
| forklift | la carretilla elevadora |
| hoist | el montacargas |
| impact wrench | la llave eléctrica |
| jackhammer | el martillo neumático |
| loader | la cargadora |
| mixer | la mezcladora |
| pulley | la polea |
| screw gun | la pistola de tornillos |
| track | el carril |
| wheelbarrow | la carretilla |
| winch | el torno |

Where's (the)…    **¿Dónde está…?**

| | |
|---|---|
| chisel | el cincel |
| hammer | el martillo |
| mallet | el mazo |
| pick | el pico |
| saw | la sierra |
| shovel | la pala |
| sledge | la almádena |

These smaller items are also required:

Bring (the)…                    **Traiga…**

| | |
|---|---|
| bolt | **el perno** |
| bracket | **la ménsula** |
| clamp | **la abrazadora** |
| clip | **la sujetadora** |
| connector | **la conexión** |
| coupling | **el enganche** |
| dowel | **la espiga** |
| fastener | **el trabe** |
| fitting | **el acoplamiento** |
| lag bolt | **el perno grande** |
| nail | **el clavo** |
| nut | **la tuerca** |
| pin | **la clavija** |
| rivet | **el remache** |
| screw | **el tornillo** |
| staple | **la grapa** |
| washer | **la arandela** |

When welding is involved, be sure you know what everyone is saying:

| | | |
|---|---|---|
| welding | **la soldadura** | **Trabaja en soldadura.** |
| arc welder | **el soldador eléctrico** | **Tiene el soldador eléctrico.** |
| spot welding | **la soldadura en puntos** | **Sabe la soldadura en puntos.** |

A welder uses a variety of specialized tools and equipment. As the metal framework is being set in place, listen for the following:

| | |
|---|---|
| bar | **la barra** |
| gas | **el gas** |
| grating | **el enrejado** |
| lead | **el plomo** |
| mesh | **la malla** |
| paste | **la pasta** |
| sheet | **la plancha** |
| wire | **el alambre** |

| He needs (the) | Necesita... |
|---|---|
| arm | el brazo |
| cable | el cable |
| clamp | las pinzas |
| electrode holder | el portaelectrodos |
| file | la lima |
| hacksaw | la sierra de arco |
| hammer | el martillo |
| hose | la manguera |
| lead line | el cable de conexión |
| mallet | el mazo |
| measuring tape | la cinta métrica |
| mold | el molde |
| nozzle | la boquilla |
| rod | la varilla |
| spacer | el separador |
| tank | el tanque |
| tongs | las tenazas |
| torch | la antorcha |
| transformer | el transformador |
| valve | la válvula |
| vice | el torno |
| wire brush | el cepillo de alambre |

| How's (the)... | ¿Cómo está...? |
|---|---|
| acetylene | el acetileno |
| alloy | la aleación |
| amperage | el amperaje |
| arc | el arqueo |
| $CO_2$ | el dióxido de carbon |
| oxygen | el oxígeno |
| voltage | el voltaje |

Look at (the)...          **Mira...**

| | |
|---|---|
| angle | **el ángulo** |
| edge | **el borde** |
| middle | **el centro** |
| position | **la posición** |
| side | **el lado** |
| tip | **la punta** |

Check (the)...          **Revise...**

| | |
|---|---|
| control | **el control** |
| current | **el corriente** |
| drippings | **el chorro** |
| flame | **la llama** |
| heat | **el calor** |
| pressure | **la presión** |
| scrap | **el desecho** |
| sparks | **las chispas** |

Study (the)...          **Estudie...**

| | |
|---|---|
| blueprint | **el cianotipo** |
| drawing | **el dibujo** |
| layout | **el diseño** |
| plan | **el plano** |
| specs | **las especificaciones** |

## JUST A SUGGESTION

When it comes to welding, it's always safety first:

| Put on (the)… | **Póngase…** |
|---|---|
| helmet | **la capucha protectora** |
| apron | **el mandil** |
| gloves | **los guantes** |
| shin guard | **las espinilleras** |
| safety glasses | **las gafas** |

TRY SOME

Translate into Spanish:

Bring the tongs and the mallet.

Bring the lumber and the rebar.

Bring the bolt and the washer.

## WORKING WORDS: ON THE JOB SITE

As you walk around, identify everyone who's been working on the project.
Begin with those you already know:

| Ask (the)… | Pregunte a… |
|---|---|
| contractor | **el contratista** |
| laborer | **el obrero** |
| truck driver | **el camionero** |
| designer | **el diseñador** |
| technician | **el técnico** |
| architect | **el arquitecto** |
| engineer | **el ingeniero** |
| plumber | **el fontanero** |
| electrician | **el electricista** |
| mason | **el albañil** |
| welder | **el soldadero** |
| machine operator | **el maquinista** |

As the job moves forward, discuss details with your crew:

| Where's (the)…? | ¿Dónde está…? |
|---|---|
| duct | **el conducto** |
| hole | **el hueco** |
| opening | **la abertura** |
| pit | **el hoyo** |
| slot | **la ranura** |

| The hole is for the… | El hueco es para… |
|---|---|
| door | **la puerta** |
| window | **la ventana** |
| stairs | **las escaleras** |

| It's for (the)… | Es para… |
|---|---|
| air conditioning | **el aire acondicionado** |
| cabling | **el cableado** |
| drainage tank | **el tanque de drenaje** |
| electrical wiring | **la instalación eléctrica** |
| gas line | **la linea de gas** |
| heating | **la calefacción** |
| insulation | **el aislamiento** |
| lighting | **la iluminación** |
| plumbing | **la tubería** |
| septic system | **el sistema séptico** |
| ventilation | **la ventilación** |
| waste pipe | **el desagüe** |

Structures are built upon flooring, so practice these key words today:

| subfloor | **el subpiso** |
|---|---|
| ground floor | **el primer piso** |
| second floor | **la segunda planta** |

Getting the correct measurement is the key to success, so take down what you need from this important selection:

| What's the…? | ¿Cuál es…? |
|---|---|
| cutting | **el corte** |
| elevation | **la altura** |
| flexibility | **la flexibilidad** |
| gauge | **el calibrador** |
| load | **la carga** |
| measurement | **la medida** |
| position | **la posición** |
| shape | **la forma** |
| size | **el tamaño** |
| strength | **la fuerza** |
| torque | **la torción** |
| weight | **el peso** |

The measurement… **La medida…**

…isn't exact. **…no es exacta.**

…must be this high. **…tiene que ser de esta altura.**

…is off by… **…le falta …**

I'm explaining (the)… **Estoy explicando…**

regulation **el reglamentario**

certification **el certificado**

requirement **el requisito**

Precautions must be taken to protect any structure:

| It's protected from… | Está protegido de… |
|---|---|
| corrosion | **la corrosión** |
| dry rot | **la podredumbre** |
| fire | **el incendio** |
| hurricane | **el huricán** |
| ice | **el hielo** |
| rain | **la lluvia** |
| rust | **el óxido** |
| snow | **la nieve** |
| storm | **la tormenta** |
| wind | **el viento** |

## JUST A SUGGESTION

Continue to combine words to create key command phrases:

| Build the forms. | **Construye los moldes.** |
|---|---|
| Install the steel. | **Instale el acero.** |
| Dig the trench. | **Excave la zanja.** |
| Use the stakes. | **Use las estacas.** |
| Cut the braces. | **Corte las riostras.** |

## TRY SOME

What do you think these words mean?

**zonas sísmicas**

**condiciónes geolólicas**

**diferencias climáticas**

# WORKING WORDS: DESCRIBING THE JOB

It's time to describe what you need done. Warm up with words that are the same in English:

**interior**

**exterior**

**lateral**

**frontal**

**diagonal**

**rectangular**

**triangular**

**hexagonal**

**perpendicular**

Now describe everything in front of you by using words you learned before:

| small | **chico** | **La viga chica** |
|-------|-----------|-------------------|
| medium | **mediano** | **El poste mediano** |
| large | **grande** | **La vigueta grande** |

Group them in sets of opposites:

It's...                    Es/Está...

| | | | |
|---|---|---|---|
| long | **largo** | thick | **grueso** |
| short | **corto** | thin | delgado |
| smooth | **liso** | loose | **flojo** |
| rough | áspero | tight | apretado |

| | | | |
|---|---|---|---|
| light | **ligero** | partial | **parcial** |
| heavy | **pesado** | complete | **completo** |
| solid | **sólido** | even | **igual** |
| hollow | **hueco** | uneven | **desigual** |
| level | **nivel** | temporary | **provisional** |
| pitched | **inclinado** | permanent | **permanente** |

Can you describe all the structural work? Note how many descriptions end with "**-ado**":

| | |
|---|---|
| sealed | **sellado** |
| secure | **seguro** |
| pointed | **en punta** |
| reinforced | **reforzado** |
| adjustable | **ajustable** |
| straight | **recto** |
| durable | **duradero** |
| galvanized | **galvanizado** |
| rolled | **enrollado** |
| cut | **cortado** |
| pre-cut | **pre-cortado** |
| hardened | **endurecido** |
| finished | **acabado** |
| semi-finished | **semi-acabado** |
| fabricated | **fabricado** |
| laminated | **laminado** |
| forged | **fundido** |
| perforated | **perforado** |
| threaded | **roscado** |
| protected | **protegido** |
| embedded | **incrustado** |
| spaced | **espaciado** |
| attached | **conectado** |
| rust-proof | **inoxidable** |
| coated | **bañado** |
| uniform | **uniforme** |
| balanced | **balanceado** |
| stable | **estable** |
| flat | **llano** |
| round | **redondo** |
| squared | **cuadrado** |
| shaped | **formado** |
| welded | **soldado** |
| butted | **a tope** |
| symmetrical | **simétrico** |

Notice how all the vocabulary fits together:

| | |
|---|---|
| side beam support | **el soporte de la viga lateral** |
| welded metal post | **el poste de metal fundido** |
| reinforced wood stud | **el barrote de madera reforzado** |

JUST A SUGGESTION

Many expressions in construction include descriptive words. Practice each as one long phrase:

maximum strength      **la fuerza máxima**

double plate      **la placa doble**

steel pipe column      **la columna tubular de acero**

TRY SOME

Find the opposite:

**llano**      _____

**parcial**      _____

**áspero**      _____

**igual**      _____

**chico**      _____

WORKING WORDS: ON-SITE ACTIONS

The following are "verbs" related to the structural phase of construction. To practice, stick in the words that you like best:

| It needs… | **Necesita…** |
|---|---|
| to interlace | **entrelazar** |
| to withstand | **aguantar** |
| to cross | **cruzar** |
| to attach | **conectar** |
| to support | **soportar** |
| to shape | **formar** |
| to overlap | **superponerse** |

| You need… | **Usted necesita…** |
|---|---|
| to adjust | **ajustar** |
| to insert | **meter** |
| to mount | **amontar** |
| to weld | **soldar** |
| to build | **construir** |
| to erect | **erigir** |
| to raise | **levantar** |
| to lower | **bajar** |
| to add | **añadir** |
| to remove | **quitar** |
| to bend | **doblar** |
| to support | **soportar** |
| to hold | **sostener** |
| to lean | **inclinar** |

| We need… | Necesitamos… |
|---|---|
| to allow | **dejar** |
| to block | **poner bloques** |
| to bore | **taladrar** |
| to crown | **poner coronas** |
| to cut | **cortar** |
| to enclose | **encerrar** |
| to glue | **pegar con pegamento** |
| to line up | **alinear** |
| to nail | **clavar** |
| to plate | **poner placas** |
| to plumb | **aplomar** |
| to screw | **tornillar** |
| to sight | **fijarse** |
| to snap line | **marcar con tiza** |
| to spread | **esparcir** |
| to stagger | **alterar** |
| to tie | **amarrar** |
| to tighten | **apretar** |
| to toenail | **clavar a un ángulo** |

And notice the difference between these two phrases:

| to straighten vertically | **enderezar** |
|---|---|
| to straighten horizontally | **poner recto** |

## JUST A SUGGESTION

This expression is used with verbs to comment on future activity:

| It's going… | **Va a…** |
|---|---|
| to twist | **torcer** |
| to fall | **caer** |
| to move | **mover** |
| to break | **romper** |
| to sag | **hundirse** |

## TRY SOME

Follow the pattern with these action words:

| **levantar postes** | **Estamos levantando postes.** | We're raising posts. |
|---|---|---|
| **mover bloques** | _____ | _____ |
| **cortar varilla** | _____ | _____ |
| **soldar acero** | _____ | _____ |
| **alterar estacas** | _____ | _____ |

## GRAMMAR TIME

In Chapter Three, we learned the "present progressive" tense, which refers to what's happening right now. Now we'll look at the "simple present" tense which refers to what happens every day. Remember that action words or basic "verbs" in Spanish end in "**ar**", "**er**" or "**ir**":

| | |
|---|---|
| TO SPEAK | **HABLAR** |
| I speak | **hablo** |
| you speak; he, she speaks | **habla** |
| you (plural), they speak | **hablan** |
| we speak | **hablamos** |

| | |
|---|---|
| TO EAT | **COMER** |
| I eat | **como** |
| you eat; he, she eats | **come** |
| you (plural), they eat | **comen** |
| we eat | **comemos** |

| | |
|---|---|
| TO WRITE | **ESCRIBIR** |
| I write | **escribo** |
| you write; he, she writes | **escribe** |
| you (plural), they write | **escriben** |
| we write | **escribimos** |

Notice how the "**ar**" verb, "**hablar**", doesn't change the same as the "**er**" and "**ir**" verbs! This tip will be helpful as you pick up more action forms later on. By the way, here are two important "irregular" verbs in Spanish. They need to be memorized:

| **querer** | to want | | |
|---|---|---|---|
| **quiero** | I want | I want the nails. | **Quiero los clavos.** |
| **quiere** | You want; He, She wants | | |
| **quieren** | You (plural), they want | | |
| **queremos** | We want | | |

| **poder** | to be able to (can) | | |
|---|---|---|---|
| **puedo** | I can | I can understand. | **Puedo entender.** |
| **puede** | You, He, She can | | |
| **pueden** | You (plural), They can | | |
| **podemos** | We can | | |

## JUST A SUGGESTION

Some irregular verbs are extremely useful in construction work.  Notice how the present tense of "to go" in Spanish can also be used to refer to future time:

| TO GO | **IR** | | |
|---|---|---|---|
| I go | **voy** | I go home. | **Voy a mi casa.** |
| you go; he, she goes | **va** | | |
| you (plural), they go | **van** | | |
| we go | **vamos** | | |

To talk about the future, all you add is a basic verb:

I'm going to finish.                    **Voy a terminar.**

| | |
|---|---|
| <u>He's going to unload.</u> | **Va a descargar.** |
| <u>We're going to weld.</u> | **Vamos a soldar.** |

TRY SOME

Change these sentences from the "present progressive" tense to the "simple present" tense. Look at the example:

| | | | |
|---|---|---|---|
| I'm working. | **Estoy trabajando.** | I work. | <u>**Trabajo.**</u> |
| I'm driving. | **Estoy manejando.** | I drive. | _____ |
| I'm cutting. | **Estoy cortando.** | I cut. | _____ |
| I'm speaking. | **Estoy hablando.** | I speak. | _____ |

THE ONE-LINERS

One of the most useful construction phrases in any language are those that direct others to a specific location. Think of all the ways these one-liners will come in handy:

It's...                                      **Está...**

| | |
|---|---|
| back to back | **de espalda con espalda** |
| downhill | **cuesta abajo** |
| from the ground up | **del suelo hacia arriba** |
| inside out | **al revés** |
| right side up | **boca arriba** |
| side by side | **al lado** |
| uphill | **cuesta arriba** |
| upside down | **boca abajo** |

| In, on, or at (the)… | En… |
|---|---|
| back part | **la parte trasera** |
| bottom part | **la parte abajo** |
| corner | **la esquina** |
| edge | **el borde** |
| end | **el fin** |
| front part | **la parte delantera** |
| middle | **el medio** |
| side | **el lado** |
| tip | **la punta** |
| top part | **la parte arriba** |

TRY SOME

Translate into Spanish:

It's upside down.    _____

Where is the place?    _____

Look at the edge.    _____

CULTURE CLASH

If you get "stuck" in the middle of a phrase or sentence, don't be afraid to send messages using hand gestures or facial expressions. Body signals are used frequently in conversations throughout the Spanish-speaking world. And remember, there's nothing wrong with repeating your message several times until you're understood!

# CHAPTER FIVE

## FRAMING

### El armazón del edificio

## WORKING WORDS: WOOD FRAMING

Here are some common words in the world of wood framing:

| | |
|---|---|
| lumber | **el madero** |
| carpenter | **el carpintero** |
| plans | **los planos** |
| | |
| structure | **la construcción** |
| frame | **el marco** |
| support | **el apoyo** |
| | |
| floor | **el piso** |
| wall | **la pared** |
| roof | **el tejado** |
| | |
| hammer | **el martillo** |
| nails | **los clavos** |
| saw | **la sierra** |

Keep going:

| We use (the)… | Usamos… |
|---|---|
| backing | **el respaldo** |
| beam | **la viga** |
| board | **la tabla** |
| brace | **la riostra** |
| cap | **la corona** |
| collar beam | **el travesaño** |
| cripple | **el refuerzo** |
| expansion bolt | **el perno de expansión** |
| fire block | **el cortafuego** |
| hanger | **el gancho** |
| header | **la cabecera** |
| hold down | **el soporte** |
| jack | **el cabrio corto** |
| joint | **la unión** |
| joist | **la vigueta** |
| lag bolt | **el tirafondo** |
| lap block | **el bloque de revestimiento** |
| ledger | **el larguero** |
| panel | **el panel** |
| post | **el poste** |
| rafter | **el cabrio** |
| ridge | **el caballete** |
| sill | **el antepecho** |
| sole plate | **la placa de solera** |
| strap | **la cubrejunta** |
| stud | **el montante** |
| tie | **la traviesa** |
| trimmer | **el moldeador** |
| truss | **la armadura** |

Add words to provide better detail:

| | |
|---|---|
| hip post | **el poste de la lima** |
| top plate | **la placa superior** |

| | |
|---|---|
| floor joist | **la vigueta del piso** |

Many of the words used in framing are also used in structural work:

| | |
|---|---|
| bearing wall | **el muro de carga** |
| rake wall | **el muro de tope inclinado** |
| shear wall | **el muro sismorresistente** |

The word "board" in Spanish has a variety of translations, but is often simply identified by its size:

| | |
|---|---|
| Bring me a 2 by 6. | **Tráigame una dos por seis.** |
| Where are the 16-footers? | **¿Dónde están las de dieciséis?** |
| I need more 4 by 4's. | **Necesito más cuatro por cuatros.** |

Here are other words that refer to wood:

| | |
|---|---|
| large board | **el tablón** |
| long beam | **el larguero** |
| rail | **el riel** |
| raw timber | **la madera cruda** |
| round timber | **el rollizo** |
| wood block | **el bloque** |

There are several types of wood used in construction. These are from nature:

| | |
|---|---|
| birch | **el abedul** |
| cedar | **el cedro** |
| cherry | **el cerezo** |
| fir | **el abeto** |
| mahogany | **el caoba** |
| maple | **el arce** |
| oak | **el roble** |
| pine | **el pino** |
| redwood | **la secoya** |
| teak | **la teca** |

| It's… | **Es…** |
|---|---|
| hard wood | **la madera brava** |
| soft wood | **la madera blanda** |

These are man-made:

| plywood | **la madera contrachapada** |
|---|---|
| pressed wood | **la madera prensada** |
| wood composite | **la madera compuesta** |

JUST A SUGGESTION

Although wood framing is common, some buildings are constructed of something else:

It's made of...                    **Está hecho de...**

| | |
|---|---|
| block | **el bloque** |
| brick | **el ladrillo** |
| cement | **el cemento** |
| iron | **el hierro** |
| aluminum | **el aluminio** |
| steel | **el acero** |
| stone | **la piedra** |

TRY SOME

Which word would be the best match?

**el acero y _____**          **la piedra**

**el cabrio y _____**         **el clavo**

**el ladrillo y _____**       **el respaldo**

**el refuerzo y _____**       **el hierro**

**el martillo y _____**       **el caballete**

WORKING WORDS: FRAMER'S TOOLS

Framers use a variety of tools, so spend some time with the list below:

| Where's (the)...? | ¿Dónde está...? |
|---|---|
| air compressor | **el compresor de aire** |
| carpenter's glue | **el adhesivo** |
| caulking | **el sellador** |
| chalk | **la tiza** |
| chisel | **el cincel** |
| drill | **el taladro** |
| extension cord | **la extension eléctrica** |
| framing square | **la escuadra** |
| hammer | **el martillo** |
| hand saw | **el serrucho** |
| ladder | **la escalera** |
| level | **el nivel** |
| mallet | **el mazo** |
| marker | **el marcador** |
| measuring tape | **la cinta métrica** |
| pencil | **el lápiz** |
| pliers | **el alicates** |
| plumb bob | **la plomada** |
| plumb line | **el hilo de plomada** |
| ratchet | **el trinquete** |
| router | **la ranuradora** |
| sander | **la lijadora** |
| screwdriver | **el desarmador** |
| shears | **las tijeras** |
| transit | **la niveladora electrónica** |
| utility knife | **la navaja** |
| vice | **la prensa** |
| wrench | **la llave inglesa** |

These three tools are also in high demand in carpentry:

| nail puller | **el sacaclavos** |
|---|---|
| pry bar | **la pata de cabra** |
| flat bar | **la palanca** |

Now just focus on the different kinds of saws:

| | |
|---|---|
| hand saw | **el serrucho** |
| hack saw | **el serrucho para cortar metal** |
| band saw | **la sierra de cinta** |
| skill saw | **la sierra circular** |
| jig saw | **la sierra de vaivén** |
| reciprocating saw (sawzall) | **la sierra alternativa** |
| miter saw | **la sierra de corte angular** |
| scroll saw | **la sierra caladora** |
| table saw | **la sierra de banco** |

## JUST A SUGGESTION

Continue to build phrases around a single word:

| | |
|---|---|
| chalk box | **la cajita de tiza** |
| chalk line | **la cuerda de tiza** |
| chalk powder | **el polvo de tiza** |

## TRY SOME

**¿Cuál es la diferencia entre…?**

**la tiza y el lápiz**

**el desarmador y la llave inglesa**

**la sierra circular y la sierra alternativa**

## WORKING WORDS: MORE TOOLS AND EQUIPMENT

Some Spanish workers will say "**pistola**" when referring to a power tool, while others might call it a "**neumática**". Notice these examples:

| | |
|---|---|
| nail gun | **la pistola de clavos** or **la clavadora neumática** |
| screw gun | **la pistola de tornillos** or **la atornilladera neumática** |
| staple gun | **la pistola de grapas** or **la engrapadora neumática** |

| We need (the)… | **Necesitamos…** |
|---|---|
| work bench | **el tablero de trabajo** |
| scaffolding | **el andamio** |
| sawhorses | **los caballetes** |

| | |
|---|---|
| crane | **la grúa** |
| conveyor | **la cinta transportadora** |
| forklift | **la carretilla elevadora** |
| flatbed | **el camión plataforma** |
| impact wrench | **la llave eléctrica** |

These smaller items are important, too:

| Look for (the)… | Busque… |
| --- | --- |
| bit | la broca |
| blade | la hoja |
| bolt | el perno |
| bracket | la ménsula |
| clamp | la abrazadora |
| clip | la sujetadora |
| nail | el clavo |
| nut | la tuerca |
| pin | la clavija |
| screw | el tornillo |
| staple | la grapa |
| washer | la arandela |

There are several kinds of nails, so be careful when you speak:

| I want (the)… | Quiero… |
| --- | --- |
| barbed nail | el clavo afilado |
| box nail | el clavo para madera |
| casing nail | el clavo de cabeza perdida |
| finishing nail | el clavo sin cabeza |
| roofing nail | el clavo para tejado |
| siding nail | el clavo para revestimiento |
| spiral nail | el clavo espiral |

Remember that framing is packed with specialized vocabulary:

| | |
| --- | --- |
| masonary nails | los clavos de mampostería |
| "J" bolts | los pernos "J" |
| decking screws | los tornillos de terraza |

## JUST A SUGGESTION

Keep it simple when you refer to nails or screws:

| | |
|---|---|
| I need more sixteens. | **Necesito mas clavos de dieciséis.** |
| Look for the three-eighths. | **Necesito los tornillos de tres octavos.** |
| The bolts are four inches long. | **Los pernos son cuatro pulgadas de largo.** |

## TRY SOME

How many kinds of scews can you name in Spanish?

How many kinds of nails?

How many pneumatic tools?

## WORKING WORDS: ON THE JOB SITE

Review these other words as you layout the project. They are the basic parts of your job site:

| Check (the)… | Revise… |
|---|---|
| cut yard | **la área para cortar** |
| entrance | **la entrada** |
| exit | **la salida** |

| | |
|---|---|
| ceiling | **el techo** |
| door | **la puerta** |
| floor | **el piso** |
| roof | **el tejado** |
| room | **el cuarto** |
| window | **la ventana** |

Now, be a bit more specific:

The _____ goes here.          _____ **va aquí.**

| | |
|---|---|
| deck | **la terraza** |
| door way | **el portal** |
| flooring | **la solería** |
| stairway | **la escalera** |
| window frame | **el marco para la ventana** |

As the job moves forward, discuss each detail with the crew:

This space is for (the)…          **Este espacio es para…**

| | |
|---|---|
| air conditioning | **el aire acondicionado** |
| bay | **el bache** |
| chimney | **la chimenea** |
| drain | **el drenaje** |
| duct | **el conducto** |
| electrical wiring | **la instalación eléctrica** |
| elevator | **el ascensor** |
| gas line | **la línea de gas** |
| heating | **la calefacción** |
| insulation | **el aislamiento** |
| lighting | **la iluminación** |
| plumbing | **la tubería** |
| skylight | **el tragaluz** |
| ventilation | **la ventilación** |

These words primarily focus on the stairs:

| | |
|---|---|
| landing | **el descanso** |
| railing | **las barandas** |
| stairs | **las escaleras** |
| stairwell | **la caja de la escalera** |
| step | **el escalón** |

Are you cleaning up as you move along?

Pick up (the)…          **Recoja…**

| | |
|---|---|
| debris | **los escombros** |
| rest· | **los restos** |
| sawdust | **el serrín** |
| scrap | **los desperdicios** |
| trash | **la basura** |

It's time to use commands with key vocabulary:

Build (the)…          **Construya…**

| | |
|---|---|
| arch | **el arco** |
| barrier | **la barrera** |
| base | **la base** |
| bridging | **el puntal** |
| overhang | **el voladizo** |
| partition | **el tabique** |

When you give commands as a framer, add words to create new phrases:

| Put (the)… | Ponga… |
|---|---|
| double | **doble** |
| double header | **la doble cabecera** |
| double beam | **la doble viga** |
| upper | **superior** |
| upper support | **el apoyo superior** |
| upper fire block | **el contrafuego superior** |
| underground | **subterráneo** |
| underground wall | **el muro subterráneo** |
| underground post | **el poste subterráneo** |

You should already know these:

| Look at (the)… | Mire… |
|---|---|
| back | **la parte atrás** |
| corner | **la esquina** |
| edge | **el borde** |
| front | **la parte adelante** |
| middle | **el centro** |
| side | **el lado** |

To avoid mistakes, don't forget anything:

| What's (the)…? | ¿Cuál es…? |
|---|---|
| pattern | **el patrón** |
| style | **el estilo** |
| design | **el diseño** |

## JUST A SUGGESTION

If possible, learn one-liners in pairs, such as words with opposite meanings:

| clockwise | **según las agujas del reloj** |
|---|---|
| counter clockwise | **en contra las agujas del reloj** |

| apart | **separados** |
|---|---|
| together | **juntos** |

| only one side | **solamente un lado** |
|---|---|
| both sides | **los dos lados** |

## TRY SOME

Find the opposites:

**entrada** _____

**separado** _____

**adelante** _____

174

Translate into Spanish:

This space is for the electrical wiring.

Pick up the scrap.

What's the pattern?

## WORKING WORDS: DESCRIBING THE JOB

When referring to wood, most descriptions end in the letter "**a**":

| It's very… | **Es muy…** | It's not… | **No es…** |
|---|---|---|---|
| long | **larga** | short | **corta** |
| thick | **gruesa** | thin | **delgada** |
| light | **ligera** | heavy | **pesada** |

This time, use "**Está**", which indicates more of a temporary condition:

| It's very… | **Está muy…** | It's not… | **No está…** |
|---|---|---|---|
| loose | **floja** | tight | **apretada** |
| smooth | **lisa** | rough | **áspera** |
| even | **igual** | uneven | **desigual** |

| It's… | Es/Está… |
|---|---|
| attached | **conectado** |
| balanced | **balanceado** |
| braced | **arriostrada** |
| cut | **cortado** |
| finished | **acabado** |
| fireproof | **incombustible** |
| flat | **llano** |
| flush | **al ras de** |
| framed | **armado** |
| graded | **clasificado** |
| inverted | **volteado** |
| laminated | **laminado** |
| overlapping | **sobrepuesto** |
| plumb | **nivel** |
| pre-cut | **pre-cortado** |
| pre-fabricated | **pre-fabricado** |
| reinforced | **reforzado** |
| round | **redondo** |
| sealed | **sellado** |
| secure | **seguro** |
| square | **cuadrado** |
| stable | **estable** |
| straight | **recto** |
| tongue & groove | **lingüeta y ranura** |
| treated | **tratado** |
| uniform | **uniforme** |

Here's how you describe lumber in further detail:

| There are… | Hay… |
|------------|------|
| bumps | **bultos** |
| cracks | **grietas** |
| gaps | **boquetes** |
| holes | **huecos** |
| knots | **nudos** |
| marks | **marcas** |
| splits | **rajadas** |
| stains | **manchas** |
| twists | **torcidos** |

| It's… | Está… |
|-------|-------|
| broken | **rota** |
| dirty | **sucia** |
| rotten | **podrida** |
| warped | **combada** |
| swollen | **hinchada** |
| wet | **mojada** |

Getting the correct measurement is the key to success, so take down what you need from this important selection:

Give me (the)…       **Deme…**

| | |
|---|---|
| angle | **el ángulo** |
| cutting | **el corte** |
| depth | **la profundidad** |
| difference | **la diferencia** |
| gauge | **el calibre** |
| grade | **la calificación** |
| height | **la altura** |
| length | **el largo** |
| measurement | **la medida** |
| number | **el número** |
| ratio | **la relación** |
| size | **el tamaño** |
| sum | **la suma** |
| width | **el ancho** |

And to be technical, follow this pattern:

| | |
|---|---|
| linear feet | **los pies lineales** |
| square inches | **las pulgadas cuadradas** |
| cubic centimeters | **los centímetros cúbicos** |

## JUST A SUGGESTION

Framers often toss in words with very specific meanings:

It has (the)…       **Tiene…**

| | |
|---|---|
| ring | **el anillo** |
| flange | **la ala** |

| | |
|---|---|
| loop | **el lazo** |
| bend | **el recado** |
| slit | **la muesca** |
| groove | **la ranura** |
| hoop | **el cincho** |

TRY SOME

Underline one word in each group that doesn't belong with the others:

**larga, delgada, grieta**

**torcido, redondo, cuadrado**

**combada, medida, hinchada**

## WORKING WORDS: ON-SITE ACTIONS

The following Spanish "verbs" often work well as parts of "action phrases".
Picture a scenario as you practice aloud:

| You have to… | **Tiene que…** |
|---|---|
| to cut | **cortar** |
| to glue | **encolar** |
| to join | **unir** |
| to nail | **clavar** |
| to remove | **sacar** |
| to screw in | **atornillar** |

| | |
|---|---|
| to stabilize | **estabilizar** |
| to support | **apoyar** |
| to tighten | **apretar** |
| to toenail | **clavar en ángulo** |
| to pound | **golpear** |
| to hold | **sostener** |
| to tack | **fijar** |
| to wrap | **forrar** |
| to add | **añadir** |
| to alter | **modificar** |
| to attach | **conectar** |
| to bypass | **evitar** |

Continue talking, but now try adding a key vocabulary word:

| We need to… | **Necesitamos…** | |
|---|---|---|
| to adjust | **ajustar** | **el cabrio** |
| to insert | **meter** | **el perno** |
| to mount | **amontar** | **la pieza** |
| to stack | **apilar** | _____ |
| to level | **nivelar** | _____ |
| to build | **construir** | _____ |
| to erect | **erigir** | _____ |
| to raise | **levantar** | |
| to lower | **bajar** | |
| to line up | **alinear** | |

| | |
|---|---|
| to enclose | **encerrar** |
| to plate | **poner placa** |
| to bore | **taladrar hueco** |
| to make | **hacer** |
| to sort | **clasificar** |
| to snap a line | **marcar la línea** |
| to clean | **limpiar** |
| to redo | **volver a hacer** |
| to sharpen | **afilar** |

With the following, talk about things that go wrong:

| It's going … | **Se va a…** |
|---|---|
| to twist | **torcer** |
| to fall over | **tumbar** |
| to move | **mover** |
| to slip | **resbalar** |
| to break | **romper** |
| to sag | **hundir** |
| to fall | **caer** |
| to spin | **girar** |
| to overlap | **superponer** |
| to sight | **fijarse** |
| to turn | **voltear** |

TRY SOME

Insert a verb from the lists above:

**La viga se va a _____ .**

**El capintero tiene que _____ la tabla.**

**Usted no necesita _____ la vigueta.**

GRAMMAR TIME

There are two ways to chat about future events in Spanish. Generally, all you do is add a few letters at the end of a basic verb. As you practice the following pattern, try to exaggerate the accented syllable:

| to speak | **hablar** |
|----------|------------|
| I'll speak | **hablaré** |
| You'll, He'll, She'll speak | **hablará** |
| You'll (pl.), They'll speak | **hablarán** |
| We'll speak | **hablaremos** |

| to eat | **comer** |
|--------|-----------|
| I'll eat | **comeré** |
| You'll, He'll, She'll eat | **comerá** |
| You'll (pl.), They'll eat | **comerán** |
| We'll eat | **comeremos** |

| | |
|---|---|
| <u>to write</u> | **escribir** |
| I'll write | **escribiré** |
| You'll, He'll, She'll write | **escribirá** |
| You'll (pl.),They'll write | **escribirán** |
| We'll write | **escribiremos** |

## JUST A SUGGESTION

You'll need to learn any "irregular" ones on your own:

| | |
|---|---|
| <u>to put</u> | **poner** |
| I'll put | **pondré** |

| | |
|---|---|
| <u>to come</u> | **venir** |
| He'll come | **vendrá** |

| | |
|---|---|
| <u>to say</u> | **decir** |
| They'll say | **dirán** |

## TRY SOME

Now, using the same formula, give these a try:

**trabajar**

_____

_____

_____

_____

**vender**

_____

_____

_____

**ir**

_____

_____

_____

_____

## THE ONE-LINERS

You may know how to greet people in Spanish, but are you ready for their response? This is what most folks say when you ask them how they're doing:

| I am... | **Estoy...** |
|---------|--------------|
| fine | **bien** |
| very well | **muy bien** |
| O.K. | **regular** |
| bored | **aburrido/a** |
| happy | **contento/a** |
| nervous | **nervioso/a** |

| | |
|---|---|
| sad | **triste** |
| sick | **enfermo/a** |
| surprised | **sorprendido/a** |
| tired | **cansado/a** |
| upset | **enojado/a** |
| worried | **preocupado/a** |
| afraid | **asustado/a** |
| frustrated | **frustrado/a** |
| uncomfortable | **incómodo/a** |
| confused | **confundido/a** |
| embarrassed | **turbado/a** |

## CULTURE CLASH

Most of Latin America is Roman Catholic, so you may notice the religious influence during your association with some Hispanics during a crisis. Using God, **Dios** (dee-'ohs) in conversation, attending daily Mass, **la misa** (lah 'mee-sah) or observing Catholic traditions are simple signs of their devout faith. Remember that respect and sensitivity are always in demand when topics center on cultural and religious beliefs or personal opinions.

# CHAPTER SIX

ROOFING

**La techumbre**

(lah teh-'choom-breh)

WORKING WORDS: THE ROOF

In Spanish, the "roof" is often called **el techo** or **el tejado**, although **el techo** may also refer to the ceiling. Although "*el rufero*" is used in Spanglish, the best translation for "roofer" is **el instalador de tejados**. A roofer's vocabulary includes the following:

| | |
|---|---|
| covering | **la cubierta** |
| framing | **el armazón** |
| flashing | **el tapajuntas** |
| coating | **la capa** |
| | |
| slope | **la cuesta** |
| edge | **el borde** |
| deck | **la terraza** |
| overhang | **el voladizo** |
| | |
| gable | **el aguilón** |
| ridge | **el caballete** |
| valley | **la limahoya** |
| hip | **la limatesa** |
| | |
| shingle | **la teja de asfalto** |
| shake | **el listón** |
| slate | **la pizarra** |
| tile | **la teja** |

There are various roofing projects, so this is only a sample:

It's...                              **Es...**

new roofing                          **la techumbre nueva**

re-roofing                           **el reemplazo de la techumbre**

built-up roofing                     **la techumbre urbanizada**

rolled roofing                       **la techumbre del rodillo**

It has a _____ roof.                **Tiene un techo _____.**

| | |
|---|---|
| flat | **plano** |
| gabled | **de dos aguas** |
| gambrel | **granjero** |
| hipped | **de varias aguas** |
| mansard | **francés** |
| pyramidal | **pirámide** |
| shed | **cobertizo** |

Use this roofing vocabulary in a sentence:

It's for (the)...      **Es para...**

| | |
|---|---|
| cornice | **la cornisa** |
| dormer | **la buhardilla** |
| drip edge | **el borde de goteo** |
| eaves | **el alero** |
| fascia | **la fachada** |
| rake board | **la moldura del techo** |
| ridge board | **la tabla del caballete** |
| soffit | **la cubierta del alero** |

Work on (the)…    **Trabaje con…**

| | |
|---|---|
| attic | **el ático** |
| balcony | **el balcón** |
| crawlspace | **el entretecho** |
| roof top | **la azotea** |
| sub-roof | **el subtecho** |
| | |
| chimney | **la chimenea** |
| downspout | **el bajante de aguas** |
| drain | **el drenaje** |
| gutter | **el canalón** |
| skylight | **la tragaluz** |

Now focus on the terminology related to ventilation:

Look at (the)…        **Mire…**

| | |
|---|---|
| hood | **la capota** |
| jack | **la rejilla** |
| duct | **el conducto** |
| air filter | **el filtro de aire** |
| air intake vent | **el aspirador** |
| fan | **la ventiladora** |
| exhaust pipe | **el tubo de escape** |
| louvers | **las persianas** |
| screen | **el mosquitero** |
| vent tube | **el tubo para ventilación** |

Don't forget the words used in framing that specifically relate to roofing:

| Check the… | Revise… |
|---|---|
| backing | **el respaldo** |
| beam | **la viga** |
| brace | **el tirante** |
| cross beam | **el travesaño** |
| doubler | **el doble** |
| header | **la cabecera** |
| joint | **la unión** |
| joist | **la vigueta** |
| panel | **el panel** |
| plate | **la placa** |
| post | **el poste** |
| rafter | **el cabrio** |
| sheathing | **el revestimiento** |
| trimmer | **el moldeador** |
| tripler | **el triple** |
| truss | **la armadura** |

See how phrases can be developed from one single word:

| collar | **el <u>amarre</u>** |
|---|---|
| collar tie | **la vigueta de <u>amarre</u>** |
| collar beam | **la viga de <u>amarre</u>** |

Roofing also requires a few location words:

| Finish (the)… | Termine con… |
|---|---|
| back | **la espalda** |
| beginning | **el principio** |
| bottom | **el pie** |
| cap | **la corona** |
| center | **el centro** |
| corner | **la esquina** |
| edge | **el borde** |
| end | **el fin** |
| face | **la cara** |
| middle | **el medio** |
| side | **el costado** |
| top | **la cima** |

## JUST A SUGGESTION

To be specific in Spanish, it usually requires a longer phrase:

| ridge tile | **la teja del caballete** |
|---|---|
| hip slate | **la pizarra de la limatesa** |
| eaves flashing | **el tapajuntas para el alero** |

## TRY SOME

Select the correct word to complete the series:

**el drenaje, el canalón, _____**          **el centro**

**la teja, la pizarra, _____**          **el bajante**

**la cima, el pie, _____**          **el listón**

# WORKING WORDS: ROOFING MATERIALS

Check off all the roofing materials you'll need for your next job:

Unload (the)…      **Descargue…**

| | |
|---|---|
| asphalt | **el asfalto** |
| boards | **las tablas** |
| bricks | **los ladrillos** |
| caulking | **la masilla** |
| connectors | **las conexiones** |
| felt | **el fieltro** |
| gravel | **la grava** |
| insulation | **el aislamiento** |
| membrane | **la membrana** |
| mortar | **la argamasa** |
| paint | **la pintura** |
| roofing paper | **el papel protector** |
| sealer | **el sellador** |
| sheeting | **la lámina** |
| shims | **las calzas** |
| tape | **la cinta** |
| tar | **la brea** |
| waterproofing | **el impermeable** |

It's made of…          **Está hecho de…**

| | |
|---|---|
| adobe | **el adobe** |
| aluminum | **el aluminio** |
| cedar | **el cedro** |
| cement | **el cemento** |
| ceramic | **la cerámica** |
| clay | **la arcilla** |
| composite | **la compuesta** |
| copper | **el cobre** |
| enamel | **el esmalte** |
| fiber | **la fibra** |
| fiberglass | **la fibra de vidrio** |
| pine | **el pino** |
| plastic | **el plástico** |
| plywood | **el contrachapado** |
| redwood | **la secoya** |
| rubber | **la goma** |
| steel | **el acero** |
| stone | **la piedra** |
| tin | **el estaño** |
| zinc | **el zinc** |

Materials can also be described as parts of complete sets:

I need (the)…          **Necesito…**

| | |
|---|---|
| coarse of shingles | **la hilera de tejas** |
| bundle of shake | **el paquete de listones** |
| box of slate | **la caja de pizarra** |
| bag of cement | **el saco de cemento** |
| tube of caulking | **el tubo de masilla** |
| pallet of plywood | **la plataforma de contrachapado** |
| bucket of tar | **la cubeta de brea** |
| roll of paper | **el rollo de papel** |
| strip of adhesive | **la tira de adhesivo** |

## JUST A SUGGESTION

Roofing can be a pretty messy job, so make sure you learn everything:

Bring (the)…        **Traiga…**

| | |
|---|---|
| mop | **la fregona** |
| rag | **el trapo** |
| brush | **el cepillo** |
| water | **el agua** |
| thinner | **el disolvente** |

## TRY SOME

Guess what these words mean in English:

**plástico**

**adhesivo**

**concreto**

**aluminio**

**cerámico**

## WORKING WORDS: EQUIPMENT AND TOOLS

The larger pieces of equipment are often unloaded first:

| We'll use (the)… | Usaremos… |
|---|---|
| conveyor | **la cinta transportadora** |
| crane | **la grúa** |
| forklift | **la carretilla elevadora** |

Now break out the lighter stuff:

| Where's (the)..? | ¿Dónde está…? |
|---|---|
| air compressor | **el compresor de aire** |
| caulking gun | **la pistola de masilla** |
| chalk box | **la cajita de tiza** |
| extension cord | **la extension eléctrica** |
| hammer | **el martillo** |
| impact wrench | **la llave eléctrica** |
| ladder | **la escalera** |
| level | **el nivelador** |
| measuring tape | **la cinta métrica** |
| nail gun | **la pistola de clavos** |
| pliers | **el alicates** |
| pry bar | **la pata de cabra** |
| saw | **la sierra** |
| scaffolding | **el andamio** |
| screw gun | **la pistola de tornillos** |
| screwdriver | **el desarmador** |
| square | **la escuadra** |
| tile cutters | **la cizalla de tejas** |
| utility knife | **la cuchilla** |

Some items are not only used by roofers, but throughout the building project:

| I want (the)… | Quiero… |
|---|---|
| bolt | **el perno** |
| clip | **la sujetadora** |
| fastener | **el sujetador** |
| nail | **el clavo** |
| nut | **la tuerca** |
| pin | **la clavija** |
| screw | **el tornillo** |
| staple | **la grapa** |
| tack | **la tachuela** |

Remember that descriptive words generally appear in reverse order in a Spanish phrase:

| corrugated metal | **el metal corrugado** |
|---|---|
| galvanized wire nail | **el clavo de alambre galvanizado** |
| plain tile | **la teja plana** |
| processed wood | **la madera procesada** |
| wood screw | **el tornillo para madera** |

## JUST A SUGGESTION

And don't forget that many items will not be translated into Spanish:

**el PVC**

**el waferboard**

**el Bitumen**

## TRY SOME

Translate these into Spanish:

I need the nail gun.                    _____

Unload the plain tiles.                 _____

We'll use the scaffolding.              _____


## WORKING WORDS: ON THE JOB SITE


Begin by giving a few tips for roofers:


Be careful with (the)…          **Tenga cuidado con…**

| | |
|---|---|
| antenna | **la antena** |
| phone lines | **las líneas del teléfono** |
| power lines | **los cables del tendido eléctrico** |
| satellite dish | **el disco de satélite** |
| television cables | **los cables para la televisión** |
| weathervane | **la veleta** |

Now use commands with more location words:


Move…          **Mueva…**

| | |
|---|---|
| above | **encima** |
| across | **de un lado al otro** |
| along | **a lo largo de** |
| around | **alrededor de** |
| backwards | **hacia atrás** |
| below | **debajo de** |
| down | **abajo** |
| forward | **adelante** |
| inside | **adentro** |
| outside | **afuera** |
| through | **por** |
| towards | **hacia** |
| up | **arriba** |

Continue to give instructions:

| Add… | **Añada…** |
|---|---|
| another coat | **otra capa** |
| another layer | **otro nivel** |
| less | **menos** |
| more | **más** |
| the same | **lo mismo** |

Check (the)…            **Revise…**

| | |
|---|---|
| angle | **el ángulo** |
| classification | **la clasificación** |
| color | **el color** |
| design | **el diseño** |
| distance | **la distancia** |
| height | **la altura** |
| length | **el largo** |
| measurement | **la medida** |
| pattern | **el patrón** |
| pitch | **el pendiente** |
| position | **la posición** |
| rise | **la distancia vertical** |
| size | **el tamaño** |
| space | **el espacio** |
| span | **la distancia horizontal** |
| style | **el estilo** |
| temperature | **la temperatura** |
| texture | **la textura** |
| width | **el ancho** |

## JUST A SUGGESTION

Practice giving measurements in Spanish, because more words are usually needed:

5/8 plywood

**la madera contrachapada de cinco octavos**

12 in. wide by 36 in. long

**doce pulgadas de ancho por treinta y seis pulgadas de largo**

550° F

**quinientos cincuenta grados Farenheit**

TRY SOME

Find the opposites:

**adentro** _____

**el largo** _____

**encima** _____

WORKING WORDS: ROOF REPAIR

Open up repair work with a few simple statements:

It needs…          **Necesita…**

| | |
|---|---|
| changes | **cambios** |
| patching | **remiendo** |
| reconstruction | **reconstrucción** |
| repair | **reparación** |
| restoration | **restauración** |

There are…          **Hay…**

| | |
|---|---|
| bubbles | **burbujas** |
| bumps | **bultos** |
| corrosion | **corrusión** |
| cracks | **grietas** |
| damage | **daño** |
| de-coloration | **decoloración** |
| dripping | **escurrimiento** |
| exposure | **exposición** |
| holes | **huecos** |
| leaks | **goteras** |
| mold | **moho** |
| pieces | **pedazos** |
| scratches | **rajaduras** |
| stains | **manchas** |
| termites | **termitas** |

It's...                 **Está...**

| | |
|---|---|
| broken | **rota** |
| chipped | **mellada** |
| dented | **abollada** |
| loose | **suelta** |
| missing | **perdida** |
| old | **vieja** |
| rusty | **oxidada** |
| warped | **combada** |
| weak | **débil** |
| worn | **gastada** |

Continue to discuss the cause for alarm:

The _____ did it.       _____ **lo hizo.**

| | |
|---|---|
| cold | **el frío** |
| hail | **el granizo** |
| heat | **el calor** |
| hurricane | **el huracán** |
| moisture | **la humedad** |
| rain | **la lluvia** |
| snow | **la nieve** |
| storm | **la tormenta** |
| sun | **el sol** |
| wind | **el viento** |

The _____ is the trouble.   _____ **es el problema.**

| | |
|---|---|
| framing | **el armazón** |
| pollution | **la contaminación** |
| tree | **el árbol** |
| water | **el agua** |
| weight | **el peso** |

JUST A SUGGESTION

Remember that the "**-ción**" ending Spanish is a lot like "-tion" in English:

| | |
|---|---|
| inspection | **la inspección** |
| certification | **la certificación** |
| classification A, B, C | **la clasificación A, B, C** |

TRY SOME

Say five words in Spanish that describe a damaged roof:

## WORKING WORDS: DESCRIBING THE JOB

Are you still learning words with opposite meanings?

| | |
|---|---|
| apart | **separados** |
| together | **juntos** |

| | |
|---|---|
| lower | **inferior** |
| upper | **superior** |

| | |
|---|---|
| first | **primero** |
| last | **último** |

Instead of "**Es**", use "**Está**", which indicates more of a temporary condition:

| It's… | **Está…** |
|---|---|
| It's not… | **No está…** |

| | |
|---|---|
| loose | **flojo** |
| tight | **apretado** |
| even | **igual** |
| uneven | **desigual** |
| dry | **seco** |
| mojado | **wet** |
| heavy | **pesado** |
| light | **liviano** |
| thick | **grueso** |
| thin | **delgado** |

| It's... | Es/Está... |
|---------|-----------|
| attached | **conectado** |
| balanced | **balanceado** |
| braced | **arriostrada** |
| crossed | **cruzado** |
| curved | **curvado** |
| decorative | **decorativo** |
| durable | **duradero** |
| finished | **acabado** |
| fire resistant | **resistente contra el fuego** |
| fireproof | **incombustible** |
| framed | **armado** |
| hollow | **hueco** |
| laminated | **laminado** |
| rustproof | **inoxidable** |
| sealed | **sellado** |
| solid | **sólido** |
| square | **cuadrado** |
| steep | **empinado** |
| sticky | **pegajoso** |
| straight | **recto** |
| synthetic | **sintético** |
| treated | **tratado** |
| uniform | **uniforme** |
| waterproof | **impermeable** |

Here's how you describe more than one thing:

They are...      **Están...**

| | |
|---|---|
| flush | **a ras de** |
| in order | **arreglados** |
| interwoven | **entretejidos** |
| lined up | **en fila** |
| parallel | **paralelo** |
| similar | **similares** |

These should be easy:

| | |
|---|---|
| diagonal | **diagonal** |
| horizontal | **horizontal** |
| perpendicular | **perpendicular** |
| rectangular | **rectangular** |
| vertical | **vertical** |

What do you know about architectural styles?

| I like… | **Me gusta el estilo…** |
|---|---|
| classic | **clásico** |
| colonial | **colonial** |
| conventional | **convencional** |
| Dutch | **holandés** |
| Spanish | **español** |

## JUST A SUGGESTION

Several roofing-specific terms have rather unusual translations, and are generally expressed in English:

| | |
|---|---|
| rake | **el borde inclinado** |
| lap | **la solapa** |
| tab | **la teja expuesta** |
| cricket | **el tapajuntas especial** |
| eyebrow | **el entretecho** |

TRY SOME

Find the opposites in Spanish:

**último**

**vertical**

**mojado**

**curvado**

**flojo**

**hueco**

## WORKING WORDS: ON-SITE ACTIONS

The following Spanish "verbs" often work well as parts of "action phrases" in roofing:

| | |
|---|---|
| It's going to… | **Se va a…** |

| | |
|---|---|
| to last | **durar** |
| to line up | **alinear** |
| to overhang | **sobresalir por encima** |
| to overlap | **superponerse** |
| to overload | **sobrecargar** |
| to protect | **proteger** |
| to reach | **alcanzar** |
| to reinforce | **reforzar** |
| to repel | **repeler** |
| to support | **apoyar** |

It's not going to…          **No se va a…**

| | |
|---|---|
| to break | **romper** |
| to drip | **escurrir** |
| to fade | **descolorar** |
| to fall over | **tumbar** |
| to move | **mover** |
| to penetrate | **penetrar** |
| to ruin | **destruir** |
| to sag | **hundir** |
| to slip | **resbalar** |
| to spill | **derramar** |
| to splatter | **salpicar** |
| to stain | **manchar** |
| to stick | **pegar** |

You need to…          **Necesita…**

| | |
|---|---|
| to apply | **aplicar** |
| to attach | **conectar** |
| to match | **armonizar** |
| to bore | **calar** |
| to build | **construir** |
| to clean | **limpiar** |
| to climb | **subir** |
| to cover | **cubrir** |
| to cut | **cortar** |
| to enclose | **encerrar** |
| to fill | **llenar** |
| to float | **elevar** (*flotar*) |
| to glue | **encolar** |
| to heat | **calentar** |
| to hook | **enganchar** |
| to hot mop | **poner brea** |
| to install | **instalar** |
| to join | **juntar** |
| to lean | **recostar** |
| to level | **nivelar** |
| to lift | **levantar** |
| to loosen | **soltar** |
| to lower | **bajar** |
| to measure | **medir** |
| to mount | **amontar** |
| to nail | **clavar** |
| to notch | mellar |
| to overlay | **revistar** |
| to patch | **remendar** |
| to place | **colocar** |
| to remove | **quitar** |
| to repair | **reparar** |
| to screw in | **atornillar** |
| to seal | **sellar** |
| to snap a line | **marcar una linea** |
| to space | **espaciar** |
| to spray | **rociar** |
| to spread | **repartir** |
| to stack | **apilar** |
| to staple | **engrapar** |
| to tape | **encintar** |
| to toenail | **clavar en ángulo** |
| to ventilate | **ventilar** |
| to waterproof | **impermeabilizar** |
| to wrap | **forar** |

# JUST A SUGGESTION

To describe an action word in Spanish, try one of these. The secret is the "**-mente**" ending:

| | |
|---|---|
| completely | **completamente** |
| quickly | **rápidamente** |
| slowly | **lentamente** |

You have to seal the pipes quickly.

**Tiene que sellar la tubería rápidamente.**

# TRY SOME

Connect the verbs that belong together:

| | |
|---|---|
| **calar** | **escurrir** |
| **conectar** | **cortar** |
| **derramar** | **juntar** |

# THE ONE-LINERS

Here's a set of expressions that should be practiced regularly. They are used to motivate the folks around you:

| How...! | ¡Qué...! |
|---------|----------|
| great | **bueno** |
| excellent | **excelente** |
| tremendous | **magnífico** |

Nothing works better than encouraging remarks!

| What a great job! | **¡Qué buen trabajo!** |
|-------------------|------------------------|
| Very good! | **¡Muy bien!** |
| Good work! | **¡Bien hecho!** |

## GRAMMAR TIME

Here's one way that Spanish speakers chat about activities that took place in the past. They simply share "what they were doing". There are two steps to putting this together, so pay attention:

## STEP ONE

First, give your "**ar**" actions the "**ando**" endings and the "**er**" or "**ir**" actions the "**iendo**" endings. You did this in a previous chapter:

| **hablar** | **hablando** |
|------------|--------------|
| **comer** | **comiendo** |
| **escribir** | **escribiendo** |

## STEP TWO

Now, change the verb "**estar**" to these simple "past tense" forms:

**estar**

| | |
|---|---|
| I, He, She was, You were | **estaba** |
| They, You (pl.) were | **estaban** |
| We were | **estábamos** |

Now, put them together. This verb form gets easier the more you practice. Concentrate as you read each line below:

| | |
|---|---|
| I was working. | **Estaba trabajando.** |
| You were eating; He, She was eating. | **Estaba comiendo.** |
| You (pl.), They were climbing. | **Estaban subiendo.** |
| We were nailing. | **Estábamos clavando.** |

## JUST A SUGGESTION

The negative and question forms are simple to create:

| | |
|---|---|
| We weren't eating. | **No estábamos comiendo.** |
| Were you guys leaving? | **¿Estaban saliendo?** |

## TRY SOME

Change these present progressive sentences to the past progressive:

**Estoy trabajando.**  **<u>Estaba trabajando.</u>**

**Está resbalando.**  _____

**Estamos revisando.**  _____

**Están limpiando.**  _____


## CULTURE CLASH

In Latin America, the extended family may include in-laws, friends, or neighbors who have lent their support to family members in the past. They may also want to know more about each other's place of employment. When dealing with a large family, it is usually a good idea to find out who is in charge. Remember, too, that Hispanic families respect the elderly, and older children are often given more responsibilities than their younger siblings.

Since the traditional Hispanic family includes more than just its immediate members, you may want to consider learning the names for "relations" outside the immediate family. Here are some examples:

| | |
|---|---|
| close friend | **el compañero** |
| girlfriend | **la novia** |
| godparents | **los padrinos** |
| neighbor | **el vecino** |
| family friends | **los tíos** |

# CHAPTER SEVEN

## MECHANICAL

### las instalaciones mecánicas

WORKING WORDS: GENERAL MECHANICAL

Begin by telling everyone what you'll be working on:

| I'm (the)… | **Soy…** |
|---|---|

| | |
|---|---|
| electrician | **el electricista** |
| plumber | **el fontanero** |
| installer | **el instalador** |
| technician | **el técnico** |
| mechanic | **el mecánico** |

| I'm here for (the)… | **Estoy aquí para…** |
|---|---|
| installation | **la instalación** |
| repair | **la reparación** |
| service | **el servicio** |

| | |
|---|---|
| plumbing | **la tubería** |
| electricity | **la electricidad** |
| heating | **la calefacción** |
| air conditioning | **el aire condicionado** |
| insulation | **el aislamiento** |

| Where's (the)…? | **¿Dónde está…?** |
|---|---|
| shut-off valve | **la válvula principal de corte** |
| shut-off switch | **el interruptor principal** |
| | |
| power | **la potencia** |
| supply | **el suministro** |
| main line | **la línea principal** |

| | |
|---|---|
| equipment | **el equipo** |
| appliance | **el aparato electrodoméstico** |
| machinery | **la maquinaria** |
| apparatus | **el aparato** |
| device | **el mecanismo** |

Now name some built-in fixtures that need your attention:

Let's work on (the)…    **Trabajamos con…**

| | |
|---|---|
| air conditioner | **el acondicionador de aire** |
| bathtub | **la tina de baño** |
| dishwasher | **el lavaplatos** |
| dryer | **la secadora** |
| garbage disposal | **el desechador** |
| heater | **la calentadora** |
| hot water heater | **el calentador para el agua** |
| light | **la luz** |
| oven | **el horno** |
| shower | **la ducha** |
| sink | **el lavabo** |
| stove | **la estufa** |
| toilet | **el excusado** |
| washer | **la lavadora** |

Be sure to include those items that require specialized skills:

Install (the)…    **Instale…**

| | |
|---|---|
| fuse box | **la caja de fusibles** |
| gas meter | **el medidor de gas** |
| water valve | **la válvula de agua** |
| | |
| security system | **el sistema de seguridad** |
| sound system | **el sistema de audio** |
| waste/vent system | **el sistema de drenaje y ventilación** |
| | |
| phone lines | **las líneas del teléfono** |
| satellite dish | **el disco de satélite** |
| television cables | **los cables para la televisión** |

| They want (the)… | **Quieren…** |
|---|---|
| blown insulation | **el aislamiento soplado** |
| central vacuuming system | **el sistema de aspiradora central** |
| garage door opener | **el abridor de garajes** |
| gas bar-b-que | **la parrilla de gas** |
| gas fireplace | **el fogón de gas** |
| intercom system | **el sistema de intercomunicación** |
| outdoor lighting | **los faroles para afuera** |
| solar panels | **los paneles solares** |
| sprinkler system | **el sistema de aspersores** |

Be sure everything is set up for installation:

| Check (the)… | **Revise…** |
|---|---|
| backing | **el respaldo** |
| brace | **el soporte** |
| cabinet | **el gabinete** |
| counter | **el mostrador** |
| flooring | **el piso** |
| footing | **el cimiento** |
| framing | **el armazón** |
| header | **el cabecero** |
| stud | **el montante** |
| wall | **la pared** |

JUST A SUGGESTION

Sometimes several words are needed to describe a system install:

integrated sound and video system

**el sistema integral de sonido y video**

closed circuit cable system

**el sistema de circuito cerrado de cable**


heating and air conditioning system

**el sistema de calefacción y aire acondicionado**


TRY SOME


Connect the worker with the appropriate household item:


| | |
|---|---|
| **el instalador** | **el excusado** |
| **el plomero** | **la luz** |
| **el electricista** | **el gabinete** |


## WORKING WORDS: MACHINE PARTS


Before installing anything, first pick up the names for fixture, machine, and product parts lying around the worksite. Pronounce a few as you hold them in your hand:

Give me (the)...    **Deme...**

| | |
|---|---|
| bar | **la barra** |
| battery | **la batería** |
| bearing | **el cojinete** |
| belt | **la banda** |
| board | **el tablero** |
| bulb | **el foco** |
| button | **el botón** |
| cartridge | **el cartucho** |
| case | **la caja** |
| cell | **el célula** |
| chamber | **la cámara** |
| chassis | **el bastidor** |
| coil | **el rollo** |
| crank | **la manivela** |
| conduit | **el conducto** |
| filter | **el filtro** |
| gauge | **el indicador** |
| gear | **el enbrague** |
| handle | **la perilla** |
| hinge | **la bisagra** |
| hood | **la capota** |
| knob | **el botón** |
| lid | **la tapadera** |
| lever | **la palanca** |
| motor | **el motor** |
| needle | **la aguja** |
| nozzle | **el pitón** |
| panel | **el panel** |
| peg | **la clavija** |
| pipe | **el tubo** |
| piston | **el émbolo** |
| plate | **la placa** |
| propeller | **la hélice** |
| pump | **la bomba** |
| rivet | **el remache** |
| rod | **la varilla** |
| roller | **el rodillo** |
| rotor | **la rueda** |
| shaft | **el astil** |
| spool | **el carrete** |
| spring | **el resorte** |
| valve | **la válvula** |

When you can't recall the name for something, use one of these words:

Bring (the)...                 **Traiga...**

| component | **el componente** |
|-----------|-------------------|
| part      | **la parte**      |
| piece     | **la pieza**      |
| section   | **la sección**    |
| thing     | **la cosa**       |

These concepts are tough to explain, but are needed to explain the machine's purpose or function:

What's (the)...?               **¿Cuál es...?**

function                       **la función**

purpose                        **el propósito**

use                            **el uso**

| load        | **la carga**                |
|-------------|-----------------------------|
| power       | **la potencia**             |
| pressure    | **la presión**              |
| speed       | **la velocidad**            |
| temperature | **la tempertura**           |
| torque      | **el esfuerzo de torsión**  |

# JUST A SUGGESTION

Location words will be required for every mechanical install. Do you know any of these?

Look at (the)...          **Mire...**

| | |
|---|---|
| back | **la parte trasera** |
| bottom | **el fondo** |
| front | **la parte delantera** |
| side | **el lado** |
| top | **la tapa** |

# TRY SOME

Try to translate the following words correctly:

**el resorte**

**la carga**

**el foco**

**la válvula**

**la cosa**

# WORKING WORDS: ELECTRICAL INSTALLATION

Here are a few of the most common words used on any project involving electrical work:

| | |
|---|---|
| electricity | **la electricidad** |
| current | **el corriente** |
| power | **la potencia** |
| cable | **el cable** |
| electric cord | **el cable de extensión** |
| wire | **el alambre** |
| switch | **el interruptor** |
| plug | **el enchufe** |
| outlet | **la toma de corriente** |
| circuit board | **el tablero de circuitos** |
| fuse box | **la caja de fusibles** |
| control panel | **el panel de control** |
| light | **la luz** |
| bulb | **el foco** |
| appliance | **el electrodoméstico** |

Install (the)…                    **Instale…**

| | |
|---|---|
| main power switch | **el interruptor principal** |
| contact plate | **la placa de contacto** |
| double wall socket | **la caja de dos enchufes** |
| switch and socket | **la caja combinada** |
| four-way socket | **la caja de cuatro enchufes** |
| three-way plug | **el enchufe de tres puntas** |
| extension plug | **la clavija macho** |
| extension socket | **la clavija hembra** |
| rotary switch | **el interruptor giratorio** |
| circuit breaker | **el cortacircuitos** |
| reset button | **el botón de reinicio** |
| dimmer switch | **el interruptor con regulador** |
| connection box | **la caja de empalmes** |
| Watthour meter | **el medidor de vatios por hora** |
| rocker switch | **el interruptor de balancín** |
| bypass switch | **el interruptor de derivación** |
| splice plate | **la placa de empalme** |
| switch plate | **la placa de interruptor** |
| distribution board | **el tablero auxiliar** |

Electricians can't do much without saying the following:

| | |
|---|---|
| watt | **el vatio** |
| wattage | **la potencia en vatios** |
| volt | **el voltio** |
| voltage | **el voltaje** |
| amp | **el ampere** |
| amperage | **el amperaje** |

Is everything hooked up?

| Connect (the)… | **Conecte…** |
|---|---|
| alarm | **la alarma** |
| doorbell | **el timbre** |
| fan | **el ventilador** |
| microphone | **el micrófono** |
| speaker | **el altavoz** |
| thermostat | **el termostato** |

And don't forget your colors:

| The cable/wire is… | **El cable/alambre es…** |
|---|---|
| green | **verde** |
| white | **blanco** |
| black | **negro** |
| red | **rojo** |
| yellow | **amarillo** |

JUST A SUGGESTION

Add these Spanish and English words to your easy-to-learn list:

**terminal**

**sensor**

**control**

**detector**

**conductor**

TRY SOME

Circle the word in each set that doesn't belong with the others:

**ventilador, voltaje, voltio**

**altavoz, micrófono, corriente**

**timbre, enchufe, interruptor**

<u>WORKING WORDS:</u> ELECTRICIAN'S TOOLS AND MATERIALS

Electricians will need the following, so use this simple command:

| Unload (the)… | Descargue… |
|---|---|
| caulking gun | la pistola de masilla |
| charger | la cargadora |
| circuit tester | el probador de circuitos |
| cutters | la cizalla |
| drop light | el foco de extensión |
| electric drill | el taladro eléctrico |
| electrician's tape | la cinta aislante |
| extension cord | la extension eléctrica |
| hammer | el martillo |
| mallet | el mazo |
| measuring tape | la cinta métrica |
| meter | el medidor |
| pinchers | las tenazas |
| pliers | el alicates |
| saw | la sierra |
| screwdriver | el desarmador |
| soldering iron | la pistola de slodar |
| step-ladder | la escalera baja |
| utility knife | la cuchilla |
| wire brush | el cepillo de alambre |
| wrench | la llave inglesa |

Remember that some tools come in a variety of forms:

## SCREWDRIVERS

| adjustable screwdriver | el desarmador ajustable |
|---|---|
| cordless screwdriver | el desarmador sin cable |
| expansive screwdriver | el desarmador de expansion |
| Phillips head screwdriver | el desarmador cruz |
| square shaft screwdriver | el desarmador de mango cuadrado |

## PLIERS

| | |
|---|---|
| channel-lock pliers | **el alicates ajustable** |
| needle-nose pliers | **el alicates de punta** |
| vise-grip pliers | **el alicates de presión** |
| wire cutters | **el alicates cortacable** |
| wire strippers | **el alicates para terminales** |

## WRENCHES

| | |
|---|---|
| box-ended wrench | **la llave fija** |
| combination wrench | **la llave combinada** |
| monkey wrench | **la llave cremallera** |
| pipe wrench | **la llave de pipa** |
| socket wrench | **la llave de vaso y juegos** |

Now grab some of these smaller things:

| | |
|---|---|
| bolt | **el perno** |
| bracket | **el soporte** |
| clip | **la clavija** |
| coupling | **el cople** |
| fastener | **la sujetadora** |
| nail | **el clavo** |
| nut | **la tuerca** |
| screw | **el tornillo** |
| staple | **la grapa** |
| washer | **la arandela** |

As you know, many tools are often named in English instead of Spanish:

**el Hex driver**

**el set screw**

**el Allen wrench**

Review more materials that are needed for the electrical job:

I need (the)…　　　　　**Necesito…**

| | |
|---|---|
| bulb | **la bombilla** |
| cable | **el cable** |
| caulking | **la masilla** |
| glue | **la cola** |
| wire | **el alambre** |

Keep going:

Bring (the)…　　　**Traiga…**

| | |
|---|---|
| adapter | **el adaptador** |
| EMT pipe | **la tubería de EMT** |
| fitting | **la conexión** |
| fuse | **el fusible** |
| insulation | **el aislamiento** |
| sealer | **el sellador** |

When the job is hi-tech, the materials are usually specialized:

| They are... | Son... |
|---|---|
| capacitors | **los capacitores** |
| condensers | **los condensadores** |
| detectors | **los detectores** |
| diodes | **los diodos** |
| insulators | **los aisladores** |
| integrated circuits | **los circuitos integrados** |
| microprocessors | **los micro-procesadores** |
| oscillators | **los osciladores** |
| processors | **los procesadores** |
| resistors | **los resistores** |
| semi-conductors | **los semi-conductores** |
| sensors | **los sensores** |
| transducers | **los transductores** |
| transformers | **los transformadores** |
| transistors | **los transistores** |

| Look at (the)... | Mire... |
|---|---|
| battery | **la batería** |
| channel | **el canal** |
| electrode | **el electrodo** |
| filament | **el filamento** |
| laser | **el láser** |
| magnet | **el imán** |
| thread | **la rosca** |

Here are other key words that electricians use:

| What's (the)…? | ¿Cuál es…? |
|---|---|
| capacity | **la capacidad** |
| density | **la densidad** |
| frequency | **la frecuencia** |
| intensity | **la intensidad** |
| memory | **la memoria** |
| polarity | **la polaridad** |
| variation | **la variedad** |

| Check (the)… | Revise… |
|---|---|
| contact | **el contacto** |
| energy | **la energía** |
| flow | **el flujo** |
| force | **la fuerza** |
| friction | **la fricción** |
| movement | **el movimiento** |
| power | **la potencia** |
| resistance | **la resistencia** |
| static | **el estático** |

And don't forget your computer:

| Fix (the)… | Repare… |
|---|---|
| cable | **el cable** |
| computer | **la computadora** |
| drive | **la disquetera** |
| hard drive | **el disco duro** |
| keyboard | **el teclado** |
| laptop | **la computadora portátil** |
| monitor | **el monitor** |
| mouse | **el ratón** |
| screen | **la pantalla** |

## JUST A SUGGESTION

As with other trades, most technical abbreviations in English stay the same in construction Spanish:

**GFI**

**DSL**

**LED**

**btu**

**UV**

## TRY SOME

List three common electrician's tools in Spanish.

List three common parts of a computer in Spanish.

List three materials that are used in most electrical projects.

# WORKING WORDS: PLUMBING INSTALLATION

A plumber is generally called **el plomero**, **el fontanero**, or **el gasfitero** in Spanish. Regardless of which word you use, all plumbers are familiar with this word list below:

| | |
|---|---|
| drinking water | **el agua potable** |
| waste water | **las aguas residuales** |
| shut-off valve | **la válvula de corte** |
| | |
| drain | **el drenaje** |
| sewer | **la alcantarilla** |
| pipe | **el tubo** |
| | |
| faucet | **el grifo** |
| toilet | **el excusado** |
| sink | **el lavabo** |

Keep focusing on the key words:

Where's (the)…?   **¿Dónde está…?**

| | |
|---|---|
| hydrant | **la bomba de incendio** |
| manhole | **la boca del alcantarillado** |
| meter box | **la caja del medidor** |
| water main | **el tubo de suministro** |
| water meter | **el medidor de agua** |

Now name a common fixture that uses water:

| Work on (the)... | Trabaje con... |
|---|---|
| bathtub | **la tina de baño** |
| shower stall | **la ducha** |
| kitchen sink | **el fregadero** |
| toilet | **el excusado** |
| bathroom sink | **el lavabo** |
| faucet | **el grifo** |
| water heater | **el calentador de agua** |
| dishwasher | **el lavaplatos** |
| washing machine | **la lavadora** |
| urinal | **el urinario** |

Worksites may also include some outdoor plumbing:

| fountain | **el fuente** |
|---|---|
| hose bib | **el grifo para la manguera** |
| pool | **la piscina** |
| spa | **el bañario** |
| sprinkler | **el aspersor** |

Use this command as you get to work:

| Check (the)... | Revise... |
|---|---|
| water level | **el nivel de agua** |
| water tank | **el depósito de agua** |
| water inlet | **la entrada del agua** |

| Give me (the)... | Deme... |
|---|---|
| fittings | **las conexiones** |

| | |
|---|---|
| tools | **las herramientas** |
| equipment | **el equipo** |

Here's a common concern:

| | |
|---|---|
| Look for (the)… | **Busque…** |
| | |
| clog | **la obstrucción** |
| leak | **la fuga** |
| break | **la rotura** |
| | |
| I need (the)… | **Necesito…** |
| | |
| hose | **la manguera** |
| plunger | **el desatascador** |
| snake | **la sonda motorizada** |

TRY SOME

Say in English where these are most likely to found:

**la ducha**

**la piscina**

**la lavadora**

**el excusado**

**el aspersor**

# WORKING WORDS: PLUMBING TOOLS AND MATERIALS

Focus on those tools that every plumber needs:

| Move (the)… | **Mueva…** |
|---|---|
| dolley | **la carretilla** |
| step ladder | **la escalera baja** |
| wet-dry vac | **la aspiradora de agua** |

| Do you have…? | **¿Tiene…?** |
|---|---|
| adhesive | **el adhesivo** |
| caulking gun | **la pistola de masilla** |
| pipejoint compound | **el compuesto para juntar tubos** |
| cordless drill | **el taladro neumática** |
| file | **la lima** |
| flashlight | **la linterna** |
| glue | **el pegamento/la cola** |
| hacksaw | **la sierra para cortar metal** |
| heating gun | **la pistola térmica** |
| knife | **la cuchilla** |
| level | **el nivel** |
| meter | **el medidor** |
| miter saw | **la sierra de cortar en ángulos** |
| pipe cutters | **el cortatubos** |
| pipe vice | **el prensatubos** |
| pipe wrench | **la llave para tubos** |
| pliers | **el alicates** |
| plumber's tape | **la cinta aislante** |
| probe | **la sonda** |
| pump | **la bomba** |
| putty | **la masilla** |
| tape measure | **la cinta métrica** |
| tube bender | **la dobladora de tubos** |
| wax | **la cera** |

In plumbing, there are usually an assortment of wrenches involved:

| | |
|---|---|
| chain wrench | **la llave de cadena** |
| disc wrench | **la llave de disco** |
| seat wrench | **la llave del grifo** |
| strap wrench | **la llave de cincho** |
| tube wrench | **la llave tubular** |

And did you bring any materials? Begin with some of these:

Install (the)…                **Instale…**

| | |
|---|---|
| drain | **el drenaje** |
| faucet | **el grifo** |
| handle | **la manija** |
| pipe | **el tubo** |
| spigot | **la llave de paso** |
| valve | **la válvula** |

Now mention the plumbing pipe:

Carry (the)…                **Lleve…**

| | |
|---|---|
| 45° elbow pipe | **el codo de cuarenta y cinco grados** |
| ABS pipe | **la tubería negra** |
| cold water pipe | **el tubo para agua fría** |
| distribution pipe | **la tubería de derivación** |
| drain pipe | **el tubo de drenaje** |
| end pipe | **el tubo de acabado** |
| hot water pipe | **el tubo para agua caliente** |
| PVC pipe | **la tubería de plástico** |
| return pipe | **el tubo de retorno** |
| riser pipe | **el tubo vertical** |
| T-pipe | **el tubo tipo T** |

Group your plumbing vocabulary into related sets:

Where's (the)…?          **¿Dónde está…?**

| | |
|---|---|
| ½ inch pipe | **el tubo de una mitad** |
| ¾ inch pipe | **el tubo de tres cuartos** |
| one inch pipe | **el tubo de una pulgada** |
| | |
| storm drain | **el drenaje para tormentas** |
| floor drain | **el drenaje del piso** |
| shower drain | **el drenaje de ducha** |
| | |
| C-clamp | **la abrazadera tipo C** |
| split ring clamp | **la abrazadera de anillo separado** |
| extension clamp | **la abrazadera de extensión** |

Keep going:

| | |
|---|---|
| angle valve | **la válvula angular** |
| ball valve | **la válvula de bola** |
| butterfly valve | **la válvula de mariposa** |
| check valve | **la válvula de antirretorno** |
| safety valve | **la válvula de seguridad** |
| waste valve | **la válvula de desagüe** |

To be specific, add the necessary descriptive words:

Do you have (the)…          **¿Tiene…?**

| | |
|---|---|
| clean out stop | **el tapón de limpieza** |
| drain plug | **el tapón del drenaje** |
| drain waste vent | **la chimenea de ventilación** |
| P-trap | **el sifón tipo P** |
| swivel tap | **el grifo giratorio** |

| Bring (the)... | Traiga... |
|---|---|
| adapter | **el adaptador** |
| ball | **la bola** |
| bolt | **el perno** |
| bracket | **el soporte** |
| connector | **el acomplamiento** |
| coupler | **el cople** |
| duct | **el conducto** |
| filter | **el filtro** |
| grating | **la rejilla** |
| hanger rod | **la barra colgante** |
| insert | **el anclaje** |
| joint | **el codo** |
| nipple | **el niple** |
| nut | **la tuerca** |
| plate | **la placa** |
| ring | **el anillo** |
| screwjoint | **el tornillo de ajuste** |
| strap | **la tira** |
| union | **la unión** |
| washer | **la arandela** |

These words target the work in the bathroom:

| Repair (the)... | Repare... |
|---|---|
| basin | **la tina** |
| float | **el flotador** |
| gasket | **el empaque** |
| head | **la cabeza** |
| nozzle | **la boquilla** |
| overflow | **el rebosadero** |
| plug | **la espiga** |
| seal | **el sello** |
| seat | **el asiento** |
| tank | **el tanque** |
| trap | **el sifón** |

Talk a bit more about your materials:

| It's… | Es… |
|---|---|
| ceramic | **cerámico** |
| chrome | **cromado** |
| graphite | **grafito** |
| metallic | **metálico** |
| plastic | **plástico** |
| porcelain | **porcelano** |
| | |
| aluminum flashing | **el tapajuntas de aluminio** |
| flexible copper | **el cobre flexible** |
| galvanized steel | **el hierro galvanizado** |

Some soldering or **soldadura** may be required, so use this vocabulary as you get started:

| We use (the)… | Usamos… |
|---|---|
| acetylene | **el acetilino** |
| brush | **la brocha** |
| $CO_2$ | **el carbón de dióxido** |
| emery cloth | **la tela de esmeril** |
| oxygen | **el oxígeno** |
| paste | **la pasta** |
| propane | **el propano** |
| regulator | **el regulador** |
| soldering wire | **el alambre de soldadura** |
| gas tank | **el cilindro de gas** |
| torch lighter | **el encendedor** |
| torch | **el soplete** |

JUST A SUGGESTION

Mechanical installation is full of simple sets of words with opposite meanings:

| | |
|---|---|
| entrance | **la entrada** |
| exit | **la salida** |
| positive | **positivo** |
| negative | **negativo** |
| open | **abierta** |
| closed | **cerrada** |
| male | **macho** |
| female | **hembra** |
| inside | **adentro** |
| outside | **afuera** |

TRY SOME

Connect the words that belong together:

**el soplete**          **la boquilla**

**la manguera**         **el perno**

**la arándela**         **el encededor**

Can you say these in Spanish?

large clamp          _____

medium clamp         _____

small clamp          _____

# WORKING WORDS: HEATING AND AIR CONDITIONING

When it comes to installing heating or AC units, or working on other mechanical projects in construction, many of the same words used in plumbing and electrical will be required.

| Where's (the)...? | ¿Dónde está...? |
|---|---|
| main water line | la tubería principal de agua |
| main gas line | la línea principal de gas |
| main power line | el cable principal de electricidad |

| Check (the)... | Revise... |
|---|---|
| air conditioner | el acondicionador de aire |
| heater | el calentador |
| heating system | el sistema de califacción |
| radiator | el radiador |
| unit | el aparato |

| What's (the)...? | ¿Cuál es...? |
|---|---|
| amount | la cantidad |
| make | la marca |
| model | el modelo |
| number | el número |
| quality | la calidad |
| shape | la forma |
| size | el tamaño |
| supply | el suministro |

| It's not… | No está… |
|-----------|----------|
| cold | **frío** |
| cool | **fresco** |
| freezing | **helado** |
| hot | **caliente** |
| warm | **tibio** |

| Use (the)… | Use… |
|------------|------|
| cable | **el cable** |
| hose | **la manguera** |
| pipe | **el tubo** |
| plug | **el enchufe** |
| switch | **el interruptor** |
| valve | **la válvula** |

This time focus on those AC and heating components that relate specifically to the job at hand:

| Look at (the)… | Mire… |
|---|---|
| air filter | **el filtro de aire** |
| air vent | **el conducto de aire** |
| circuit board | **el tablero de circuitos** |
| compressor | **el compresor** |
| defroster | **el descongelador** |
| fan | **el ventilador** |
| flashing | **el tapajuntas** |
| flexible duct | **el conducto flexible** |
| flow switch | **el interruptor de flujo** |
| grill | **la rejilla** |
| humidifier | **el humidificador** |
| ignitor | **el encendidor** |
| insulation | **el aislamiento** |
| lens | **el lente** |
| lock | **la cerradura** |
| mounting screws | **el tornillo de fijación** |
| pilot | **el piloto** |
| pump | **la bomba** |
| purifier | **el purificador** |
| regulator | **el regulador** |
| remote control | **el control remoto** |
| return | **el conducto de retorno** |
| seal | **el sello** |
| thermometer | **el termómetro** |
| thermostat | **el termostato** |
| timer | **el reloj** |
| transformer | **el transformador** |

Try out this new terminology by using the plural form:

| See (the)… | Vea… |
| --- | --- |
| burners | **los quemadores** |
| coils | **los rollos** |
| condensers | **los condensadores** |
| heating elements | **los elementos calefactores** |
| sensors | **los sensores** |

## JUST A SUGGESTION

Name brands are usually pronounced about the same in both languages:

| | |
| --- | --- |
| Teflon | **el teflón** |
| Latex | **el látex** |
| Silicone | **la silicona** |

## TRY SOME

Name three parts of an AC unit and three parts of a heater in Spanish.

## WORKING WORDS: OTHER MECHANICAL

Mechanical work involves a variety of specialized vocabulary and commands:

Work on (the)…    **Trabaje con…**

| | |
|---|---|
| chimney | **la chimenea** |
| skylight | **la tragaluz** |
| vent tubes | **los tubos para ventilación** |
| well | **el pozo** |
| cesspool | **el silo** |
| cooler | **el cuarto de refrigeración** |
| furnace | **el horno** |
| boiler | **la caldera** |

Notice the pattern in these phrases:

soft water system    **el sistema de suavizar el agua**

filtration system    **el sistema de filtrar el agua**

sewage system    **el sistema de alcantarilla**

Now, break your vocabulary into groups based on the specific job:

It's the pool _____.                **Es _____ para la piscina.**

| | |
|---|---|
| drain | **el drenaje** |
| filter | **el filtro** |
| heater | **el calentador** |
| light | **la luz** |
| pump | **la bomba** |

Now focus on the installation:

| Where's (the)…? | ¿Dónde está…? |
|---|---|
| gap | **el hueco** |
| hole | **el hoyo** |
| opening | **la abertura** |
| slit | **la ranura** |
| space | **el espacio** |

| It has (the)… | Tiene… |
|---|---|
| aluminum | **el aluminio** |
| brass | **el latón** |
| drywall | **el enyesado** |
| fiberglass | **la fibra de vidrio** |
| foam | **la espuma** |
| glass | **el vidrio** |
| iron | **el hierro** |
| lead | **el plomo** |
| plywood | **el contrachapado** |
| rubber | **la goma** |
| steel | **el acero** |
| wood | **la madera** |

We need (the)…    **Necesitamos…**

| | |
|---|---|
| acid | **el ácido** |
| battery | **la batería** |
| catalyst | **el catalizador** |
| cell | **la célula** |
| chemical | **el químico** |
| chlorine | **el cloro** |
| coal | **el carbón** |
| compound | **el compuesto** |
| diesel | **el diesel** |
| dye | **el tinte** |
| fluid | **el fluido** |
| fuel | **el combustible** |
| gasoline | **la gasolina** |
| liquid | **el líquido** |
| mixture | **la mezcla** |
| natural gas | **el gas natural** |
| oil | **el aceite** |
| propane | **el propano** |
| water | **el agua** |

What's (the)…?    **¿Cuál es…?**

| | |
|---|---|
| area | **la área** |
| circumference | **la circunferencia** |
| color | **el color** |
| diameter | **el diámetro** |
| height | **la altura** |
| length | **el largo** |
| model | **el modelo** |
| percentage | **el porcentaje** |
| size | **el tamaño** |
| temperature | **la temperatura** |
| volume | **el volumen** |
| width | **la anchura** |

| How many…? | ¿Cuántos…? |
|---|---|
| degrees | **grados** |
| inches | **pulgadas** |
| ounces | **onzas** |

| Look at (the)… | **Mire…** |
|---|---|
| angle | **el ángulo** |
| distance | **la distancia** |
| fall | **el pediente** |
| pattern | **el patrón** |
| position | **la posición** |
| program | **el programa** |

| Pay attention to (the)… | **Preste atención a…** |
|---|---|
| arrow | **la flecha** |
| cycle | **el ciclo** |
| dial | **la esfera** |
| line | **la linea** |
| signal | **la señal** |
| sound | **el sonido** |
| time | **el tiempo** |

## JUST A SUGGESTION

Remember that several prefixes are also the same in both languages:

**mili-**

**kilo-**

**giga-**

**mega-**

**centi-**

TRY SOME

These are similar in Spanish and should be easy to translate:

chimney

distance

temperature

diameter

liquid

program

## WORKING WORDS: MECHANICAL PROBLEMS

Mechanical work involves plenty of checking and testing. These one-liners will help resolve problems:

| | |
|---|---|
| Let's check it. | **Vamos a revisarla.** |
| Something is wrong. | **Algo está mal.** |
| Start over. | **Empiece de nuevo.** |
| We have to make sure. | **Tenemos que estar seguros.** |
| You need to fix it. | **Necesita repararlo.** |

Do a _____ test.　　　**Haga una prueba de _____.**

| | |
|---|---|
| continuity | **continuidad** |
| diagnostic | **diagnóstico** |
| pressure | **presión** |
| safety | **seguridad** |
| static | **estático** |
| voltage | **voltaje** |

Keep addressing your concerns:

Let's talk about (the)…    **Hablamos de…**

| | |
|---|---|
| advice | **el aviso** |
| danger | **el peligro** |
| precaution | **la precaución** |
| prevention | **la prevención** |
| suggestion | **la sugerencia** |
| warning | **la advertencia** |

It's (the)…    **Es…**

| | |
|---|---|
| regulation | **el reglamento** |
| law | **la ley** |
| code | **el código** |

Be sure to include these words in your safety instructions:

Be careful with (the)…          **Tenga cuidado con…**

| | |
|---|---|
| ground wire | **el cable de tierra** |
| heating elements | **los elementos calefactores** |
| power lines | **los cables del tendido eléctrico** |
| service drop | **la toma de suministro eléctico** |
| service entrance head | **la entrada principal de servicio** |
| service mast | **el mastil de servicio eléctrico** |
| service panel | **el tablero de servicio** |

Keep going:

| | |
|---|---|
| electric shock | **el shock eléctrico** |
| explosion | **la explosión** |
| heat | **el calor** |
| flame | **la llama** |
| smoke | **el humo** |
| sparks | **las chispas** |
| steam | **el vapor** |

If water is a concern, use these descriptive words:

Is it…?          **¿Es/Está…?**

| | |
|---|---|
| frozen | **congelado** |
| moist | **húmedo** |
| soaked | **empapado** |
| waterproof | **impermeable** |
| watertight | **hermético** |
| wet | **mojado** |

And if more problems arise, keep it short using words you already know:

There's trouble with (the)…     **Hay problemas con…**

| piece | **la pieza** |
|---|---|
| connection | **la acometida** |
| system | **el sistema** |
| | |
| support | **el apoyo** |
| strength | **la resistencia** |
| movement | **el movimiento** |
| | |
| condition | **la condición** |
| shape | **la forma** |
| age | **la edad** |

There are…     **Hay…**

| bubbles | **burbujas** |
|---|---|
| bumps | **bultos** |
| cracks | **grietas** |
| fumes | **escape** |
| holes | **huecos** |
| knots | **nudos** |
| loops | **lazos** |
| pressure loss | **caída de presión** |
| puddles | **charcos** |
| water leaks | **fugas** |

Clean up (the)…     **Limpie...**

| grease | **la grasa** |
|---|---|
| waste | **la basura** |
| dirt | **la sucuedad** |

And use (the)…     **Y use…**

| | |
|---|---|
| bucket | **el balde** |
| mop | **el trapeador** |
| rag | **el trapo** |
| sponge | **la esponja** |
| towel | **la toalla** |

It's…     **Está…**

| | |
|---|---|
| bent | **doblado** |
| broken | **descompuesto** |
| burned | **quemado** |
| contaminated | **contaminado** |
| corroded | **corroido** |
| cracked | **agrietado** |
| damaged | **dañado** |
| defective | **defectuoso** |
| eroded | **erosionado** |
| loose | **suelto** |
| old | **viejo** |
| scratched | **roscado** |
| stained | **manchado** |
| weak | **débil** |
| worn | **gastado** |

Call the _____ company.     **Llame la compañía de _____.**

| | |
|---|---|
| cable | **cable** |
| electric | **electricidad** |
| gas | **gas** |
| phone | **teléfono** |
| water | **agua** |

# JUST A SUGGESTION

The secret to learning a foreign language is to find as many words as you can that look like English as possible. In mechanical work, this terminology is everywhere:

| | |
|---|---|
| conduction | **la conducción** |
| operation | **la operación** |
| lubrication | **la lubricación** |
| contamination | **la contaminación** |
| production | **la producción** |
| connection | **la conexión** |
| purification | **la purificación** |
| concentration | **la concentración** |
| filtration | **la filtración** |
| acclimatization | **la climatización** |
| refrigeration | **la refrigeración** |
| calibration | **la calibración** |
| | |
| dimension | **la dimensión** |
| tension | **la tensión** |
| absorbsion | **la absorbsión** |
| transmission | **la transmisión** |
| precision | **la precisión** |
| | |
| polarity | **la polaridad** |
| intensity | **la intensidad** |
| security | **la seguridad** |

TRY SOME

Choose the best word to complete each sentence below:

**Haga un prueba de...**                    **las chispas**

| | |
|---|---|
| **Tenga cuidado con…** | **cable** |
| **Está…** | **la continuidad** |
| **Limpie…** | **congelado** |
| **Llame la compañía de…** | **la suciedad** |

Translate these:

| | |
|---|---|
| **corriente eléctrico** | electric current |
| **alto voltaje** | _____ |
| **el alambre vivo** | _____ |
| **la caja metálica** | _____ |

## WORKING WORDS: DESCRIBING THE JOB

Say these words to describe everything around you:

It's…        **Es…**

| | |
|---|---|
| double | **doble** |
| single | **sencillo** |
| | |
| curved | **curvado** |
| straight | **recto** |
| | |
| flat | **plano** |
| round | **redondo** |

Now use "**Está**" instead of "**Es**" to indicate more of a temporary condition:

| It's… | Está… |
|-------|-------|
| loose | **floja** |
| tight | **apretada** |
| | |
| dry | **seco** |
| mojado | **wet** |
| | |
| hot | **caliente** |
| cold | **frío** |
| | |
| live | **vivo** |
| dead | **muerto** |
| | |
| turned on | **prendido** |
| turned off | **apagado** |

| It looks… | Se ve… |
|-----------|--------|
| crossed | **cruzado** |
| in series | **en serie** |
| interwoven | **entretejidos** |
| lined up | **arreglados** |
| parallel | **paralelo** |

| It's… | Es/Está… |
|-------|----------|
| durable | **duradero** |
| fire resistant | **resistente contra el fuego** |
| grounded | **aterrizado** |
| leak-proof | **que no se gotea** |
| rustproof | **inoxidable** |
| sealed | **sellado** |
| shock-proof | **antigolpes** |
| treated | **tratado** |
| underground | **subterráneo** |
| waterproof | **impermeable** |

Here's a selection that generally refers to lighting:

| It's… | Es… |
|---|---|
| decorative | **decorativo** |
| incandescent | **incandescente** |
| luminescent | **luminiscente** |
| neon | **neón** |
| reflective | **reflectivo** |
| shiny | **luminoso** |

Again, record any descriptive terminology that is similar to English:

| | |
|---|---|
| alternating | **alternative** |
| automated | **automatizado** |
| centralized | **centralizado** |
| continuous | **contínuo** |
| fabricated | **fabricado** |
| filtered | **filtrado** |
| functional | **funcional** |
| installed | **instalado** |
| integrated | **integrado** |
| monitored | **monitoreado** |
| mounted | **montado** |
| programmed | **programado** |
| soldered | **soldado** |

By the way, here's the pattern for English words ending in "-ic":

| | |
|---|---|
| metallic | **metálico** |
| plastic | **plástico** |
| optic | **óptico** |
| electronic | **electrónico** |
| hydraulic | **hidráulico** |
| automatic | **automático** |
| hydronic | **hidrónica** |
| metric | **métrico** |
| magnetic | **magnético** |
| synthetic | **sintético** |
| diagnostic | **diagnóstico** |
| schematic | **esquemático** |
| electromagnetic | **electromagnético** |
| electro-mechanic | **electromecánico** |
| electro-chemical | **electroquímico** |
| electro-thermal | **electrotérmico** |
| electro-acoustic | **electroacústico** |

## JUST A SUGGESTION

Not all words follow the same consistent pattern when translating from one language to the other. Look at these examples:

| | | |
|---|---|---|
| insulated | **aislante** | Not "insulado" |
| environmental | **ambiental** | Not "environmental" |
| interchangeable | **intervariable** | Not "interchangeable" |

## TRY SOME

Pronounce these Spanish descriptive words correctly:

| | | |
|---|---|---|
| similar | horizontal | circular |
| rectangular | vertical | semicircular |
| manual | diagonal | central |
| digital | lateral | modular |
| universal | frontal | exterior |
| reversible | posterior | interior |

## WORKING WORDS: ON-SITE ACTIONS

Review these sets of opposites that all relate to activities in mechanical installation:

| You need… | Necesita… |
|---|---|
| to push | **empujar** |
| to pull | **jalar** |
| | |
| to tighten | **apretar** |
| to loosen | **aflojar** |
| | |
| to empty | **vaciar** |
| to fill | **llenar** |
| | |
| to put inside | **meter** |
| to take out | **sacar** |
| | |
| to lift | **levantar** |
| to lower | **bajar** |
| | |
| to open | **abrir** |
| to close | **cerrar** |

As you know, "**des-**" is added some verbs in order to create an opposite:

| | |
|---|---|
| to plug in | **enchufar** |
| to unplug | **desenchufar** |
| | |
| to connect | **conectar** |
| to disconnect | **desconectar** |
| | |
| to assemble | **armar** |
| to disassemble | **desarmar** |

This selection of "verbs" refer to most mechanical installations, so as always, take down the ones you'll be using right away:

| It's necessary… | **Es necesario…** |
|---|---|
| to adjust | **ajustar** |
| to align | **alinear** |
| to amplify | **amplificar** |
| to apply | **aplicar** |
| to bond | **adherir** |
| to bore | **calar** |
| to carry | **llevar** |
| to caulk | **calafatear** |
| to check | **revisar** |
| to circulate | **circular** |
| to connect | **conectar** |
| to control | **controlar** |
| to convert | **convertir** |
| to cool | **refrescar** |
| to correct | **corregir** |

| | |
|---|---|
| to cover | **cubrir** |
| to cut | **cortar** |
| to distribute | **distribuir** |
| to divert | **desviar** |
| to fill | **llenar** |
| to filter | **filtrar** |
| to flip | **voltear** |
| to glue | **encolar** |
| to heat | **calentar** |
| to install | **instalar** |
| to join | **unir** |
| to lubricate | **lubricar** |
| to measure | **medir** |
| to modify | **modificar** |
| to mount | **amontar** |
| to move | **mover** |
| to operate | **operar** |
| to place | **colocar** |
| to program | **programar** |
| to protect | **proteger** |
| to put | **poner** |
| to reach | **alcanzar** |
| to reduce | **reducir** |
| to remove | **quitar** |
| to repair | **reparar** |
| to replace | **sustituir** |
| to roll up | **enrollarse** |

| | |
|---|---|
| to screw in | **atornillar** |
| to seal | **sellar** |
| to splice | **empalmar** |
| to stretch | **estirar** |
| to support | **apoyar** |
| to thread | **roscar** |
| to transmit | **transmitir** |
| to test | **probar** |
| to turn on | **encender** |
| to twist | **torcer** |
| to untangle | **desenredar** |
| to upgrade | **subir de categoría** |
| to use | **usar** |
| to wrap | **forar** |

| | |
|---|---|
| It needs… | **Necesita…** |

| | |
|---|---|
| to return | **regresar** |
| to absorb | **absorber** |
| to thaw | **descongelar** |
| to ventilate | **ventilar** |
| to start up | **arrancar** |
| to produce | **producir** |
| to function | **funcionar** |
| to flow | **fluir** |

| | |
|---|---|
| It's going… | **Se va a…** |

| | |
|---|---|
| to overflow | **rebosar** |
| to overheat | **recalentar** |
| to overload | **sobrecargar** |
| to drip | **gotear** |
| to stick | **pegar** |
| to interrupt | **interrumpir** |
| to break | **romper** |

## JUST A SUGGESTION

Don't forget that some English verbs, such as "to turn on" may have more than one translation in Spanish:

**prender**
**encender**
**alumbrar**

## TRY SOME

Can you recall the meanings of the verbs listed below? Notice how the sentences incorporate some of the verb tenses presented in the book thus far. Simply match each sentence with its appropriate ending:

| | |
|---|---|
| **No está goteando…** | **…ahorita** |
| **Usaré el alicates…** | **…ayer** |
| **Estaba funcionando bien…** | **…mañana** |

# GRAMMAR TIME

Spanish has two basic "past tenses"- the "preterit" and the "imperfect".

The "preterit" is a little more common, because it refers to actions that were completed in past time. It kind of reports, narrates, or sums up activities that were completed in the past. We'll get to the "imperfect" tense a little later on.

Let's take a look at a simple formula that shows how to create "preterit" forms with most action words.

For regular "**ar**" verbs, change the endings just like the example:

| | |
|---|---|
| <u>to work</u> | <u>**trabajar**</u> |
| I worked | **trabajé** |
| You, He, She worked | **trabajó** |
| You (pl.), They worked | **trabajaron** |
| We worked | **trabajamos** |

In other words, drop the "**ar**" and add one of these:

**trabaj ___    -e    -o    -aron    -amos**

| | |
|---|---|
| I worked yesterday. | **Trabajé ayer.** |
| Did they work? | **¿Trabajaron?** |

| We didn't work. | **No trabajamos.** |

For regular "**er**" and "**ir**" actions, change the forms to look like these:

| to eat | **comer** |
|---|---|
| I ate | **comí** |
| You, He, She ate | **comió** |
| You (pl.), They ate | **comieron** |
| We ate | **comimos** |

Again, keep things simple.  These are the letters you'll need to know:

**com** ___          **-í**    **-ió**    **-ieron**    **-imos**

| They ate last night. | **Comieron anoche.** |
|---|---|
| Did you eat? | **¿Comió usted?** |
| I didn't eat. | **No comí.** |

Most "**ir**" verbs are handled the same as the "**er**" verbs.  Notice the resemblance:

| to write | **escribir** |
|---|---|
| I wrote | **escribí** |
| You, He, She wrote | **escribió** |
| You (pl.), They wrote | **escribieron** |
| We wrote | **escribimos** |

**escrib \_\_\_**     **-í**    **-ió**    **-ieron**    **-imos**

I wrote the list two weeks ago.   **Escribí la lista hace dos semanas.**

He did not write the list.        **No escribió la lista.**

Did you guys write the list?      **¿Escribieron ustedes la lista?**

## THE ONE-LINERS

In order to create one-liners in Spanish, one clever technique is to attach a few words to a simple preposition:

| with | **con** | with the ladder | **con la escalera** |
|------|---------|-----------------|---------------------|
| without | **sin** | without water | **sin el agua** |
| to | **a** | to the kitchen | **a la cocina** |
| from, of | **de** | from the street | **de la calle** |
| in, on, at | **en** | in the box | **en la caja** |
| for | **para** | for the machine | **para la máquina** |
| by, through | **por** | through the pipes | **por la tubería** |

However, remember that there are two "contractions" in the language:

| of, from, the | **del** | It's from the other one | **Es del otro** |
|---------------|---------|-------------------------|-----------------|
| to the | **al** | It goes to the room | **Va al cuarto** |

By the way, almost everyone struggles with the differences between "**por**" and "**para**" in Spanish. Generally speaking, "**para**" means "to", "in order to", and "for the purpose of", while "**por**" means "by", "through", "because of" and "on account of".  Listen to how each are used in conversations, and you'll get a feel for them in no time.

CULTURE CLASH

To avoid problems at the workplace, post important signage in two languages today!

| | |
|---|---|
| Open | **ABIERTO** |
| Closed | **CERRADO** |
| Pull | **JALE** |
| Push | **EMPUJE** |
| | |
| Danger | **PELIGRO** |
| Out of Order | **DESCOMPUESTO** |
| Restrooms | **SANITARIOS** |
| No Smoking | **NO FUMAR** |
| | |
| Authorized Personnel Only | **Solo para personas autorizadas** |
| No Food Allowed | **No pasar con alimentos** |
| Emergency Exit | **Salida de emergencia** |
| Wet Floor | **Piso mojado** |
| High Power Cables | **Cables de alto voltaje** |
| Do Not Block Entrance | **No obstruir la entrada** |
| Follow The Arrow | **Siga la flecha** |
| Use Other Door | **Favor de utilizar la otra puerta** |
| Employee Parking | **Estacionamiento para empleados** |

# CHAPTER EIGHT

## THE EXTERIOR

### el exterior

(ehl ehks-teh-ree-'ohr)

WORKING WORDS: THE BUILDING'S EXTERIOR

Name the exterior parts of a typical home:

Go to (the)…       **Vaya a…**

front yard         **el jardín enfrente**
backyard           **el jardín trasero**
side yard          **el jardín al lado**

| courtyard | **el patio** |
|-----------|--------------|
| deck | **la terraza** |
| garden | **el jardín** |
| porch | **el pórtico** |
| patio | **el patio** |

Now name a few parts of the building itself. Follow the pattern as you give directions:

It's next to (the) _____          **Está al lado de _____**

entrance          **la entrada**

exit          **la salida**

| | |
|---|---|
| steps | **los escalones** |
| garage | **el garaje** |
| carport | **la cochera** |
| walkway | **el camino** |
| stairs | **las escaleras** |
| driveway | **la entrada para carros** |
| parking lot | **el estacionamento** |

Focus on what you are going to be specifically working on:

We'll work on (the) _____.          **Trabajaremos con _____.**

| | |
|---|---|
| siding | **el revestimiento** |
| stucco | **el estuco** |
| painting | **la pintura** |
| masonry | **la mampostería** |
| carpentry | **la carpentería** |
| installation | **la instalación** |
| finishing | **el acabado** |
| framing | **el armazón** |

We'll install (the) _____.          **Instalaremos _____.**

| | |
|---|---|
| door | **la puerta** |
| window | **la ventana** |
| flooring | **el piso** |
| wall | **la pared** |
| roof | **el tejado** |
| gate | **el portón** |
| fence | **la cerca** |

Continue to name exterior features:

| Go to (the)… | **Vaya a…** |
|---|---|
| bar-b-que | **la parrilla** |
| bench | **la banca** |
| bridge | **el puente** |
| fire pit | **la fogota** |
| flower box | **la plantera** |
| fountain | **el fuente** |
| gazebo | **el belvedere** |
| greenhouse | **el invernadero** |
| hot tub | **el jacuzzi** |
| mailbox | **el buzón** |
| pool | **la piscina** |
| shed | **el cobertizo** |

It's easier if you practice new words in sets of threes:

| Look at (the)… | **Mire…** |
|---|---|
| curb | **el bordillo** |
| sidewalk | **la vereda** |
| street | **la calle** |
| | |
| awning | **el toldo** |
| balcony | **el balcón** |
| doorway | **el portal** |

| | |
|---|---|
| eaves | **el alero** |
| fascia | **la fachada** |
| soffit | **la cubierta del alero** |
| | |
| downspout | **la bajada de aguas** |
| drain | **el drenaje** |
| gutter | **el canalón** |
| | |
| block wall | **el muro de bloque** |
| brick wall | **el muro de ladrillo** |
| stone wall | **el muro de piedras** |
| | |
| arch | **el arco** |
| column | **la columna** |
| post | **el poste** |
| | |
| chimney | **la chimenea** |
| light fixture | **el farol** |
| skylight | **el tragaluz** |
| | |
| barrier | **la barrera** |
| railing | **la baranda** |
| ramp | **la rampa** |
| | |
| tennis court | **la cancha de tenis** |
| basketball court | **la cancha de básquetbol** |
| fish pond | **la pesquera** |

Exterior jobs include the same vocabulary as other projects:

It needs (the)…                    **Necesita…**

| | |
|---|---|
| assembly | **el montaje** |
| brace | **el soporte** |
| coping | **el borde decorativo** |
| frame | **el marco** |
| insulation | **el aislamiento** |
| joint | **la unión** |
| lathing | **el listón** |
| trim | **el adorno** |
| wrapping | **el forro** |

Check (the)…                    **Revise…**

| | |
|---|---|
| beams | **las vigas** |
| cables | **los cables** |
| faucets | **los grifos** |
| footings | **las zapatas** |
| outlets | **los enchufes** |
| pipes | **los tubos** |
| vents | **los conductos** |
| wires | **los alambres** |

Now explain everything in detail:

| It's made of … | Es hecho de… |
|---|---|
| alloy | **la aleación** |
| aluminum | **el aluminio** |
| brass | **el latón** |
| brick | **el ladrillo** |
| cement | **el cemento** |
| ceramic | **la cerámica** |
| clay | **la arcilla** |
| composite | **el compuesto** |
| drywall | **el enyesado** |
| felt | **el fieltro** |
| fiberglass | **la fibra de vidrio** |
| glass | **el vidrio** |
| iron | **el hierro** |
| membrane | **la membrana** |
| mesh | **la malla** |
| plastic | **el plástico** |
| plywood | **el contrachapado** |
| rubber | **la goma** |
| steel | **el acero** |
| stone | **la piedra** |
| tin | **el estaño** |
| vinyl | **el vinilo** |
| wood | **la madera** |

Exterior work involves a variety of metals and wood:

| | |
|---|---|
| magnesium | **el magnesio** |
| zinc | **el cinc** |
| bronze | **el bronce** |
| | |
| cedar | **el cedro** |
| fir | **el abeto** |
| pine | **el pino** |

JUST A SUGGESTION

Some Spanish words have a variety of meanings in English:

**el enyesado**   =   drywall, sheetrock, plasterboard, gypsum board, etc.

TRY SOME

Name three outdoor features of a typical home in Spanish.

Name three outdoor construction projects in Spanish.

Name three different kinds of metal in Spanish.

WORKING WORDS: TOOLS AND MATERIALS

Most standard tools are needed for work on the exterior of a building:

Bring (the)…           **Traiga…**

| | |
|---|---|
| air compressor | **el compresor** |
| caulking gun | **la pistola de masilla** |
| charger | **la cargadora** |
| circular saw | **la sierra circular** |
| cordless drill | **el taladro inalámbrica** |
| cutters | **la cizalla** |
| duct tape | **la cinta ploma** |
| extension cord | **la extension eléctrica** |
| file | **la lima** |
| glue | **el pegamento/la cola** |
| hammer | **el martillo** |
| heating gun | **la pistola térmica** |
| level | **el nivel** |
| mallet | **el mazo** |
| masking tape | **la cinta pegajosa** |
| measuring tape | **la cinta métrica** |
| miter saw | **la sierra de cortar en ángulos** |
| nail gun | **la pistola de clavos** |
| pliers | **el alicates** |
| ratchet wrench | **la llave de trinquete** |
| rope | **la soga** |
| sandpaper | **el papel de lija** |
| scraper | **el raspador** |
| screwdriver | **el desarmador** |
| step-ladder | **la escalera baja** |
| utility knife | **la cuchilla** |
| wrench | **la llave inglesa** |

Now grab some of these smaller things:

Pick up (the)…     **Recoja…**

| | |
|---|---|
| adapter | **el adaptador** |
| bit | **la broca** |
| blade | **la hoja** |
| bolt | **el perno** |
| bracket | **el soporte** |
| clamp | **la abrazadora** |
| connector | **el acomplamiento** |
| fastener | **el sujetador** |
| insert | **el anclaje** |
| joint | **la unión** |
| nail | **el clavo** |
| nut | **la tuerca** |
| pin | **la clavija** |
| plate | **la placa** |
| rod | **la barra** |
| screw | **el tornillo** |
| staple | **la grapa** |
| strap | **la tira** |
| washer | **la arandela** |

There are many different kinds of screws. Review your vocabulary:

They are _____ screws.     **Son tornillos para _____.**

| | |
|---|---|
| decking | **terrazas** |
| drywall | **enyesado** |
| fastening | **sujetar** |
| laminating | **laminar** |
| lathing | **listones** |
| masonry | **mampostería** |
| roofing | **tejado** |
| self-drilling | **autotaladrar** |

These heavier items may also be required:

Where's the…?    **¿Dónde está…?**

| | |
|---|---|
| cement mixer | **la mezcladora** |
| crane | **la grúa** |
| extension ladder | **la escalera de extensión** |
| forklift | **la carretilla elevadora** |
| scaffolding | **el andamio** |
| skid-steer loader | **la cargadora Bobcat** |

Review names for specialized tools by listing them under different trades.

## CARPENTRY

| | |
|---|---|
| carpenter's hammer | **el martillo de carpintero** |
| chalk | **la tiza** |
| chisel | **el cincel** |
| flat pencil | **el lápiz plano** |
| framing square | **la escuadra** |
| hand saw | **el serrucho** |
| plane | **el cepillo** |
| plumb bob | **la plomada** |
| plumb line | **el hilo de plomada** |
| sander | **la lijadora** |
| stud finder | **el buscador de montantes** |
| vice | **la prensa** |

## MASONRY

| | |
|---|---|
| brick cutting saw | **la sierra para cortar ladrillos** |
| broom | **la escoba** |
| bull float | **la llana mecánica** |
| edger | **la llana para bordes** |
| finishing broom | **el cepillo de acabado** |
| joint compound | **la pasta para las uniones** |
| jointer | **el marcador de juntas** |
| masonry hammer | **la maceta del albañil** |
| pick | **el pico** |
| pump | **la bomba** |
| shovel | **la pala** |
| stretcher | **el tensor** |
| tie | **el sujetador** |
| tongs | **las tenazas** |
| trowel | **la paleta** |
| wheelbarrow | **la carretilla** |

Give me (the)...    **Deme...**

| | |
|---|---|
| asphalt | **el asfalto** |
| black paper | **el papel negro** |
| block | **el bloque** |
| brick | **el ladrillo** |
| cement | **el cemento** |
| chicken wire | **el alambre de gallinera** |
| compound | **el compuesto** |
| flashing | **el tapajuntas** |
| grating | **la rejilla** |
| lamination | **la lámina** |
| lumber | **el madero** |
| pipe | **la tubería** |
| plaster | **el yeso** |
| rebar | **la varilla** |
| sand | **la arena** |
| sheet metal | **la chapa de metal** |
| wire mesh | **la malla metálica** |

Now, specify exactly what you need:

We need (the)…     **Necesitamos…**

slump stone        **el bloque de hormigón**

cinderblock        **el ladrillo grande de cemento**

cultured stone     **la piedra prefabricada**

Combine these words with your materials:

| | |
|---|---|
| bag | **el saco** |
| board | **la tabla** |
| bucket | **el balde** |
| bundle | **el bulto** |
| coarse | **la hilada** |
| pallet | **la plataforma** |
| panel | **el pánel** |
| row | **la hilera** |
| sheet | **la hoja** |
| stack | **el montón** |
| strip | **la tira** |

JUST A SUGGESTION

Create specialized names for one specific item:

They are…          **Son…**

cap blocks         **bloques de remate**

| | |
|---|---|
| corner blocks | **bloques de esquina** |
| decorative blocks | **bloques decorativos** |
| planter blocks | **bloques para planteras** |
| step blocks | **bloques para pisadas** |

## TRY SOME

Translate:

**la malla metálica** _____

**el sujetador**_____

**la llana mecánica** _____

**el bloque de hormigón** _____

**el buscador de montantes** _____

## WORKING WORDS: DOOR AND WINDOW INSTALLATION

First mention any specialized item that will be needed for the job:

Give me (the)...      **Deme...**

| | |
|---|---|
| door hanger | **la colgadora de puertas** |
| glass cutter | **la cortavidrios** |
| hinge templates | **las plantillas para bisagras** |
| lock mortiser | **la embutidora de cerraduras** |
| lubricant | **el lubricante** |
| scraper | **el raspador** |
| sealant | **el sellador** |
| utility knife | **la cuchilla** |

## DOORS

When it comes to installing doors, these words will be required first:

| It's for (the)… | Es para… |
|---|---|
| entry door | **la puerta de la entrada** |
| back door | **la puerta falsa** |

| double doors | **la doble puerta** |
|---|---|
| Dutch door | **la puerta cortada** |
| French door | **la puerta de dos hojas** |
| garage door | **la puerta de la cochera** |
| revolving door | **la puerta giratoria** |
| sliding door | **la puerta corrediza** |
| storm door | **la contrapuerta** |
| swinging door | **la puerta rotante** |

| They are _____ doors. | Son puertas de _____. |
|---|---|
| aluminum | **aluminio** |
| fiberglass | **fibra de vidrio** |
| hollow | **hueco** |
| solid wood | **madera maciza** |
| steel | **acero** |
| vinyl | **vinilo** |
| wood clad | **madera forrada** |

| It has (the)… | Tiene… |
|---|---|
| grille | **el enrejado** |
| hardware | **el herraje** |
| louvers | **las persianas** |
| mail slot | **la placa del buzón** |
| panels | **los paneles** |
| transom | **el tragaluz** |

Here's (the)…　　　**Aquí tiene…**

| | |
|---|---|
| casing | **el marco** |
| deadbolt | **el pestillo** |
| hinge | **la bisagra** |
| jamb | **la jamba** |
| molding | **la moldura** |
| pin | **el perno** |
| pivot | **el pivote** |
| screen | **el mosquetero** |
| seal | **el sello** |
| stop | **el tope** |
| threshold | **el umbral** |
| toe kick | **la tabla de pie** |
| weather stripping | **el gualdrín** |

Now work on the lock alone:

Use (the)…　　　**Use…**

| | |
|---|---|
| connecting screw | **el tornillo conector** |
| cylinder | **el cilindro** |
| key | **la llave** |
| latch | **el cerrojo** |
| lock casing | **el cuerpo del pestillo** |
| lock nut | **la tuerca de seguridad** |
| plate | **la placa guía** |
| shaft | **el eje** |

Even the garage door has specialized vocabulary:

| Install (the)… | **Instale…** |
|---|---|
| cables | **los cables** |
| drums | **los tambores** |
| opener | **el abrepuerta automático** |
| pulley | **la polea** |
| rails | **los rieles** |
| rollers | **los rodillos** |
| sectional | **el seccional** |
| spring | **el resorte de torsión** |

Stay with short expressions which include related vocabulary:

| Check (the)… | **Revise…** |
|---|---|
| balance | **el equilibrio** |
| clearance | **la distancia de seguridad** |
| slope | **el declive** |

| It's… | **Está…** |
|---|---|
| level | **nivelado** |
| plumb | **justo en medio** |
| square | **cuadrado** |

| Be careful with (the)… | **Tenga cuidado con…** |
|---|---|
| lites | **cristales** |
| divided lites | **cristales divididas** |
| sidelites | **cristales laterals** |

Where's (the)…?   **¿Dónde está…?**

| | |
|---|---|
| door bell | **el timbre** |
| door knob | **la perilla** |
| door knocker | **el picaporte** |

## JUST A SUGGESTION

Sometimes you'll need several words to describe a common door:

| | |
|---|---|
| left hand in-swing | **la puerta de apertura interior hacia la izquierda** |
| right hand out-swing | **la puerta de apertura exterior hacia la derecha** |

## WINDOWS

Now, talk about the window installation:

Install (the)…        **Instale…**

| | |
|---|---|
| awning window | **la ventana marquesina** |
| bay window | **la ventana sastrong** |
| bow window | **la ventana en forma de curva** |
| casement window | **la puertaventana** |
| cellar window | **el respirador** |
| double pane window | **la ventana con doble cristal** |
| fixed window | **la ventana fija** |
| hung window | **la ventana guillotina** |
| sliding window | **la ventana corrediza** |
| storm window | **la guardaventana** |

Bring (the)…          Traiga…

| | |
|---|---|
| arm | **el brazo** |
| balance | **el contrapeso** |
| breast | **el alfeízar** |
| clip | **el sujetador** |
| cord | **el cordón** |
| crank | **la manivela** |
| flashing | **el verteaguas** |
| guide | **la guía** |
| handle | **la manija** |
| head | **la cabecera** |
| hook | **el gancho** |
| housing | **la cubierta** |
| latch | **el trinquete** |
| lever | **la palanca** |
| lintel | **el dintel** |
| lock | **la cerradura** |
| mounting screw | **el tornillo de montaje** |
| mullion | **el montante** |
| operator | **el operador** |
| pane glass | **la hoja de vidrio** |
| pulley | **la polea** |
| reveal | **la jamba** |
| roller | **el rodillo** |
| rubber stripping | **la tira de goma** |
| sash | **la vidriera** |
| sill | **el antepecho** |
| spring | **el resorte** |
| track | **la carrilera** |
| vinyl casing | **el marco de vinilo** |
| weather stripping | **el gualdrín** |

Remember that some hardware is not translated into Spanish:

**los cams**

**los keepers**

**los strikes**

Keep talking about the window itself:

| It's… | **Es/ Está…** |
|---|---|

| | |
|---|---|
| double pane | **de double hoja** |
| insulated | **insulada** |
| noise resistant | **resistente al ruído** |
| sealed | **sellada** |
| self-closing | **cerrada con mecanismo automático** |
| steel reinforced | **reforzada con acero** |
| tinted | **tintada** |
| treated | **tratada** |

| Unload (the)… | **Descargue…** |
|---|---|

| | |
|---|---|
| accessory | **el accesorio** |
| assembly | **el montaje** |
| kit | **el equipo** |
| package | **el paquete** |
| part | **la pieza** |
| set | **el juego** |

## JUST A SUGGESTION

Phrases with numbers and letters are usually translated into Spanish:

| 16-penny nail | **el clavo de dieciséis** |
|---|---|

| 25 gauge steel | **el acero de caliber veinte y cinco** |
| 36-inch door | **la puerta de treinta y seis pulgadas** |
| A-frame | **la forma de A** |
| R-20 insulation | **el aislamiento de veinte** |
| V-groove | **la ranura en V** |
| Z-flashing | **el verteaguas en Z** |

TRY SOME

Delete the word that doesn't belong with the others:

**el declive, el juego, el equipo**

**la llave, el pestillo, el timbre**

**la polea, la cubeta, el resorte**

## WORKING WORDS: STUCCO AND PAINT

The building is wrapped for stucco. Make sure you know these words before you begin:

It has (the)…                    Tiene…

| black paper | **el papel negro** |
| chicken wire | **el alambre de gallinera** |
| membrane | **la membrana** |
| | |
| nails | **los clavos** |
| hooks | **los ganchos** |
| screws | **los tornillos** |
| | |
| scratch coat | **la primera capa** |
| brown coat | **la segunda capa** |
| finish coat | **la capa final** |

It needs (the)…        Necesita…

| additives | **los aditivos** |
| color | **el color** |
| gravel | **la grava** |
| lime | **el cal** |
| mixture | **la mezcla** |
| mortar | **la argamasa** |
| plaster | **el yeso** |
| sand | **la arena** |
| water | **el agua** |

They are…            Son…

| casing beads | **molduras de contramarca** |
| control joints | **juntas de control** |
| corner beads | **bordones de esquina** |
| drip screeds | **maestras de gotea** |
| slip joints | **juntas deslizantes** |
| weep screeds | **maestras inferiors** |

| Check (the)… | Revise… |
|---|---|
| amount | **la cantidad** |
| consistency | **la consistencia** |
| hydration | **la hidratación** |
| surface | **la superficie** |
| texture | **la textura** |
| thickness | **el espesor** |

| Remove (the)… | Quite… |
|---|---|
| blisters | **las ampollas** |
| chalking | **el álcalis** |
| chemical | **la química** |
| dirt | **la suciedad** |
| dust | **el polvo** |
| mold | **el moho** |
| oil | **el aceite** |
| old paint | **la pintura vieja** |
| rust | **el óxido** |
| wax | **la cera** |

It's time for some painting, so begin with some common tools and materials:

Unload (the)...                    **Descargue...**

| | |
|---|---|
| bucket | **el balde** |
| caulking | **el sellador** |
| compressor | **el compresor** |
| drop cloth | **la lona** |
| exterior paint | **la pintura para el exterior** |
| hose | **la manguera** |
| masking tape | **la cinta adhesiva** |
| paint brush | **la brocha para pintar** |
| paint sprayer | **la pistola pintadora** |
| pan | **el plato** |
| putty knife | **la espátula** |
| putty | **la masilla** |
| roller | **el rodillo** |
| sander | **la lijadora** |
| sandpaper | **el papel de lija** |
| scraper | **el raspador** |
| spackling | **el mástique** |
| utility knife | **la cuchilla** |

All materials need to be identified:

I have (the)...                    **Tengo...**

| | |
|---|---|
| acrylic | **el acrílico** |
| enamel | **el esmalte** |
| epoxy | **el epoxi** |
| lacquer | **la laca** |
| primer | **el imprimador** |
| stain | **el tinte** |
| varnish | **el barniz** |

It needs (the)…              **Necesita…**

| | |
|---|---|
| another coat | **otra capa** |
| cleaning | **una limpiada** |
| sanding | **una lijada** |
| stain-block | **antimanchas** |
| texture coat | **una capa de textura** |
| washing | **una lavada** |
| waterproofing | **impermeabilizante** |

And don't forget these:

| | |
|---|---|
| thinner | **el disolvente** |
| turpentine | **la trementina** |
| mineral spirits | **el solvente** |

Painters must know these basic colors, and may need the others that follow:

They want _____ paint.  **Quieren la pintura _____.**

| | |
|---|---|
| black | **negra** |
| blue | **azul** |
| brown | **café** |
| green | **verde** |
| grey | **gris** |
| orange | **anaranjada** |
| pink | **rosada** |
| purple | **morada** |
| red | **roja** |
| white | **blanca** |
| yellow | **amarilla** |

The color is…              **El color es…**

| | |
|---|---|
| aqua marine | **verde mar** |
| copper | **cobrizo** |
| cream | **crema** |
| dark green | **verde oscuro** |
| golden | **dorado** |
| light blue | **azul claro** |
| navy blue | **azul marino** |
| silver | **plateado** |
| sky blue | **celeste** |
| tan | **café claro** |

Many paint colors are similar to their equivalents in English:

| | |
|---|---|
| emerald | **esmeralda** |
| lilac | **lila** |
| olive | **oliva** |
| rose | **rosa** |
| scarlet | **escarlata** |
| turquoise | **turquesa** |
| violet | **violeta** |

Exterior painting requires care, so use all the words you know:

Look at (the)…                **Mire…**

| | |
|---|---|
| design | **el diseño** |
| pattern | **el patrón** |
| pigment | **el pigmento** |
| plan | **el plano** |
| shade | **el matiz** |
| style | **el estilo** |
| type | **el tipo** |

These are descriptive words that are heard used around exterior paint:

| It looks… | Se ve… |
|---|---|
| bright | **brillante** |
| clean | **limpio** |
| decorative | **decorativo** |
| dirty | **sucio** |
| dry | **seco** |
| fast drying | **rápido para secar** |
| flat | **mate** |
| glossy | **lustroso** |
| opaque | **opaco** |
| satin | **satinada** |
| semi-gloss | **semi-lustroso** |
| sticky | **pegajoso** |
| synthetic | **sintético** |
| thick | **espeso** |
| thin | **aguado** |
| wet | **mojado** |

## JUST A SUGGESTION

Painting jobs get messy, so use words that refer to cleaning:

| Use (the)… | Use… |
|---|---|
| mop | **la fregona** |
| rag | **el trapo** |
| towel | **la toalla** |
| sponge | **la esponja** |
| bucket | **el balde** |

Translate into English:

**Quite el óxido.**

**Necesita más arena.**

**Traiga la pintura del color celeste.**

WORKING WORDS: OTHER EXTERIOR WORK

First remember the names for those who are working around you:

Speak with (the) _____.  **Hable con _____.**

| | |
|---|---|
| plumber | **el fontanero** |
| electrician | **el electricista** |
| painter | **el pintero** |
| welder | **el soldadero** |
| landscaper | **el jardinero** |
| carpenter | **el carpintero** |
| mason | **el albañil** |
| worker | **el obrero** |
| bricklayer | **el ladrillero** |
| drywaller | **el yesero** |
| installer | **el instalador** |
| architect | **el arquitecto** |

Can you guess what these Spanglish words mean?

**los sheetroqueros**

**los ruferos**

**los freimers**

## SIDING

They want (the)…          **Quieren…**

| | |
|---|---|
| fascia board | **la moldura del alero** |
| paneling | **los paneles** |
| plank | **el tablón** |
| shake | **el listón** |
| sheathing | **el entablado** |
| sheeting | **la lamina** |
| shutter | **la contraventana** |
| trim | **el adorno** |
| veneer | **la chapa** |
| wall tile | **el azulejo** |

Use (the)…          **Use…**

particle board          **la madera aglomerada**

fiber board          **la madera de fibra**

vinyl board          **la tabla de vinilo**

It's…          **Es…**

seamless          **sin costura**

tapered          **ahusado**

wrapped          **forrado**

It's…          **Está…**

overlapped          **superpuesto**

| | |
|---|---|
| straight | **recto** |
| aligned | **alineado** |

Look closer at the siding material:

| | |
|---|---|
| I see (the)… | **Veo…** |

| | |
|---|---|
| bevel | **el bisel** |
| tongue and groove | **el lengüete y ranura** |
| channel | **el acanalado** |

## JUST A SUGGESTION

The word "board" is "**la tabla**" in Spanish, but generally changes when it becomes part of a specialized material:

| | |
|---|---|
| ledger board | **el larguero** |
| strand board | **el bambú** |
| mortar board | **el birrete** |
| chip board | **el aglomerado** |
| clap board | **la tablilla** |

## FLOORING

Most outdoor flooring involves the following materials:

Let's use (the)…    **Usamos…**

| | |
|---|---|
| bricks | **los ladrillos** |
| cobblestones | **los adoquines** |
| concrete pads | **las losas de concreto** |
| pavers | **los pavers** |
| pebbles | **los guijarros** |

Bring (the)…    **Traiga…**

| | |
|---|---|
| cast stone | **la piedra moldeada** |
| flagstone | **la losa de piedra** |
| floor tile | **la baldosa** |
| granite | **el granite** |
| limestone | **la piedra caliza** |
| marble | **el mármol** |
| masonry tile | **el ladrillo cerámico** |
| natural stone | **la piedra natural** |
| quartzite | **la cuarcita** |
| sandstone | **la piedra arenisca** |
| slate | **la pizarra** |
| stepping stone | **la pisada** |
| travertine | **la piedra travertine** |

Here are some other kinds of outdoor flooring:

We have (the)…    **Tenemos…**

| | |
|---|---|
| artificial grass | **el césped artificial** |
| carpet | **la alfombra** |
| matting | **las esteras** |
| rubber tiles | **las tejas de goma** |
| wood decking | **el entarimado de madera** |

Now name a few tools and materials that are needed when working with outdoor materials:

| | |
|---|---|
| adhesive | **el adhesive** |
| epoxy | **la resina epoxi** |
| grout | **la lechada** |
| masonry saw | **la sierra de mampostería** |
| notched trowel | **la llana dentada** |
| rubber grout float | **la llana de goma** |
| rubber mallet | **el mazo de goma** |
| spacers | **los esparcidores** |

And describe what you see:

| They are… | **Están…** |
|---|---|
| clear | **claros** |
| colored | **coloreados** |
| dark | **oscuros** |
| fixed | **fijas** |
| loose | **flojas** |
| polished | **pulidos** |
| porous | **poroso** |

There is/are......   **Hay...**

| | |
|---|---|
| condensation | **condesación** |
| corrosion | **corrosión** |
| deterioration | **deterioro** |
| discoloration | **descoloramiento** |
| imperfections | **imperfecciones** |
| | |
| bubbles | **burbujas** |
| bumps | **bultos** |
| cracks | **grietas** |
| dents | **melladuras** |
| holes | **huecos** |
| knots | **nudos** |
| loops | **lazos** |

These words will help you with another outdoor concern:

It's...            **Es/Está...**

| | |
|---|---|
| frozen | **congelado** |
| moist | **húmedo** |
| soaked | **empapado** |
| waterproof | **impermeable** |
| watertight | **hermético** |
| wet | **mojado** |

## JUST A SUGGESTION

Words refering to chemicals are similar in both languages:

| | |
|---|---|
| polyethylene | **polietileno** |

| | |
|---|---|
| polystyrene | **poliestireno** |
| polymer | **polímero** |
| polyurethane | **poliuretano** |
| polychrome | **policromo** |

## TRY SOME

Name three words that relate to the installation of siding in Spanish.

Name three professionals who work on the exterior of a home in Spanish.

Name three different kinds of exterior flooring in Spanish.

## WORKING WORDS: DESCRIBING THE JOB

Start off with these pairs of opposites. They can be used to describe work on the exterior:

| | |
|---|---|
| cramped | **estrecho** |
| spacious | **amplio** |
| | |
| loose | **flojo** |
| tight | **apretado** |
| | |
| hollow | **hueco** |
| solid | **macizo** |
| | |
| coarse | **áspero** |
| smooth | **liso** |
| | |
| exposed | **expuesto** |
| hidden | **oculto** |

Here are more words you should already know:

The _____ piece.          **La pieza _____.**

| | |
|---|---|
| corner | **de la esquina** |
| edge | **del borde** |
| inside | **interior** |
| lower | **inferior** |
| outside | **exterior** |
| side | **lateral** |
| surface | **de la superficie** |
| upper | **superior** |

When on the job, pull words that you need today:

It isn't…          **No es/ está…**

| | |
|---|---|
| corrugated | **corrugado** |
| double | **doble** |
| even | **nivelado** |
| insulated | **aislante** |
| manufactured | **prefabricado** |
| painted | **pintado** |
| parallel | **paralelo** |
| perforated | **perforado** |
| pre-painted | **pintado adelantado** |
| protected | **protegido** |
| single | **sencillo** |
| synthetic | **sintético** |

As you know, many Spanish words resemble their equivalents in English.
Here are some more:

| | |
|---|---|
| applied | **aplicado** |
| configured | **configurado** |
| formed | **formado** |
| protected | **protegido** |
| specified | **especificado** |

This time, give detail to the building itself:

| The style is… | **El estilo es…** |
|---|---|
| classic | **clásico** |
| coastal | **playera** |
| colonial | **colonial** |
| contemporary | **contemporario** |
| country | **campestre** |
| French | **francés** |
| Italian | **italiano** |
| Mediterranean | **mediteráneo** |
| rustic | **rústico** |
| Spanish | **español** |
| traditional | **tradicional** |
| Tudor | **inglés** |
| Victorian | **victoriano** |

| It's… | **Es…** |
|---|---|
| circular | **circular** |
| diagonal | **diagonal** |
| half-circular | **medio-circular** |
| hexagonal | **hexagonal** |
| horizontal | **horizontal** |
| octagonal | **octagonal** |
| quarter-circular | **cuarto-circular** |
| square | **cuadrado** |
| triangular | **triangular** |
| vertical | **vertical** |

| It will be… | Será… |
|---|---|
| custom-built | **hecho a la orden** |
| custom-designed | **diseñado a la orden** |
| custom-painted | **pintado a la orden** |

And don't forget the building materials:

| It's… | Es/Está… |
|---|---|
| sealed | **sellado** |
| treated | **tratado** |
| rustproof | **inoxidable** |
| durable | **duradero** |
| waterproof | **impermeable** |
| leak-proof | **que no se gotea** |
| lead free | **sin plomo** |
| anti-corrosive | **resistente a la corrosion** |
| stainless | **anti-corrosivo** |
| galvanized | **galvanizado** |
| fire-rated | **resistente al fuego** |

TRY SOME

What is the opposite of the following Spanish words?

**apretado** _____

**superior** _____

**doble** _____

# WORKING WORDS: ON-SITE ACTIONS

Write down only those "verbs" that you use time and again:

| You have to… | Tiene que … | |
|---|---|---|
| to adjust | **ajustar** | **Tiene que ajustar los rodillos.** |
| to align | **alinear** | |
| to apply | **aplicar** | |
| to bond | **adherir** | |
| to bore | **calar** | |
| to caulk | **calafatear** | |
| to check | **revisar** | |
| to clean | **limpiar** | |
| to connect | **conectar** | |
| to correct | **corregir** | |
| to cover | **cubrir** | |
| to cut | **cortar** | |
| to distribute | **distribuir** | |
| to divert | **desviar** | |
| to erect | **eregir** | |
| to glue | **encolar** | |
| to heat | **calentar** | |
| to hold | **sostener** | |
| to inlay | **embutir** | |
| to install | **instalar** | |
| to join | **juntar** | |

| | |
|---|---|
| to level | **nivelar** |
| to loosen | **soltar** |
| to lubricate | **lubricar** |
| to measure | **medir** |
| to modify | **modificar** |
| to mount | **amontar** |
| to operate | **operar** |
| to paint | **pintar** |
| to pour | **verter** |
| to pre-drill | **pretaladrar** |
| to prep | **preparar** |
| to press | **apretar** |
| to probe | **sondear** |
| to protect | **proteger** |
| to put | **poner** |
| to reach | **alcanzar** |
| to reduce | **reducir** |
| to refill | **rellenar** |
| to remove | **quitar** |
| to repair | **reparar** |
| to replace | **sustituir** |
| to sand | **lijar** |
| to screw in | **atornillar** |
| to seal | **sellar** |
| to separate | **separar** |
| to set | **colocar** |
| to smooth | **alisar** |

| | |
|---|---|
| to soak | **remojar** |
| to straighten | **enderezar** |
| to stretch | **estirar** |
| to support | **apoyar** |
| to touch up | **retocar** |
| to wash | **lavar** |
| to wet | **mojar** |
| to wipe | **pasar un trapo** |
| to wrap | **forar** |

Be as detailed as you like:

| It's important… | **Es importante…** |
|---|---|
| to pressure wash | **lavar a presión** |
| to pry | **levantar con palanca** |
| to rabbet | **cortar ranura** |

| It's going … | **Va a …** |
|---|---|
| to break | **romperse** |
| to peel | **pelarse** |
| to split | **partirse** |
| to squirt | **sacarse a chorro** |
| to stick | **pegarse** |

| It needs … | Necesita… |
|---|---|
| to breathe | **respirar** |
| to cure | **curar** |
| to dry | **secar** |
| to expand | **ampliar** |
| to harden | **endurecer** |

## JUST A SUGGESTION

In Spanish, several words can be "formed" from basic action words. Notice the pattern:

| to ventilate | **ventilar** |
|---|---|
| ventilating | **ventilatando** |
| ventilation | **la ventilación** |
| ventilated | **ventilado** |
| vent | **el ventilador** |

## TRY SOME

Follow the pattern as you create new words:

| to form | **formar** | **formacíon** | **formado** |
|---|---|---|---|
| to penetrate | **penetrar** | _____ | _____ |
| to renovate | **renovar** | _____ | _____ |
| to install | **instalar** | | |
| to repair | **reparar** | | |
| to apply | **aplicar** | | |

| | |
|---|---|
| to classify | **clasificar** |
| to insulate | **insular** |

## GRAMMAR TIME

Unlike the preterit, which expresses a completed action, the "imperfect" tense in Spanish expresses a continued, customary, or repeated action in the past. In other words, it's used to express "what was happening" or "what used to happen" before.

Let's take a look at a simple formula that shows how to create "imperfect" forms with most action words. Fortunately, it's a whole lot easier than the preterit. To get a feel for its usage, pay extra attention to the English translations.

For regular "**ar**" actions, change the endings just like this example:

<u>to work</u>                                                          <u>**trabajar**</u>

| | |
|---|---|
| I was working | **trabajaba** |
| You were working; He, She was working | **trabajaba** |
| You (pl.), They were working | **trabajaban** |
| We were working | **trabajábamos** |

Check out these translations. These "actions" were never really "started and completed":

| | |
|---|---|
| I used to work in Mexico. | **Trabajaba en Mexico.** |
| Were they working? | **¿Trabajaban?** |
| We wouldn't work there. | **No trabajábamos allí.** |

For regular "**er**" and "**ir**" actions, the endings are formed differently:

| | |
|---|---|
| <u>to eat</u> | **<u>comer</u>** |

| | |
|---|---|
| I was eating. | **comía** |
| You were eating; He, She was eating. | **comía** |
| You (pl.), They were eating | **comían** |
| We were eating | **comíamos** |

## JUST A SUGGESTION

Practice by listening carefully to Spanish speakers. Knowing the difference between the preterit and imperfect can be important:

| | |
|---|---|
| We were finishing. | **Terminábamos.** |
| We finished. | **Terminamos.** |

## TRY SOME

Fill in the English. You don't need any help:

| | |
|---|---|
| <u>to write</u> | **<u>escribir</u>** |

**I used to write.**

_____

_____

_____

**escribía**

**escribía**

**escribían**

**escribíamos**

THE ONE-LINERS

Learn these common one-liners and how they are used. Notice the "**el - la**" business:

that one        **ese** or **esa**

these ones   **estos**  or **estas**

this one        **este** or **esta**

those ones   **esos** or **esas**

When you don't care to be specific, use "**esto**" and "**eso**":

What's this?        **¿Qué es esto?**

What's that?        **¿Qué es eso?**

When the object of discussion is far away, try these:

That martillo is mine.        **Aquel martillo es mío.**

Those hammers are mine.        **Aquellos martillos son míos.**

That saw is mine.        **Aquella sierra es mía.**

Those saws are mine.        **Aquellas sierras son mías.**

Once a co-worker or employee establishes a friendly relationship, it's not uncommon for native Hispanics to use nicknames when referring to others. It is meant to show intimacy, and not disrespect. Besides, it might be fun to look up the translations for any terms of endearment that you hear.

# CHAPTER NINE

THE INTERIOR

**el interior**

(ehl een-teh-ree-'ohr)

WORKING WORDS: THE BUILDING'S INTERIOR

First explain what you're going to be doing with the interior:

I'm working on (the)…          **Trabajo en…**

| | |
|---|---|
| carpentry | **la carpentería** |
| drywall | **el enyesado** |
| finishing | **el acabado** |
| flooring | **la instalación del suelo** |
| insulation | **el aislamiento** |
| painting | **la pintura** |
| plumbing | **la fontanería** |
| wiring | **la instalación eléctrica** |
| lighting | **la iluminación** |

It needs (the)…          **Necesita…**

| | |
|---|---|
| windows | **las ventanas** |
| doors | **las puertas** |
| cabinets | **los gabinetes** |
| fixture | **el artefacto** |
| appliance | **el electrodoméstico** |
| light | **la luz** |
| assembly | **el montaje** |
| repair | **la reparación** |
| installation | **la instalación** |

Now, name the interior features of a typical American home:

That is (the)…          **Eso es…**

| | |
|---|---|
| attic | **el ático** |
| balcony | **el balcón** |
| basement | **el sótano** |
| bathroom | **el baño** |
| bedroom | **la recámara** |
| breakfast room | **el ante-comedor** |
| den | **la sala de familia** |
| dining room | **el comedor** |
| dressing room | **el vestuario** |
| foyer | **el vestíbulo** |
| garage | **el garaje** |
| greenhouse | **el invernadero** |
| guest room | **el cuarto de visitas** |
| hallway | **el pasillo** |
| kitchen | **la cocina** |
| laundry room | **la lavandería** |
| library | **la biblioteca** |
| living room | **la sala** |
| loft | **el desván** |
| nursery | **el cuarto de los niños** |
| office | **la oficina** |
| playroom | **la sala de juegos** |
| storeroom | **el depósito** |
| studio | **el estudio** |
| sunroom | **el solario** |
| utility room | **la despensa** |

Look over these other indoor items:

Look at (the)…     **Mire…**

| | |
|---|---|
| ceiling | **el techo** |
| wall | **la pared** |
| floor | **el piso** |
| | |
| closet | **el ropero** |
| counter | **el mostrador** |
| drawer | **el cajón** |
| | |
| steps | **los escalones** |
| stairs | **las escaleras** |
| railings | **las barandas** |
| | |
| bookshelf | **el librero** |
| fireplace | **el fogón** |
| bar | **el bar** |
| | |
| doorway | **el portal** |
| column | **la columna** |
| partition | **el tabique** |

You'll find these in the bathroom:

| | |
|---|---|
| shower | **la ducha** |
| toilet | **el excusado** |
| bathtub | **la tina de báno** |
| bathroom sink | **el lavabo** |
| mirror | **el espejo** |
| medicine chest | **el botiquín** |
| faucet | **el grifo** |

Industrial buildings have their own names for interior features:

| Go to (the)… | Vaya a… |
|---|---|
| ground floor | la planta baja |
| first floor | el primer piso |
| second floor | el segundo piso |
| | |
| entrance | la entrada |
| exit | la salida |
| lobby | el vestíbulo |
| | |
| restroom | el servicio |
| elevator | el ascensor |
| carport | el cobertizo para carros |

Be specific when you refer to an indoor project:

| It needs (the)… | Necesita… |
|---|---|
| baseboard | el zócalo |
| counter top | la cubierta del mostrador |
| mantle | la repisa de la chimenea |
| moulding | la moldura |
| paneling | el panelado |
| shelf | el estante |
| soffit | la cubierta del alero |
| trim | el adorno |
| veneer | la chapa |
| wall tile | el azulejo |

JUST A SUGGESTION

How many household items can you identify in Spanish? Many of these are used in home décor:

They have (the) . . .                    **Tienen . . .**

| antificial plant | **la planta artificial** |
|---|---|
| basket | **la canasta** |
| candelabra | **el candelabro** |
| curtain | **la cortina** |
| drawing | **el dibujo** |
| flowerpot | **la maceta** |
| lampshade | **la pantalla** |
| mat | **el tapete** |
| mirror | **el espejo** |
| painting | **la pintura** |
| pedestal | **el pedestal** |
| photograph | **el foto** |
| picture | **el cuadro** |
| portrait | **el retrato** |
| pottery | **la alfarería** |
| statue | **la estatua** |
| tapestry | **el tapiz** |
| vase | **el florero** |

## WORKING WORDS: TOOLS AND MATERIALS

Most of these tools are needed for work on the interior of a building:

Bring (the)…            **Traiga…**

| | |
|---|---|
| air compressor | **el compresor** |
| caulking gun | **la pistola de masilla** |
| chisel | **el cincel** |
| circular saw | **la sierra circular** |
| cordless drill | **el taladro inalámbrica** |
| crowbar | **la pata de cabra** |
| dolly | **la plataforma con ruedas** |
| duct tape | **la cinta ploma** |
| extension cord | **la extension eléctrica** |
| file | **la lima** |
| framing square | **la escuadra** |
| glue | **la cola** |
| hammer | **el martillo** |
| level | **el nivel** |
| masking tape | **la cinta adhesiva** |
| miter saw | **la sierra de cortar en ángulos** |
| nail gun | **la pistola de clavos** |
| pliers | **el alicates** |
| plumb bob | **la plomada** |
| ratchet wrench | **la llave de trinquete** |
| sandpaper | **el papel de lija** |
| scraper | **el raspador** |
| screwdriver | **el desarmador** |
| shears | **las tijeras** |
| step-ladder | **la escalera baja** |
| stud finder | **el buscador de montantes** |
| tape measure | **la cinta métrica** |
| utility knife | **la cuchilla** |
| wet-dry vac | **la aspiradora de agua** |
| wrench | **la llave inglesa** |

I'm missing (the)…        **Me falta…**

| | |
|---|---|
| nail | **el clavo** |
| staple | **la grapa** |
| screw | **el tornillo** |
| fastener | **el sujetador** |
| nut | **la tuerca** |
| washer | **la arandela** |
| bolt | **el perno** |
| pin | **la clavija** |
| bracket | **el soporte** |
| clamp | **la abrazadora** |
| plate | **la placa** |
| joint | **el codo** |
| insert | **el anclaje** |
| connector | **el acomplamiento** |
| adapter | **el adaptador** |
| flange | **la ala** |
| bolt | **el perno** |
| bit | **la broca** |

On any job with the interior, there's always need for these materials:

Use the)…        **Use…**

| | |
|---|---|
| glass | **el vidrio** |
| lumber | **la madera** |
| paint | **la pintura** |
| pipe | **la tubería** |
| plaster | **el yeso** |
| wire | **el alambre** |
| cement | **el cemento** |

TRY SOME

Translate:

I need the scraper.          **Necesito el raspador.**

I need the plaster.          _____

I need the stud-finder.       _____

I need the nut.              _____


WORKING WORDS: DRYWALL


Before hanging sheetrock, name some of a drywaller's tools and supplies:


Give me (the)…          **Deme…**

| | |
|---|---|
| C-clamp | **la prensa de tornillo** |
| corner trowel | **la llana para esquinas** |
| drywall hammer | **el martillo para tablarroca** |
| drywall tape | **la cinta adhesiva** |
| electric screwdriver | **el destornillador eléctrico** |
| level | **el nivel** |
| mud mixer | **la mezcladora de masilla** |
| pencil | **el lápiz** |
| plane | **el cepillo de mano** |
| power drill | **el taladro eléctrico** |
| pump | **la bomba** |
| putty knife | **la espátula** |
| rasp | **la raspadora** |
| router | **el acanalador** |
| sponge | **la esponja** |
| stapler | **la grapadora** |
| straightedge | **la regla metálica** |
| stud finder | **el detector de vigas** |
| tape measure | **la cinta métrica** |
| taping knife | **la cuchilla para cinta adhesiva** |
| tin snips | **las tijeras para hojalata** |
| trowel hawk | **la llana enyesadora** |
| wallboard square | **la escuadra para paneles** |

Note the translation for these important items:

Do you have (the)...?    **¿Tiene usted...?**

| drywall compound | **la masilla premexclada** |
| drywall hammer | **el martillo para enyesado** |
| drywall nails | **los clavos para enyesado** |
| drywall screws | **los tornillos para enyesado** |
| drywall spackle | **el mastique para resanar** |

To learn the names for some tools, it's best to group them into smaller sets:

I brought (the)...    **Traje...**

| plumb bob | **la plomada** |
| chalk | **la tiza** |
| chalk line | **el cordón de tiza** |
| | |
| keyhole saw | **el serrucho de calar** |
| wallboard saw | **el serrucho corto** |
| saber saw | **la sierra de vaivén** |
| | |
| hand sander | **la lijadora de mano** |
| sanding pole | **la lijadora de mango** |
| power sander | **la lijadora eléctrica** |

When drywall is involved, these other materials will be in demand:

Unload (the)…    **Descargue…**

| | |
|---|---|
| backer board | **el respaldo** |
| control joint | **la junta de control** |
| corner bead | **el bordón de esquina** |
| flex strip | **la tira flexible** |
| J bead | **el bordón de J** |
| L bead | **el bordón de L** |
| mud | **el barro** |
| panel | **el panel** |
| reveal | **el telar** |
| trim tab | **la aleta de contramarco** |
| wall angle | **el ángulo de pared** |

Check (the)…    **Revise…**

| | |
|---|---|
| crack | **la grieta** |
| hole | **el hueco** |
| joint | **la unión** |
| opening | **la abertura** |
| seam | **la costura** |

It needs (the)…    **Necesita…**

| | |
|---|---|
| finish | **el acabado** |
| coat | **la capa** |
| texture | **la textura** |

JUST A SUGGESTION

Installers need to double check their measurements:

| | |
|---|---|
| 90° angle | **el ángulo de noventa grados** |
| one inch bullnose | **la esquina boleada de una pulgada** |
| #10 screws | **los tornillos de número diez** |
| ¾ inch diameter | **un diámetro de tres cuartos de una pulgada** |
| forty inches high | **de cuarenta pulgadas de alto** |

TRY SOME

Name three tools that are needed for drywall installation in Spanish.

Name three materials that are needed for drywall installation in Spanish.

## WORKING WORDS: CABINET INSTALLATION

| Bring (the) _____ cabinets. | **Traiga los gabinetes _____.** |
|---|---|

| | |
|---|---|
| custom | **personalizados** |
| stock | **de almacenamiento** |
| | |
| face-frame | **con marco visible** |
| frameless | **sin marco** |
| | |
| base | **de base** |
| wall | **de pared** |

Cabinets are found throughout the average home:

319

They're in (the)…                    **Están en…**

| | |
|---|---|
| bathroom | **el lavabo** |
| bedroom | **la dormitorio** |
| garage | **el garaje** |
| hallway | **el pasillo** |
| home office | **la oficina en casa** |
| kitchen | **los gabinetes para la cocina** |
| storage room | **el almacenamiento** |

Here are other things that may include some cabinetry:

Work on (the)…                       **Trabaje con…**

| | |
|---|---|
| closet | **el ropero** |
| entertainment center | **el centro de entretenimiento** |
| wall unit | **la unidad de pared** |
| window seat | **el asiento de ventana** |
| staircase | **las escaleras** |
| desk | **el escritorio** |
| bookshelf | **el librero** |
| filing cabinet | **el archivero** |

These items are generally installed in the kitchen cabinet area:

They want (the)…          **Quieren…**

| | |
|---|---|
| cutting board | **la tabla para cortar** |
| island workspace | **la isla de trabajo para la cocina** |
| Lazy Susan | **la bendeja giratoria** |
| pantry cupboard | **el armario de la despensa** |
| pullout trash container | **el bote de basura extraíble** |

It's time to name parts of the cabinet itself:

| Here's (the)... | Aquí tiene... |
|---|---|
| back plate | **la placa** |
| bolt | **el perno** |
| cabinet screw | **el tornillo de fijación** |
| catch | **la cerradura** |
| door | **la puerta** |
| drawer | **el cajón** |
| hinge | **la bisagra** |
| knob | **el botón** |
| mounting screw | **el tornillo de montaje** |
| nut | **la tuerca** |
| divider | **el divisor** |
| pull | **el tirador** |
| shelf | **el estante** |
| slide | **la corredera** |
| trim | **el adorno** |
| washer | **la arandela** |
| tray | **la bandeja** |
| clip | **la abrazadera** |
| pegboard | **el tablero de clavijas** |
| shelf pin | **la clavija para estantes** |
| bracket | **la ménsula** |

Now provide details about the materials you are working with:

| It's made of... | Es hecho de... |
|---|---|
| brass | **el latón** |
| bronze | **el bronce** |
| chrome | **el cromo** |
| copper | **el cobre** |
| iron | **el hierro** |
| nickel | **el níquel** |
| pewter | **el peltre** |
| veneer | **la chapa** |
| laminate | **la lámina** |
| vinyl | **el vinilo** |

| The wood is… | La madera es… |
|---|---|
| cherry | **el cerezo** |
| birch | **el abedul** |
| spruce | **la picea** |
| cypress | **el ciprés** |
| cedar | **el cedro** |
| oak | **el roble** |
| pine | **el pino** |
| walnut | **el nogal** |
| maple | **el arce** |
| MDF | **la sintética** |

| The style is… | Es de estilo… |
|---|---|
| cathedral | **cathedral** |
| contemporary | **contemporáneo** |
| mission | **misión** |
| Roman | **romano** |
| traditional | **tradicional** |

| It's… | Está… |
|---|---|
| arched | **con arco** |
| rectangular | **rectangular** |
| square | **cuadrado** |

Be sure to mention the cabinet hinge:

| They're… | Son… |
|---|---|
| butterfly | **mariposas** |
| European | **europeas** |
| H-style | **de estilo "H"** |
| inset | **insertas** |
| offset | **con saliente** |
| overlay | **superpuestas** |
| pin | **de perno** |
| T-style | **de estilo "T"** |
| wrap-around | **envolventes** |

| It's… | Es… |
|---|---|
| antique | **antiguo** |
| brushed | **mate** |
| ceramic | **cerámico** |
| enameled | **esmaltado** |
| metallic | **metálico** |
| polished | **pulido** |
| satin | **de raso** |
| shiny | **brillante** |
| silver plated | **plateado** |

TRY SOME

Delete the word in each set that doesn't belong with the other two:

**el pino, el adorno, el cedro**

**el hueco, la abertura, el barro**

**cerámico, cuadrado, metálico**

**el antiguo, el escritorio, el librero**

**el látón, el cobre, el cajón**

WORKING WORDS: INTERIOR DOOR INSTALLATION

The following tools and materials are used for hanging the interior door:

Use (the)…          **Use…**

| clamp | **la abrazadera** |
|-------|------------------|
| door hanger | **la colgadora de puertas** |
| finishing nails | **los clavos sin cabeza** |
| lock mortiser | **la embutidora de cerraduras** |
| miter box | **la caja de ángulos** |
| miter saw | **la sierra para cortar ángulos** |
| plane | **el cepillo** |
| power sander | **la lijadora** |
| screws | **los tornillos** |
| shims | **las calzas** |
| vice | **la prensa** |

Grab (the)…          **Agarre…**

| casing | **el marco** |
|---|---|
| deadbolt | **el pestillo** |
| door knob | **la perilla** |
| hardware | **el herraje** |
| hinge | **la bisagra** |
| jamb | **la jamba** |
| molding | **la moldura** |
| pin | **el perno** |
| pivot | **el pivote** |
| screen | **el mosquetero** |
| seal | **el sello** |
| stop | **el tope** |
| threshold | **el umbral** |
| toe kick | **la tabla de pie** |
| weather stripping | **el gualdrín** |

It needs (the)…          **Necesita…**

| connecting screw | **el tornillo conector** |
|---|---|
| cylinder | **el cilindro** |
| latch | **el cerrojo** |
| lock casing | **el cuerpo del pestillo** |
| lock nut | **la tuerca de seguridad** |
| shaft | **el eje** |
| strike plate | **el cajetín** |

Specifically name what the job calls for:

Install (the)…          **Instale…**

| | |
|---|---|
| double doors | **la doble puerta** |
| Dutch door | **la puerta cortada** |
| folding door | **la puerta plegadiza** |
| French door | **la puerta de dos hojas** |
| multifold door | **la puerta de acordeón** |
| pre-hung door | **la puerta prefabricada** |
| sliding door | **la puerta corrediza** |
| swinging door | **la puerta de vaivén** |

It's a/an...          **Es una...**

| | |
|---|---|
| inswing door | **puerta que abre hacia adentro** |
| outswing door | **puerta que abre hacia afuera** |
| | |
| left-hand door | **puerta de la mano izquierda** |
| right-hand door | **puerta de la mano derecha** |

It has (the)...          **Tiene...**

| | |
|---|---|
| louvers | **las persianas** |
| panels | **los paneles** |
| springs | **los resortes** |
| tracks | **los carriles** |
| trim | **los adornos** |
| wheels | **las ruedecillas** |

It's made of...          **Es de...**

| | |
|---|---|
| aluminum | **aluminio** |
| fiberglass | **fibra de vidrio** |
| glass | **vidrio** |
| hollow core | **hueca** |
| solid core | **maciza** |
| solid wood | **madera sólida** |
| stainless steel | **acero inoxidable** |
| vinyl | **vinilo** |
| wood clad | **madera forrada** |

Include a few wood products:

| I like (the)… | **Me gusta…** |
|---|---|
| birch | **el abedul** |
| hardwood | **la madera dura** |
| mahogany | **la caoba** |
| oak | **el roble** |
| pine | **el pino** |
| plywood | **el contrachapado** |
| veneer | **la chapa** |

Now get to work on the installation:

| Check (the)… | **Revise…** |
|---|---|
| doorway | **el vano** |
| floor | **el piso** |
| frame | **el marco** |
| sub-floor | **el subpiso** |
| wall | **la pared** |

| Look at (the)… | Mire… |
|---|---|
| balance | **el equilibrio** |
| chalk line | **la línea de marcar** |
| clearance | **la distancia de seguridad** |
| corner | **la esquina** |
| dimensions | **las dimensiones** |
| size | **el tamaño** |
| slope | **el declive** |
| style | **el estilo** |

| Make sure it's… | Asegúrese que está… |
|---|---|
| level | **nivelado** |
| plumb | **justo en medio** |
| square | **cuadrado** |

TRY SOME

Choose the correct ending to each sentence below:

**La puerta de vinilo…**          **…tiene carriles.**

**La puerta cerrediza…**          **…necesita muchas bisagras.**

**La puerta de acordeón…**        **…no es de madera sólida.**

## WORKING WORDS: APPLIANCES AND FIXTURES

Begin by reviewing the indoor work that still needs to be completed. Stick with those words you already know:

It needs (the)…          **Necesita…**

| | |
|---|---|
| cable | **el cable** |
| pipe | **el tubo** |
| wire | **el alambre** |

Finish the…          **Termine con…**

| | |
|---|---|
| air conditioning | **el aire acondicionado** |
| electrical | **la electricidad** |
| heating | **la calefacción** |
| insulation | **el aislamiento** |
| lighting | **la iluminación** |
| plumbing | **la fontanería** |

Check (the)…        **Revise…**

| | |
|---|---|
| digital cable | **el cable digital** |
| fusebox | **la caja de fusibles** |
| gas meter | **el medidor de gas** |
| satellite dish | **el disco de satellite** |
| water valve | **la válvula de agua** |
| bathtub | **la tina de baño** |
| boiler | **la caldera** |
| dryer | **la secadora** |
| furnace | **el horno** |
| heater | **el calentador** |
| shower | **la ducha** |
| toilet | **el excusado** |
| washer | **la lavadora** |
| water heater | **el calentador para el agua** |

Keep going:

Did you see…?     **¿Vió…?**

| | |
|---|---|
| alarms | **las alarmas** |
| fans | **los ventiladores** |
| faucets | **los grifos** |
| lights | **las luces** |
| vents | **los conductos** |

Now review some built-in appliances in the kitchen:

Turn on (the)…    **Prenda…**

| | |
|---|---|
| cook top | **la hornilla** |
| dishwasher | **el lavaplatos** |
| freezer | **el congelador** |
| garbage disposer | **el triturador de basura** |
| microwave | **el horno de microonda** |
| refrigerator | **el refrigerador** |
| stove | **la estufa** |
| trash compactor | **el compactor de basura** |
| wall oven | **el horno de pared** |
| warming drawer | **el calentador de comida** |
| water filter | **el filtro de agua** |

Try to break up your interior work into three-word selections:

Where's (the)…          **¿Dónde está…?**

| | |
|---|---|
| thermostat | **el termostato** |
| electrical outlet | **la toma de corriente** |
| light switch | **el interruptor** |
| | |
| drain | **el drenaje** |
| clean-out | **el registro** |
| septic tank | **la fosa séptica** |
| | |
| medicine cabinet | **el botiquín** |
| vanity unit | **el lavabo empotrado** |
| utility cabinet | **el gabinete de servicios** |
| | |
| entertainment center | **el centro de entrenamiento** |
| audio system | **el sistema de audio** |
| home theater | **el cine en hogar** |

Home offices are often filled with built-in features:

| It has (the)... | **Tiene...** |
|---|---|

| | |
|---|---|
| antenna | **la antena** |
| camera | **la cámara** |
| clock | **el reloj** |
| computer | **la computadora** |
| lamp | **la lámpara** |
| monitor | **el monitor** |
| player | **el tocador** |
| printer | **el imprimidor** |
| receiver | **el receptor** |
| recorder | **la grabadora** |
| scanner | **el escáner** |
| screen | **la pantalla** |
| speaker | **el parlante** |
| telephone | **el teléfono** |
| television | **el televisor** |

To practice the names for these interior items, point them out in Spanish:

Try (the)…                  **Pruebe…**

| | |
|---|---|
| undercabinet lighting | **las luces debajo del gabinete** |
| track lights | **las luces en rieles** |
| chandelier | **la lámpara de araña** |
| | |
| ceiling fan | **el ventilador de techo** |
| dimmer switch | **el potenciómetro** |
| control panel | **el tablero de control** |
| | |
| smoke detector | **el detector de humo** |
| sprinkler | **el aspesor** |
| skylight | **el tragaluz** |

Install (the)…              **Instale…**

| | |
|---|---|
| curtains | **las cortinas** |
| draperies | **las colgaduras** |
| blinds | **las persianas** |
| | |
| rolling shutters | **las persianas enrollables** |
| folding shutters | **las contraventanas** |
| plantation shutters | **las persianas de plantación** |
| | |
| grills | **las rejillas** |
| registers | **los registros** |
| plates | **las placas** |

Provide more information about the indoor lighting:

It's…                       **Es…**

| | |
|---|---|
| flourescent | **flourescente** |
| Halogen | **halógena** |
| incandescent | **incandescente** |

JUST A SUGGESTION

Remember your English:

**el TV**

**el DVD**

**el VCR**

**el DVR**

**el TiVO**

TRY SOME

Which of the following statements are TRUE?

**La tina de baño require una caja de fusibles.**

**El televisor está en el centro de entrenamiento.**

**La luces en rieles pueden tener el potenciómetro.**

WORKING WORDS: PAINTING THE INTERIOR

Start by unloading the painting tools and materials:

Unload (the)…                **Descargue…**

| | |
|---|---|
| steel wool | **la lana de acero** |
| rag | **el trapo** |
| bucket | **la cubeta** |
| caulking | **el sellador** |
| compressor | **el compresor** |
| drop cloth | **la lona** |
| exterior paint | **la pintura para el exterior** |
| hose | **la manguera** |
| masking tape | **la cinta adhesiva** |
| paint brush | **la brocha** |
| paint sprayer | **la pistola pintadora** |
| pan | **el plato** |
| putty knife | **la espátula** |
| putty | **la masilla** |
| roller | **el rodillo** |
| sander | **la lijadora** |
| sandpaper | **el papel de lija** |
| scraper | **el raspador** |
| spackling | **el mástique** |
| utility knife | **la cuchilla** |

Use (the)…          **Use…**

| | |
|---|---|
| enamel | **la esmalte** |
| finish | **el acabado** |
| interior paint | **la pintura para el interior** |
| lacquer | **la laca** |
| oil-based paint | **la pintura de aceite** |
| primer | **el imprimador** |
| sealer | **el sellador** |
| stain | **el tinte** |
| thinner | **el disolvente** |
| varnish | **el barniz** |
| water-based paint | **la pintura de agua** |

Give me (the)…          **Deme…**

| | |
|---|---|
| gallon | **el galón** |
| half gallon | **el medio galón** |
| quart | **el cuarto** |

Check (the)…     **Revise…**

| | |
|---|---|
| amount | **la cantidad** |
| color | **el color** |
| consistency | **la consistencia** |
| design | **el diseño** |
| pattern | **el patrón** |
| pigment | **el pigmento** |
| shade | **el matiz** |
| sheen | **la luminosidad** |
| style | **el estilo** |
| surface | **la superficie** |

It needs…     **Necesita…**

| | |
|---|---|
| a cleaning | **una limpiada** |
| a sanding | **una lijada** |
| a touch up | **un retoque** |
| a washing | **una lavada** |
| another coat | **otra capa/mano** |
| base coat | **la capa de base** |
| stain-block | **la antimanchas** |
| texture coat | **la capa de textura** |
| waterproofing | **el impermeabilizante** |

It looks…     **Se ve…**

| | |
|---|---|
| bright | **brillante** |
| eggshell | **semi-mate** |
| fast drying | **rápido para secar** |
| flat | **mate** |
| glossy | **lustroso** |
| opaque | **opaco** |
| satin | **satinada** |
| semi-gloss | **semi-lustroso** |

Be careful with (the)…        **Tenga cuidado con…**

splashing        **las salpicaduras**

spillage        **el derrame**

dripping        **el chorreo**

Learn other colors of paint besides the basics:

Open the can of _____ .        **Abra la lata de _____ .**

| | |
|---|---|
| copper | **cobriza** |
| cream | **crema** |
| golden | **dorada** |
| navy blue | **azul marino** |
| silver | **plateada** |
| sky blue | **celeste** |

Always stick with words you know:

The paint is …        **La pintura está…**

| | |
|---|---|
| thick | **espesa** |
| thin | **aguada** |
| | |
| wet | **mojada** |
| dry | **seca** |
| | |
| dirty | **sucia** |
| clean | **limpia** |

## JUST A SUGGESTION

Don't forget the wallpaper:

| | |
|---|---|
| The wallpaper has… | **El papel de pared tiene…** |
| | |
| stripes | **rayas** |
| plaid | **cuadrados** |
| polka dots | **lunares** |

## TRY SOME

Name at least three procedures related to interior painting in Spanish.

Name three different colors of interior paint in Spanish.

Name three tools that are used on an interior paint job in Spanish.

## WORKING WORDS: INDOOR FLOORING

Practice the names for indoor flooring material:

| Unload (the)… | **Descargue…** |
|---|---|
| brick | **el ladrillo** |
| carpet | **la alfombra** |
| cast stone | **la piedra moldeada** |
| ceramic tile | **el ladrillo cerámico** |
| cultured stone | **la piedra prefabricada** |
| flagstone | **la losa de piedra** |
| floor tile | **la baldosa** |
| granite | **el granite** |
| hardwood | **la madera dura** |
| laminate | **el tablero laminado** |
| limestone | **la piedra caliza** |
| linoleum | **el linóleo** |
| marble | **el mármol** |
| mosaic | **el mosáico** |
| parquet | **el piso de parque** |
| quartzite | **la cuarcita** |
| sandstone | **la piedra arenisca** |
| slate | **la pizarra** |
| stone | **la piedra** |
| throw rug | **el tapete** |
| travertine | **la piedra travertine** |

| It's made of … | **Está hecho de…** |
|---|---|
| hardwood | **la madera dura** |
| mahogany | **la caoba** |
| oak | **el roble** |
| cherry | **el cerezo** |
| beech | **la haya** |
| poplar | **el álamo** |

List what you'll need to get the material installed:

| Give me (the)… | **Deme…** |
|---|---|

| | |
|---|---|
| adhesive | **el adhesive** |
| compound | **el compuesto** |
| fastener | **el sujetador** |
| felt | **el fieltro** |
| filler | **la masilla para el suelo** |
| glue | **la cola** |
| grout | **la lechada** |
| mastic | **el mastique** |
| moulding | **la moldura** |
| sealer | **el sellador** |
| shim | **la calza** |
| solvent | **el disolvente** |
| spacer | **el esparcidor** |
| tack strip | **la tira de tachuelas** |
| tape | **la cinta** |
| underlayment | **el base de piso** |
| moisture barrier | **la protectora de humedad** |

Use (the)…        **Use…**

| | |
|---|---|
| carpet roller | **el rodillo para alfombras** |
| carpet stretcher | **el estirador de alfombras** |
| chisel | **el cincel** |
| coping saw | **la sierra de arco** |
| finish nails | **los clavos sin cabeza** |
| floor leveler | **el nivelador de piso** |
| grinder | **la esmeriladora** |
| masonry saw | **la sierra de mampostería** |
| notched trowel | **la llana dentada** |
| pneumatic nailer | **la clavadora neumática** |
| rubber grout float | **la llana de goma** |
| rubber mallet | **el mazo de goma** |
| tile cutter | **el cortador de azulejos** |
| tile nippers | **las pinzas cortazulejo** |

Prepare (the)…        **Prepare…**

| | |
|---|---|
| floor | **el piso** |
| ground | **el suelo** |
| slab | **la losa** |
| sub floor | **el subsuelo** |
| surface | **la superficie** |

Look at (the)…      **Mire…**

| | |
|---|---|
| distance | **la distancia** |
| expansion gap | **la junta de dilatación** |
| high spot | **la punta alta** |
| length | **el largo** |
| line | **la línea** |
| low spot | **la punta baja** |
| width | **la anchura** |

These words focus on the carpet installation:

Check (the)…      **Revise…**

| | |
|---|---|
| cork | **el corcho** |
| foam | **la espuma** |
| liner | **el revestimiento** |
| material | **la tela** |
| padding | **el relleno** |
| patch | **el parche** |
| seam | **la costura** |
| thread | **el hilo** |

JUST A SUGGESTION

Many interior construction materials are easy to pronounce:

| | |
|---|---|
| acrylic | **el acrílico** |
| epoxy | **el epoxi** |
| resin | **la resina** |
| silicon | **el silicón** |
| Teflon | **el teflón** |

TRY SOME

Translate these into English:

**Use el cortador de azulejos.**

**Prepare la superficie.**

**Mira la punta alta.**

WORKING WORDS: ON THE JOB

You should know everyone who is working on the interior:

Talk to (the)…      **Hable con…**

| | |
|---|---|
| plumber | **el plomero** |
| electrician | **el electricista** |
| painter | **el pintero** |
| carpenter | **el carpintero** |
| drywaller | **el yesero** |
| installer | **el instalador** |
| cabinet maker | **el ebanista** |
| locksmith | **el cerrajero** |
| designer | **el diseñador** |

Now have them check everything as you review:

Check (the)…                 Revise…

| outlets | los enchufes |
| faucets | los grifos |
| lights | las luces |
| vents | los conductos |
| fixtures | los artefactos |
| appliances | los electrodomésticos |
| cabinets | los gabinetes |
| doors | las puertas |
| windows | las ventanas |
| floors | los pisos |

It has (the) _____ countertop.        Tiene el mostrador de _____.

| ceramic tile | el azulejo |
| Corian | la corian |
| Formica | la formica |
| granite | el granito |
| laminate | la lámina |
| marble | el mármol |
| natural stone | la piedra natural |
| stainless steel | el acero inoxidable |

Are you still breaking your vocabulary into usable sets?

Tell me the _____.        Dígame _____.

| percentage | el porcentage |
| square footage | los pies cuadrados |
| sum | la suma |

| Where are the…? | ¿Dónde están…? |
|---|---|
| rolls | **los rollos** |
| sheets | **las hojas** |
| stacks | **las pilas** |

| Make (the)… | Haga… |
|---|---|
| grooves | **las ranuras** |
| holes | **los huecos** |
| mortise slots | **las mortajas** |

| Fix (the)… | Repare… |
|---|---|
| rattle | **el traqueteo** |
| rumble | **el estruendo** |
| squeak | **el chirrido** |

## JUST A SUGGESTION

Jobs on the interior often include framing vocabulary:

| Look at (the)… | Mire… |
|---|---|
| beams | **las vigas** |
| joists | **las viguetas** |
| studs | **los travesaños** |

## TRY SOME

Fill in the blank with a word that makes sense:

**Tiene el mostrador de _____.**

**Es el instalador de _____.**

**Repare _____.**

## WORKING WORDS: DESCRIBING THE JOB

First review a few words with opposite meanings:

Give me (the) _____ piece.     **Deme la pieza _____.**

| | |
|---|---|
| front | **frontal** |
| back | **trasera** |
| | |
| outside | **exterior** |
| inside | **interior** |
| | |
| lower | **inferior** |
| upper | **superior** |

Now say words that describe everything around you:

| It's… | Es… |
|---|---|
| acoustic | **acústico** |
| bull nosed | **esquina boleada** |
| butted | **bien pegado** |
| custom-built | **hecho a la orden** |
| decorative | **decorativo** |
| even | **nivelado** |
| exact | **preciso** |
| fitted | **encajado** |
| floating | **flotante** |
| flush | **a tope** |
| folding | **plegable** |
| half round | **media caña** |
| hinged | **abisagrado** |
| measured | **medido** |
| notched | **dentado** |
| portable | **portátil** |
| quarter round | **cuarta caña** |
| refinished | **re-acabado** |
| recessed | **empotrado** |
| self-closing | **auto-cerrable** |
| splayed | **achaflanada** |
| standard | **estándar** |
| textured | **texturizado** |

Use the following to describe worthless material:

It looks…                **Se ve…**

| | |
|---|---|
| bowed | **combado** |
| chipped | **mellado** |
| curved | **curvado** |
| damaged | **dañado** |
| ripped | **roto** |
| stained | **manchado** |
| tarnished | **delustrado** |

The following can be used to describe your tools and materials:

| The tool is… | **La herramienta es…** |
|---|---|
| adjustable | **ajustable** |
| airless | **sin presión** |
| lightweight | **ligera** |
| pneumatic | **neumática** |
| pressurized | **pulverizada** |

| The thing is… | **Es/Está…** |
|---|---|
| asbestos-free | **sin asbesto** |
| sealed | **sellado** |
| treated | **tratado** |
| rustproof | **inoxidable** |
| durable | **duradero** |
| waterproof | **impermeable** |
| leak-proof | **que no se gotea** |
| lead free | **sin plomo** |
| anti-corrosive | **resistente a la corrosion** |
| stainless | **anti-corrosivo** |
| galvanized | **galvanizado** |
| fire-resistant | **resistente al fuego** |

Also be prepared to discuss the interior style or design:

The type of design is... **El diseño es tipo...**

| | |
|---|---|
| bungalow | **búngalo** |
| colonial | **colonial** |
| contemporary | **contemporario** |
| country | **campestre** |
| French | **francés** |
| high tech | **de alta tecnología** |
| Italian | **italiano** |
| Mediterranean | **mediteráneo** |
| Southwestern | **suroeste** |
| traditional | **tradicional** |
| Victorian | **victoriano** |

Create your own set of descriptive phases. All of these focus on the ceiling:

It needs (the)... **Necesita...**

| | |
|---|---|
| acoustic ceiling | **el techo acústico** |
| beamed ceiling | **el techo vigado** |
| conventional ceiling | **el techo tradicional** |
| false ceiling | **el techo falso** |
| suspended ceiling | **el techo suspendido** |
| textured ceiling | **el techo de textura** |
| vaulted ceiling | **el techo abovedado** |

And here's what happens when other items are described in Spanish. Notice how the word "**de**" is used:

347

| | |
|---|---|
| strand board | **la tabla de bambú** |
| particle board | **la tabla aglomerada** |
| fiber board | **la tabla de fibra** |
| | |
| spray gun | **la pistola pintadora** |
| caulking gun | **la pistola del sellador** |
| nail gun | **la pistola de clavos** |
| | |
| leftover pieces | **las piezas sobrantes** |
| plastic pieces | **las piezas de plástico** |
| missing pieces | **las piezas perdidas** |

Keep going:

stainless steel range hood

**la campana de la estufa de acero inoxidable**

mosaic backsplash

**la contra salpicaduras de mosáico**

hanging wrought iron rack

**el colgadero de hierro forrado**

JUST A SUGGESTION

Make a list of everything related to interior work:

| Work on (the)... | Trabaje con... |
|---|---|
| chimney flue | **el conducto de humo en la chimenea** |
| shower grab bars | **las barras de apoyo en la ducha** |
| stair landing | **el descanso de las escaleras** |
| walk-in closet | **el ropero vestidor** |
| wall safe | **la caja fuerte para la pared** |

## TRY SOME

Name three different kinds of ceilings in Spanish.

Name three different interior styles or designs in Spanish.

Name three Spanish words that describe damaged or worthless material.

## WORKING WORDS: ON-SITE ACTIONS

Add a key phrase to your interior action words:

| We're going... | Vamos a... |
|---|---|
| to add | **añadir** |
| to adjust | **ajustar** |
| to align | **alinear** |
| to apply | **aplicar** |
| to bond | **adherir** |
| to bore | **calar** |
| to caulk | **calafatear** |
| to center | **centrar** |
| to check | **revisar** |

| | |
|---|---|
| to clean | **limpiar** |
| to coat | **cubrir** |
| to connect | **conectar** |
| to correct | **corregir** |
| to cover | **cubrir** |
| to cross | **atravesar** |
| to cut | **cortar** |
| to deliver | **repartir** |
| to distribute | **distribuir** |
| to expand | **ampliar** |
| to fasten | **fijar** |
| to fill | **llenar** |
| to form | **formar** |
| to glue | **pegar** |
| to hide | **esconder** |
| to hold | **sostener** |
| to install | **instalar** |
| to insulate | **insular** |
| to join | **juntar** |
| to level | **nivelar** |
| to lift | **levantar** |
| to loosen | **soltar** |
| to measure | **medir** |
| to modify | **modificar** |
| to mount | **amontar** |
| to nail | **clavar** |
| to operate | **operar** |

| | |
|---|---|
| to paint | **pintar** |
| to patch | **reparar** |
| to perforate | **perforar** |
| to place | **colocar** |
| to polish | **pulir** |
| to pour | **verter** |
| to pre-drill | **pretaladrar** |
| to prep | **preparar** |
| to press | **presionar** |
| to protect | **proteger** |
| to putty | **enmasillar** |
| to reduce | **reducir** |
| to repair | **reparar** |
| to replace | **sustituir** |
| to sand | **lijar** |
| to scrape | **raspar** |
| to screw in | **atornillar** |
| to seal | **sellar** |
| to smooth | **alisar** |
| to stagger | **alternar** |
| to straighten | **enderezar** |
| to stretch | **estirar** |
| to take down | **retirar** |
| to tighten | **apretar** |
| to touch up | **retocar** |
| to trace | **trazar** |
| to unroll | **desenrollar** |

| to ventilate | **ventilar** |
|---|---|
| to wallpaper | **empapelar** |

These specialized actions may require a bit more practice:

| You need… | **Necesita…** |
|---|---|
| to mask off | **poner cinta** |
| to mud | **poner yeso** |
| to pull wire | **jalar alambre** |
| to shim | **colocar la calza** |
| to snap the line | **marcar con linea de tiza** |
| to spray paint | **pintar a presión** |
| to wipe | **pasar un trapo** |

## JUST A SUGGESTION

Don't forget those verbs that express a problem or concern:

| It's going (to)… | **Va a…** |
|---|---|
| to splash | **salpicar** |
| to drip | **derramar** |
| to stain | **manchar** |
| | |
| to slide | **resbalarse** |
| to swell | **hincharse** |
| to split | **agrietarse** |

GRAMMAR TIME

Here's still another way to talk about the past in Spanish. It's a two-part form with a fancy name – the present perfect, and it expresses action that "has been done":

Have you started?  **¿Ha comenzado?**  Yes, I've finished. **Sí, he terminado.**

In most cases, the present perfect is formed by changing the endings of your "**-ar**" verbs to "**-ado**" and your "**-er**" or "**-ir**" verbs to "**-ido**":

> trabajar (to work)  **trabajado** (driven)
>
> comer (to eat)  **comido** (eaten)

And then adding these unique forms of "**haber**" (to have):

| | |
|---|---|
| I have | **he** |
| You have; He, She has | **ha** |
| You (pl.), They have | **han** |
| We have | **hemos** |

This is what they're like when you put them together:

| | | |
|---|---|---|
| **TRABAJAR** (to work) | **Yo he trabajado.** | I have worked. |
| **TERMINAR** (to finish) | **No hemos terminado.** | We haven't finished. |
| **COMER** (to eat) | **Pablo ha comido.** | Pablo has eaten. |
| **SALIR** (to leave) | **¿Han salido?** | Have they left? |

## JUST A SUGGESTION

A few irregular "past participles" break all the rules, so you'll have to memorize them. Check out these examples:

**ver** (to see)

**visto** (seen)                 **He visto el dueño.** I've seen the owner.

**poner** (to put)

**puesto** (put)                 **He puesto todo aquí.** I've put everything here.

**hacer** (to do, to make)

**hecho** (done, made)           **He hecho el trabajo.** I've done the job.

**abrir** (to open)

**abierto** (opened)             **He abierto la puerta.** I've opened the door.

**romper** (to break

**roto** (broken)                **He roto la pieza.** I've broken the piece.


## TRY SOME

These phrases are for you to translate:

**Hemos comenzado.**            _____

**No he terminado.**            _____

**¿Han comido?**                _____

# THE ONE-LINERS

In conversational Spanish, you'll often hear a little one-liner at the end of a statement, which is meant to confirm, question, or emphasize the message. Try out one of these examples:

| | |
|---|---|
| It's your hammer, right? | **Es su martillo, <u>no</u>?** |
| | **Es su martillo, <u>verdad</u>?** |
| | **Es su martillo, <u>no es cierto</u>?** |

# CULTURE CLASH

Absences from work are often due to traditional commitments to family or friends. Moreover, much of the paycheck is spent on the following:

| I have (the)… | **Tengo…** |
|---|---|
| anniversary | **el aniversario** |
| birth | **el nacimiento** |
| birthday | **el cumpleaños** |
| engagement | **el compromiso** |
| funeral | **el funeral** |
| 15-year old daughter's "coming out" party | **la quinceñera** |
| visit | **la visita** |

| I'm going to (the)... | **Voy a...** |
|---|---|
| court | **la corte** |
| hospital | **el hospital** |
| school | **la escuela** |

# CHAPTER TEN

## LANDSCAPING

### la construcción en el jardín

WORKING WORDS: SOFTSCAPE AND HARDSCAPE

Begin with basic words related to landscaping:

| | |
|---|---|
| irrigation | **la irrigación** |
| drainage | **el drenaje** |
| sprinklers | **los aspersores/los rociadores** |
| | |
| lawn | **el césped** |
| plants | **las plantas** |
| tree | **el árbol** |
| | |
| trench | **la zanja** |
| dirt | **la tierra** |
| path | **el sendero** |
| | |
| wheelbarrow | **la carretilla** |
| lawnmower | **la cortadora de césped** |
| rototiller | **la aflojadora de tierra** |

Now mention the folks who show up to work on the landscaping project:

| He's the . . . | Él es . . . |
|---|---|
| carpenter | **el carpintero** |
| contractor | **el contratista** |
| electrician | **el electricista** |
| gardener | **el jardinero** |
| geologist | **el geólogo** |
| installer | **el instalador** |
| laborer | **el trabajador** |
| landscaper | **el paisajista** |
| painter | **el pintor** |
| plumber | **el plomero** |
| stonemason | **el albañil** |

Though some of these items are found on exterior jobs, the landscape plans call for work all over the place:

| Where is (the)...? | ¿Dónde está...? |
|---|---|
| awning | **el toldo** |
| balcony | **el balcón** |
| barbeque | **la parrilla** |
| barrier | **la barrera** |
| bench | **la banca** |
| bird bath | **la bañera de pájaros** |
| bridge | **el puente** |
| column | **la columna** |
| covering | **la cubierta** |
| deck | **la terraza** |
| dock | **el muelle** |
| driveway | **el camino de entrada** |
| fence | **la cerca** |
| firepit | **la fogato** |
| fish pond | **la pesquera** |
| flagpole | **el asta de bandera** |
| flower pot | **la maceta** |
| fountain | **la fuente** |
| garden | **el jardín** |
| gate | **el portón** |
| gazebo | **la pérgola** |
| greenhouse | **el invernadero** |
| hammock | **la hamaca** |
| Jacuzzi | **el jacuzzi** |
| lawn | **el césped** |
| light post | **el farol** |
| path | **el sendero** |
| patio | **el patio** |
| planter | **el macetero** |
| pool | **la piscina** |
| porch | **el portal** |
| ramp | **la rampa** |
| shed | **el cobertizo** |
| sidewalk | **la acera** |
| spa | **el balneario** |
| sprinkler | **el aspersor** |
| stairs | **las escaleras** |
| statue | **la estátua** |
| steps | **los escalones** |
| tower | **el torre** |
| trellis | **el enrejado** |
| umbrella | **la sombrilla** |
| walkway | **el sendero** |
| wall | **el muro** |

Use commands as you practice words you already know:

Check (the) …                **Revise…**

| | |
|---|---|
| alarm | **la alarma** |
| electrical outlet | **la toma del corriente** |
| fusebox | **la caja de fusibles** |
| gas meter | **el medidor de gas** |
| lighting | **el sistema de luces** |
| security system | **el sistema de seguridad** |
| water valve | **la válvula de agua** |

## JUST A SUGGESTION

Build your language skills over time. For now, utilize general terms when you can't remember specific vocabulary.

I can't find…            **No puedo encontrar…**

| | |
|---|---|
| the guy | **el señor** |
| the machine | **la máquina** |
| the place | **el lugar** |
| the thing | **la cosa** |
| the tool | **la herramienta** |

## TRY SOME

What is the difference between "**los escalones**" and "**las escaleras**"?

What is the difference between "**la maceta**" and "**el macetero**"?

What is the difference between "**el muro**" and "**la cerca**"?

# WORKING WORDS: MORE MATERIALS

Now, let everyone know what materials will be needed for the job:

| Use (the) . . . | Use . . . |
|---|---|
| asphalt | **el asfalto** |
| block | **el bloque de hormigón** |
| board | **la tabla** |
| brick | **el ladrillo** |
| cement | **el cemento** |
| edge trim | **el reborde** |
| floor tile | **la baldosa** |
| gravel | **la grava** |
| lumber | **el madero** |
| marble | **el mármol** |
| mortar | **el mortero** |
| paint | **la pintura** |
| pipe | **la tubería** |
| plaster | **el yeso** |
| plywood | **la madera contrachapada** |
| rope | **la cuerda** |
| sand | **la arena** |
| screen | **la malla** |
| stake | **la estaca** |
| stone | **la piedra** |
| stucco | **el estuco** |
| tar | **la brea** |
| wall tile | **el azulejo** |
| wire | **el alambre** |
| wood | **la madera** |

This time, describe the project in full detail:

| It's made of . . . | Está hecho de . . . |
|---|---|
| alloy | **la aleación** |
| aluminum | **el aluminio** |
| brass | **el latón** |
| bronze | **el bronce** |
| burlap | **la lona** |
| cardboard | **el cartón** |
| chicken wire | **el alambre de gallinera** |
| cloth | **la tela** |
| copper | **el cobre** |
| foam | **la espuma** |
| glass | **el vídrio** |
| iron | **el hierro** |
| leather | **el cuero** |
| linoleum | **el linóleo** |
| mesh | **la malla de acero** |
| metal | **el metal** |
| plastic | **el plástico** |
| rubber | **la goma** |
| steel | **el acero** |
| wood | **la madera** |

| It's . . . | Está . . . |
|---|---|
| assembled | **ensamblado** |
| capped | **coronado** |
| covered | **cubierto** |
| decorated | **decorado** |
| designed | **diseñado** |
| filled | **rellenado** |
| finished | **acabado** |
| inlaid | **incrustado** |
| painted | **pintado** |
| paved | **pavimentado** |
| pre-cast | **preformado** |
| prefabricated | **prefabricado** |

It doesn't take much to communicate important ideas in landscaping. These tell everyone what you are thinking:

| It's... | Está... |
|---|---|
| level | **nivelado** |
| uneven | **desigual** |
| twisted | **torcido** |
| straight | **recto** |
| parallel | **paralelo** |
| square | **cuadrado** |
| round | **redondo** |
| at an angle | **en un ángulo** |
| on the line | **en la línea** |
| in the groove | **en la muesca** |

JUST A SUGGESTION

Develop complete sentences on the job with these important words:

| corner | **la esquina** | **Ponga el poste en la esquina.** |
|---|---|---|
| edge | **el borde** | **El borde de la terraza no está pintada.** |
| end | **la punta** | **El jardín va hasta la punta.** |

TRY SOME

Remove the word that doesn't belong with the others:

**nivelado, recto, acabado**

**esquina, cuero, tela**

**malla, alambre, muesca**

# WORKING WORDS: LANDSCAPING TOOLS

These are popular items in almost any landscaping scenario:

We'll need (the)...                 **Necesitaremos...**

| | |
|---|---|
| auger | **el barrenador mecánico** |
| ax | **el hacha** |
| blower | **la sopladora** |
| cement mixer | **la mezcladora** |
| chain | **la cadena** |
| chainsaw | **la motosierra** |
| compressor | **el compresor de aire** |
| fuel | **el combustible** |
| gloves | **los guantes** |
| grinder | **el molinillo** |
| hose | **la manguera** |
| masonary saw | **la serrucho de piedra** |
| pliers | **el alicates** |
| post digger | **la excavadora para postes** |
| putty | **la masilla** |
| rope | **la soga** |
| roto-hammer | **el martillo eléctrico** |
| rototiller | **la aflojadora de tierra** |
| hand saw | **el serrucho** |
| screwdriver | **el desarmador** |
| shovel | **la pala** |
| sprayer | **el rociador** |
| stake | **la estaca** |
| string | **el hilo** |
| tape | **la cinta** |
| tile cutter | **la cortadora de baldosa** |
| tractor | **el tractor** |
| trash can | **el bote de basura** |
| utility knife | **la cuchilla** |
| wrench | **la llave inglesa** |
| wheelbarrow | **la carretilla** |

Most landscaping projects also involve work with a gardener. The following list includes other words you should know:

| Bring (the)… | **Traiga…** |
|---|---|
| lodge pole | **el palo de apoyo** |
| tree tie | **el amarre para el árbol** |
| root barrier | **la hoja de plástico** |

| | |
|---|---|
| broom | **la escoba** |
| edger | **la caladora** |
| fertilizer | **el fertilizante** |
| hedge trimmer | **la podadora** |
| hoe | **el azadón** |
| insecticide | **la insecticida** |
| mulch | **el esteriécol** |
| pruners | **el cortador de ramas** |
| rake | **el rastrillo** |
| weedwacker | **el desyerbador** |

To learn the specific names for flowers, bushes, trees, and any other foliage, it would be best to ask a Spanish-speaker. The word for nursery is **el semillero** or **el vivero**:

| Remove (the)… | Saque… |
|---|---|
| bark | **la corteza** |
| bush | **el arbusto** |
| flower | **la flower** |
| grass | **el pasto** |
| hedge | **el seto** |
| plant | **la planta** |
| sod | **el tepe** |
| tree | **el árbol** |
| vine | **la enrededera** |
| weed | **la mala yerba** |

| Pick up (the)… | Recoja… |
|---|---|
| branches | **las ramas** |
| leaves | **las hojas** |
| roots | **los raíces** |
| seeds | **las semillas** |
| twigs | **los ramitos** |

## JUST A SUGGESTION

Continue to practice words in pairs, and then memorize the differences in meanings:

| | |
|---|---|
| field | **el campo** |
| yard | **el jardín** |
| | |
| ground | **el suelo** |
| floor | **el piso** |

| | |
|---|---|
| land | **el terreno** |
| earth | **la tierra** |
| | |
| mud | **el lodo** |
| clay | **la arcilla** |

TRY SOME

Connect the words that belong together best:

| | |
|---|---|
| **el lodo** | **el piso** |
| **el ramito** | **el hilo** |
| **el rociador** | **la hoja** |
| **el suelo** | **la manguera** |
| **la soga** | **la arcilla** |

## WORKING WORDS: ON THE JOB SITE

A good landscaper uses clear and simple statements to avoid confusion. This phrase works well with the words you know:

| The . . . goes here. | . . . va aquí. |
|---|---|

| | |
|---|---|
| channel | **el canal** |
| control box | **la caja de control** |
| dirt | **la tierra** |
| trench | **la zanja** |
| divider | **el divisor** |
| drainage | **el drenaje** |
| furrow | **el surco** |
| hole | **el hoyo** |
| irrigation | **la irrigación** |
| lawn | **el césped** |
| path | **el sendero** |
| slope | **el declive** |
| sprinkler | **la aspersor** |

All construction work requires accurate measurement, so use these expressions to make sure there are no mistakes:

| | |
|---|---|
| What size is it? | **¿De qué tamaño es?** |
| How much does it weigh? | **¿Cuánto pesa?** |
| What are the measurements? | **¿Cuáles son las medidas?** |

Keep going:

| | |
|---|---|
| How close? | **¿Qué tan cerca?** |
| How deep? | **¿Qué tan profundo?** |
| How far? | **¿Qué tan lejos?** |
| How high? | **¿Qué tan alto?** |
| How long? | **¿Qué tan largo?** |
| How low? | **¿Qué tan bajo?** |
| How thick? | **¿Qué tan grueso?** |
| How thin? | **¿Qué tan delgado?** |
| How wide? | **¿Qué tan ancho?** |

Remember to respond using words which indicate an amount:

| | | |
|---|---|---|
| foot | **el pie** | <u>**Son dos pies.**</u> |
| gallon | **el galón** | <u>**Necesito un galón.**</u> |
| inch | **la pulgada** | _____ |
| ounce | **la onza** | _____ |
| pint | **la pinta** | _____ |
| pound | **la libra** | _____ |
| quart | **el cuarto** | _____ |
| ton | **la tonelada** | _____ |
| yard | **la yarda** | _____ |

Add commands to your words as the landscaping job continues:

Give me (the) …    **Deme …**

| | |
|---|---|
| bag | **la bolsa** |
| box | **la caja** |
| bucket | **el balde** |
| can | **la lata** |
| container | **el recipiente** |
| handful | **la puñada** |
| jar | **la jarra** |
| load | **la carga** |
| scoop | **la cucharilla** |
| shovelful | **la palada** |
| tray | **la bandeja** |

Now review the basic location words, and don't be afraid to point:

| Move it … | Muévala … |
|---|---|
| above | **encima** |
| along | **a lo largo** |
| around | **alrededor** |
| at the bottom | **en el fondo** |
| back | **para atrás** |
| behind | **detrás** |
| between | **entre** |
| down | **abajo** |
| far | **lejos** |
| forward | **adelante** |
| here | **aquí** |
| in front | **enfrente** |
| in the middle | **en medio** |
| inside | **adentro** |
| near | **cerca** |
| next to | **al lado** |
| outside | **afuera** |
| over | **sobre** |
| straight ahead | **adelante** |
| there | **allí** |
| to the left | **a la izquierda** |
| to the right | **a la derecha** |
| towards | **hacia** |
| under | **debajo** |
| underground | **subteráneo** |
| up | **arriba** |
| way over there | **allá** |

## JUST A SUGGESTION

If you're working outdoors, there might be some animals around, so study these today:

| \Beware of the . . . | Tengan cuidado con . . . |
|---|---|
| ant | **la hormiga** |
| bee | **la abeja** |
| beetle | **el escarabajo** |
| cat | **el gato** |
| dog | **el perro** |
| horse | **el caballo** |
| lizard | **la lagartija** |
| snake | **la culebra** |
| spider | **la araña** |
| termite | **la termita** |
| wasp | **la avispa** |

TRY SOME

Translate these landscaping phrases into Spanish:

How wide is the ditch?         _____

Give me a scoop of dirt.       _____

The hole goes there.           _____

Move the sprinkler back.       _____

I need a ton of bricks.        _____

## WORKING WORDS: ON-SITE ACTIONS

Most of the verbs you'll learn can be used with other trades in construction.
For now, talk only about landscaping:

| We need… | Necesitamos … | |
|---|---|---|
| to align | **alinear** | <u>**Necesitamos alinear los aspersores.**</u> |
| to apply | **aplicar** | |
| to assemble | **asamblar** | |
| to bore | **calar** | |
| to chop | **tajar** | |
| to clean | **limpiar** | |
| to combine | **combinar** | |
| to connect | **conectar** | |
| to cover | **cubrir** | |
| to cut | **cortar** | |
| to dig | **excavar** | |
| to divide | **dividir** | |
| to edge | **cortar el borde del césped** | |
| to erect | **eregir** | |
| to frame | **formar** | |
| to glue | **encolar** | |
| to hold | **sostener** | |
| to install | **instalar** | |
| to join | **unir** | |
| to level | **nivelar** | |
| to lubricate | **lubricar** | |
| to measure | **medir** | |
| to modify | **modificar** | |
| to mount | **amontar** | |
| to mow | **cortar el césped** | |

| | |
|---|---|
| to organize | **organizar** |
| to paint | **pintar** |
| to plant | **plantar** |
| to position | **situar** |
| to pour | **verter** |
| to pre-drill | **pretaladrar** |
| to prep | **preparar** |
| to reach | **alcanzar** |
| to remove | **quitar** |
| to replace | **sustituir** |
| to sand | **lijar** |
| to score | **marcar** |
| to screw in | **atornillar** |
| to seal | **sellar** |
| to seed | **semillar** |
| to separate | **separar** |
| to set | **colocar** |
| to smooth | **alisar** |
| to soak | **remojar** |
| to straighten | **enderezar** |
| to support | **apoyar** |
| to tie in | **conectar** |
| to touch up | **retocar** |
| to trim | **podar** |
| to wash | **lavar** |
| to water | **regar** |
| to wipe | **pasar un trapo** |

## JUST A SUGGESTION

You'll become more fluent in Spanish if you learn several words that mean the same thing. For example, "to fix" can be translated as **reparar**, **componer**, or **arreglar**:

I'm fixing something.     **Estoy reparando algo.**

**Estoy componiendo algo.**

**Estoy arreglando algo.**

For fun, look up the definitions of these word pairs which have similar meanings:

**unir/juntar**              _____

**cubrir/tapar**             _____

**presionar/apretar**        _____

## TRY SOME

Take some of the verb forms that were presented in this book and put them to use today:

to check                     **revisar**

I'm checking.               **Estoy revisando.**

I will check.               **Revisaré.**

| | |
|---|---|
| I checked. | **Revisé.** |
| I was checking. | **Estaba revisando.** |
| I have checked. | **He revisado.** |

## GRAMMAR TIME

The following "pronouns" can be used in Spanish to indicate who or what is receiving the action in a sentence. Notice the position of each pronoun in these examples:

**Me**

| | |
|---|---|
| He told <u>me</u> what happened. | **Me dijo qué pasó.** |
| Speak to me in Spanish. | **Hábleme en español.** |

**Nos**

| | |
|---|---|
| He told <u>us</u> what happened. | **Nos dijo qué pasó.** |
| Speak to <u>us</u> in Spanish. | **Háblenos en español.** |

**Le**

| | |
|---|---|
| He told <u>him/her</u> what happened. | **Le dijo qué pasó.** |
| Speak to <u>him/her</u> in Spanish. | **Háblele en español.** |

**Les**

| | |
|---|---|
| He told <u>them</u> what happened. | **Les dijo qué pasó.** |
| Speak to <u>them</u> in Spanish. | **Hábleles en español.** |

These words usually refer to objects instead of people. "**Lo**" indicates a masculine item and "**La**" indicates the feminine:

**Lo**

The hammer? He has it.  **¿El martillo? Lo tiene.**

**La**

The ladder? He has it.  **¿La escalera? La tiene.**

JUST A SUGGESTION

Whether it's "**le**", "**lo**", or "**la**", don't forget it always goes at the tail end of an affirmative command. Notice the accent marks:

**Háble<u>le</u> en español.**  Talk to him in Spanish.

**Muéva<u>la</u> mañana.**  Move it tomorrow.

**¡Tráiga<u>las</u>!**  Bring them!

And the same goes for "**me**" and "**nos**":

**Enséñe<u>me</u>, por favor.**  Show me, please.

**Díga<u>nos</u> todo.**  Tell us everything.

Now put them all together! Insert the "people" pronouns before the others. By the way, sometimes the "**le**" and "**les**" must change to "**se**":

**Hágamelo.** Do it for me.  **Dígaselo.** Tell it to him.

TRY SOME

Create a few commands on your own. Simply add "**le**" to the end of each command:

| | |
|---|---|
| Explain | **Explique** |
| Explain to him. | **<u>Explíquele.</u>** |

| | |
|---|---|
| Speak | **Hable** |
| Speak to him. | _____ |

| | |
|---|---|
| Listen | **Escuche** |
| Listen to him. | _____ |

THE ONE-LINERS

Read over this next set of one-liners. You never know when you'll need them:

| | |
|---|---|
| Above all... | **Sobre todo...** |
| At first... | **Al principio...** |
| At last... | **Por fin...** |
| At least... | **Por lo menos...** |
| By the way... | **A propósito...** |
| For example... | **Por ejemplo...** |
| In general... | **En general...** |

In other words...          **Es decir...**

On the other hand...          **En cambio...**


TRY SOME


Read everything aloud:


**En general, me gusta el trabajo.**

In general, I like the job.


**A propósito, necesita hablar con el jefe.**

By the way, you need to talk to the boss.


**Al principio, estaba limpiando.**

At first, I was cleaning.


**En cambio, _____** (fill blank)

On the other hand, _____.


**Por ejemplo, _____** (fill blank)

For example, _____.


**Es decir, _____** (fill blank)

In other words, _____.

## CULTURE CLASH

Did your Latino employee or co-worker just move to this country? Are they a bit confused about our language and culture? When you find the time, share a few insights on U.S. customs toward laws, dress, taxes, holidays, and basic social skills. Make them feel welcome by respecting their perspective, and watch your relationship grow!

YOU'RE DONE!

**¡Ya terminó!**

Well, you've just completed training in the SPANISH FOR CONSTRUCTION WORKERS guidebook.  Hopefully, much of what you've read has already been put into practice, and you're excited about learning more.  The vocabulary lists and grammar presentations, along with the other language and culture tips, were specifically designed to get you started. So now, fellow Spanish-speakers, the rest is up to you.

Below are some key pages that you can easily access by turning to the end of the book. Some are designed for quick-reference, while others will take a little more time to review. Either way,  you should find the material useful.

So what are you waiting for? You've still got some work to do!

**Adiós, amigo, y muy buena suerte**,

Bill Harvey

# BUSINESS MATTERS

## THE NEW EMPLOYEE
**El nuevo empleado**

Before you hire anyone, review some of the friendly greetings found in Chapter One. Remember that in the Latino culture, plenty of respect and courtesy is required when two adults discuss any business-related matters for the first time. Now you're ready to use these sample sentences to discuss what's on your mind:

My name is _____.
**Me llamo _____.**

I'm from the _____ company.
**Soy de la compañia de _____.**

We do…
**Hacemos…**

I'm the boss/owner/contractor.
**Soy el jefe/dueño/contratista.**

| I would like ... | **Quisiera ...** |
|---|---|
| to ask you some questions | **hacerle unas preguntas** |
| to call you later | **llamarle más tarde** |
| to check on everything | **averiguarlo todo** |

| | |
|---|---|
| to describe the position | **describir el puesto** |
| to discuss the details | **discutir los detalles** |
| to explain the job | **explicar el trabajo** |
| to give you a test | **darle una prueba** |
| to give you the opportunity | **darle la oportunidad** |
| to give you an interview | **darle una entrevista** |
| to have some information | **tener alguna información** |
| to hire you | **contratarle** |
| to interview you | **darle una entrevista** |
| to know if you're interested | **saber si tenga interés** |
| to offer you a job | **ofrecerle un trabajo** |
| to recommend a place | **recomendar un sitio** |
| to see if you're available | **ver si está disponible** |
| to see your references | **ver su currículum** |
| to send you somewhere | **mandarle a otro sitio** |
| to talk to your boss | **hablar con su jefe** |

## PLEASE FILL OUT THIS FORM

**Favor de llenar este formulario**

Once your prospective employee understands your intentions, hand them the proper application forms. To gather all the information you can, start off with a standard questionnaire. In Spanish, the structure is a breeze. Simply continue with the basic pattern, (and use the pronunciation guide for help):

| | |
|---|---|
| What is your...? | **¿Cuál es su...?** (kwahl ehs soo) |

| | |
|---|---|
| address | **dirección** (dee-rehk-see-'ohn) |
| age | **edad** (eh-'dahd) |
| area code | **código de área** ('koh-dee-goh deh áh-reh-ah) |
| date of birth | **fecha de nacimiento** ('feh-chah deh nah-see-mee-'ehn-toh) |
| first name | **primer nombre** (pree-'mehr 'nohm-breh) |
| full name | **nombre completo** ('nohm-breh kohm-'pleh-toh) |
| last name | **apellido** (ah-peh-'yee-doh) |
| license number | **número de licencia** ('noo-meh-roh deh lee-'sehn-see-ah) |
| marital status | **estado civil** (eh-'stah-doh see-'beel) |
| nationality | **nacionalidad** (nah-see-oh-nah-lee-'dahd) |
| place of birth | **lugar de nacimiento** (loo-'gahr deh nah-see-mee-'ehn-toh) |
| relationship | **relación** (reh-lah-see-'ohn) |
| social security number | **número de seguro social** ('noo-meh-roh deh seh-'goo-roh soh-see-'ahl) |
| telephone number | **número de teléfono** ('noo-meh-roh deh teh-'leh-foh-noh) |
| cell number | **número de teléfono celular** |
| e-mail address | **correo electrónico** |
| zip code | **zona postal** ('soh-nah pohs-'tahl) |
| | |
| last place of employment | **último lugar de empleo** ('ool-tee-moh loo-'gahr deh ehm-'pleh-oh) |

## JUST A SUGGESTION

These words might come in handy:

| Are you…? | ¿Es usted…? |
|---|---|
| Hispanic | **hispano** |
| Latin American | **latino** |
| Mexican | **mejicano** |
| Puerto Rican | **puertorriqueño** |
| Cuban | **cubano** |
| Guatemalen | **gualtemateco** |

## A FEW MORE QUESTIONS
### Unas preguntas más

| What's your…? | ¿Cuál es su…? |
|---|---|
| skill | **habilidad** |
| field | **campo de trabajo** |
| title | **título** |
| specialty | **especialidad** |
| level | **nivel** |
| pay | **pago** |
| salary | **salario** |
| fee | **precio** |

| | |
|---|---|
| Who's your ...? | **¿Quién es su ...?** |
| closest relative | **pariente mas cercano** |
| friend | **amigo** |
| neighbor | **vecino** |
| spouse | **esposo/a** |
| family physician | **médico familiar** |
| reference | **referencia** |
| previous employer | **empresario previo** |

These questions are short and can be used different ways:

| | |
|---|---|
| How much...? | **¿Cuánto/a...?** |
| time | **tiempo** |
| work | **trabajo** |
| experience | **experiencia** |
| education | **educación** |
| training | **entrenamiento** |

| | |
|---|---|
| When...? | **¿Cuándo...?** |
| did you learn | **aprendió** |
| did you start | **empezó** |
| did you leave | **salió** |
| did you work there | **trabajó ahí** |
| did you quit | **renunció** |

| | |
|---|---|
| can you work | **puede trabajar** |
| can you start | **puede empezar** |
| can you meet | **puede reunirse** |

| | |
|---|---|
| Where ...? | **¿Dónde...?** |

| | |
|---|---|
| were you born | **nació** |
| did you study | **estudió** |
| did you work before | **trabajó antes** |
| do you work now | **trabaja ahora** |
| do you live | **vive** |
| did you learn | **aprendió** |

| | |
|---|---|
| Why...? | **¿Por qué ...?** |

| | |
|---|---|
| were you fired | **le despidieron** |
| should I hire you | **debo contratarle** |
| are you applying | **está solicitando trabajo** |
| are you quitting | **está renunciando** |
| aren't you working | **no está trabajando** |

## JUST A SUGGESTION

Some important questions are pretty personal, so be respectful as you probe:

| | |
|---|---|
| Do you drink? | **¿Toma licor?** |
| Do you smoke? | **¿Fuma?** |

| | |
|---|---|
| Do you take drugs? | **¿Toma drogas?** |
| Let's talk about (the)... | **Vamos a hablar de...** |
| physical requirements | **los requisitos físicos** |
| language proficiency | **la competencia en el lenguaje** |
| medical problems | **los problemas médicos** |

DO YOU HAVE IT?

**¿Lo tiene?**

"**TENER**" (to have) is a powerful verb in Spanish. As you speak, listen for the answers, "**sí**" or "**no**" to this question:

| | |
|---|---|
| Do you have ...? | **¿Tiene...?** |
| an appointment | **una cita** |
| application | **la solicitud** |
| card | **la tarjeta** |
| certificate | **el certificado** |
| contract | **el contrato** |
| equipment | **el equipo** |
| experience | **experiencia** |
| form | **el formulario** |
| I.D. | **identificación** |
| insurance | **el seguro** |
| license | **la licencia** |

| | |
|---|---|
| record | **el record** |
| résumé | **el currículum** |
| schedule | **el horario** |
| tools | **herramientas** |
| transportation | **transporte** |
| uniform | **el uniforme** |

| | |
|---|---|
| I have (the)… | **Tengo…** |

| | |
|---|---|
| tool _____ | _____ **de herramientas** |

| | |
|---|---|
| belt | **el cinturón** |
| bag | **la bolsa** |
| bucket | **el balde** |
| box | **la caja** |
| kit | **el juego** |

## JUST A SUGGESTION

In some cases, it's OK to chat about one's citizenship:

Do you have a green card?

**¿Tiene usted una tarjeta verde?**

Are you a U.S. citizen?

**¿Es usted un ciudadano de los estados unidos?**

What's your resident number?

**¿Cuál es su número de residente?**

Are you a naturalized citizen?

**¿Es usted un ciudadano naturalizado?**

Do you have a work permit?

**¿Tiene usted un permiso de trabajo?**

HAVE YOU HAD EXPERIENCE?

**¿Ha tenido experiencia?**

Be careful with your pronunciation as you try out the new patterns below:

| Have you...? | ¿Ha...? |
|---|---|
| had training | **tenido entrenamiento** |
| completed high school | **terminado la escuela secundaria** |
| taken courses in college | **tomado cursos en la univeridad** |
| been arrested before | **estado arrestado alguna vez** |
| used that machine | **usado esa máquina** |
| worked here before | **trabajado aquí antes** |

DO YOU KNOW?

**¿Sabe?**

In Spanish, there are two primary ways to say "to know". "To know something" requires the verb "**saber**," while "to know someone" requires the verb "**conocer**." Instead of working on all the conjugated forms of these new verbs, why not put them to practical use. Next time you need "to know," pull a line from the sentences below:

| | |
|---|---|
| I don't know. | **No sé.** |
| I don't know you. | **No le conozco.** |
| Do you know English? | **¿Sabe hablar inglés?** |
| Do you know him? | **¿Le conoce a él?** |
| I didn't know it. | **No lo sabía.** |
| I didn't know them. | **No le conocía a ellos.** |

Obviously, "**saber**" works wonders at an interview. Ask your candidates about their professional skills:

Do you know how...?  **¿Sabe cómo...?**

to add  **sumar**

| | |
|---|---|
| to multiply | **multiplicar** |
| to subtract | **restar** |
| to divide | **dividir** |

Do you know how to read and write?

**¿Sabe leer y escribir**

Do you know how to do it?

**¿Sabe hacerlo?**

Do you know what you have to do today?

**¿Sabe lo que tiene que hacer ahora?**

THE BUSINESS

**El negocio**

Feel free to discuss business using these lists of popular words and expressions:

| | |
|---|---|
| business card | **la tarjeta de negocios** |
| office location | **la localidad de la oficina** |
| contact person | **la persona de contacto** |
| work schedule | **el horario de trabajo** |
| work experience | **la experiencia con el trabajo** |
| hours of business | **las horas de negocio** |
| equal opportunities | **la igualdad de oportunidades** |

| You receive (the)... | Recibe usted... |
|---|---|
| paycheck | **la paga** |
| payment | **el pago** |
| salary | **el salario** |
| check | **el cheque** |
| wages | **el sueldo** |
| raise | **el aumento de sueldo** |
| hourly pay | **la paga por hora** |
| invoice | **la factura** |
| time card | **la tarjeta** |
| receipt | **el recibo** |

| You'll have... | Tendrá... |
|---|---|
| breaks | **las pausas para descansar** |
| medical insurance | **el seguro médico** |
| parking space | **el espacio para estacionar** |
| sick leave | **los días pagados por la enfermedad** |
| time off | **los días de descanso** |
| back pay | **los pagos atrasados** |
| holiday | **el día feriado** |

| It's... | Es... |
|---|---|
| Workman's Compensation | **la compensación de obrero** |
| Social Security Insurance | **el seguro de seguridad social** |

| Union dues | **la cuota para el sindicato** |

| The job doesn't include... | **El trabajo no incluye...** |

| disability insurance | **el seguro de incapacidad** |
| dental insurance | **el seguro dental** |
| home insurance | **el seguro para la casa** |
| auto insurance | **el seguro para el carro** |
| unemployment insurance | **el seguro para desempleo** |

## JUST A SUGGESTION

Learn these two essential expressions right away. You never know when they'll be needed!

| You are... | **Usted está...** |

| hired | **contratado** |
| fired | **despedido** |

## TRY SOME

Join each English word with its correct Spanish translation:

| appointment | **la entrevista** |
| interview | **la tarjeta** |
| date | **la fecha** |

| | |
|---|---|
| card | **el seguro** |
| insurance | **la cita** |

Write in the translation as quickly as you can. These are real easy:

| | |
|---|---|
| **la referencia** | _____ |
| **la identificación** | _____ |
| **el problema** | _____ |
| **el uniforme** | _____ |
| **la experiencia** | _____ |

## THE TOP TEN

**Las diez preguntas más importantes**

Now that you've got a list of questions to use when hiring Spanish-speakers, why not prepare for the <u>key questions that they might ask you</u>. Here are the "top ten" that are asked all the time, but not necessarily in the same order:

| | |
|---|---|
| How much do you pay? | **¿Cuánto pagan?** |
| When can I start? | **¿Cuándo puedo empezar?** |
| Is it part-time or full-time? | **¿Es tiempo completo o tiempo parcial?** |
| Are there any benefits? | **¿Hay algunos beneficios?** |
| What are my days off? | **¿Cuáles son mis días de descanso?** |
| How many hours a week? | **¿Cuántas horas por semana?** |
| What tools do I need? | **¿Cuáles herramientas necesito?** |
| When is pay day? | **¿Cuál es el día de pago?** |

| Where is the job site? | ¿Dónde está el sitio de trabajo? |
| Will I have a work truck? | ¿Me dan un camión de trabajo? |

BAD NEWS!
**¡Malas noticias!**

Not everyone gets the job, so be sure you learn how to share the bad news, too:

| I'm sorry, | **Lo siento,** |
| --- | --- |
| we hired someone else | **le contratamos a otra persona** |
| we're not hiring | **no estamos contratando** |
| try back next month | **regrese el próximo mes** |
| you need more experience | **necesita más experiencia** |
| we're looking for a ____ | **estamos buscando un/a _____** |
| you could try another company | **podría encontrar otra compañía** |
| maybe later | **quizás más tarde** |

| It is … | **Es…** |
| --- | --- |
| an announcement | **un aviso** |
| a rule | **una regla** |
| a warning | **una advertencia** |

Learn all the one-liners you can!

| | |
|---|---|
| Think about it. | **Piense en eso.** |
| Call me at this number. | **Llámeme a este número.** |
| Sign this agreement. | **Firme este contrato.** |

AT WORK

**En el trabajo**

Talk to your Spanish-speaking employees about the job itself:

| | |
|---|---|
| We have (the)… | **Tenemos…** |
| | |
| job | **el trabajo** |
| task | **la tarea** |
| project | **el proyecto** |
| errand | **el encargo** |
| order | **el mandato** |
| chore | **el quehacer** |
| favor | **el favor** |

| | |
|---|---|
| The first/second/third step… | **El primer/segundo/tercer paso…** |
| After…/ Then…/ Later… | **Después…/ Entonces…/ Luego…** |
| When you finish… | **Cuando termine…** |

| | |
|---|---|
| Talk to (the)… | **Hable con…** |
| | |
| apprentice | **el aprendiz** |
| boss | **el jefe** |

| | |
|---|---|
| general contractor | **el contratista principal** |
| foreman | **el capataz** |
| inspector | **el inspector** |
| interpreter | **el intérprete** |
| project manager | **el gerente del trabajo** |
| journeyman | **el artezano** |
| lead man | **el líder** |
| owner | **el dueño** |
| subcontractor | **el sub-contratista** |
| supervisor | **el supervisor** |

Now repeat any phrase that gets your message across:

| | |
|---|---|
| Do you need anything? | **¿Necesita algo?** |
| Is everything OK? | **¿Está bien todo?** |
| Can I help? | **¿Puedo ayudar?** |

| | |
|---|---|
| Do it by hand. | **Hágalo a mano.** |
| Remember this. | **Recuerde esto.** |
| This is the procedure. | **Este es el procedimiento.** |
| This is what I want. | **Esto es lo que quiero.** |
| This way. | **De esta manera.** |
| Like this. | **Como así.** |

Keep going, and stick with your favorites:

| | |
|---|---|
| Just a moment. | **Un momento.** |
| It doesn't matter. | **No importa.** |
| Keep going. | **Siga.** |
| Pay attention. | **Preste atención.** |
| It looks good. | **Se ve bien.** |

Sometimes all you need is a simple word or two:

| | |
|---|---|
| Different. | **Diferente.** |
| Lo mismo. | **The same.** |
| | |
| Both. | **Ambos.** |
| Only one. | **Solamente uno.** |
| | |
| Either one. | **Cualquiera.** |
| Neither one. | **Ninguno.** |
| | |
| Alone. | **Solo.** |
| Together. | **Juntos** |
| | |
| Almost. | **Casi.** |
| Plenty. | **Bastante.** |

## JUST A SUGGESTION

Always be clear but respectful when your crew messes up:

It's wrong.                  **Está mal.**

| | |
|---|---|
| You made a mistake. | **Se equivocó.** |
| Please, do it again. | **Hágalo otra vez, por favor.** |

| | |
|---|---|
| Turn down the music. | **Bajen la música.** |
| Try to lower your voices. | **Traten de bajarse las voces.** |
| Stop standing around. | **No se queden parados.** |

THE TELEPHONE

**El teléfono**

Here are some great lines to remember when you're forced to speak Spanish on the phone:

| | |
|---|---|
| Hello! | **¡Bueno!** |
| I'm…from… | **Soy….de…** |
| May I speak with…? | **Puedo hablar con…** |
| More slowly, please. | **Más despacio, por favor.** |
| I don't speak much Spanish. | **No hablo mucho español.** |
| Please wait a moment. | **Espere un momento, por favor.** |
| Please don't hang up. | **No cuelgue, por favor.** |
| I'll call back later. | **Llamaré más tarde.** |

Is there someone there who speaks English?

**¿Hay alguien allí que habla inglés?**

May I leave a message?

**¿Puedo dejar un mensaje?**

When will he/she return?

**¿Cuándo regresa?**


I am calling about work.

**Estoy llamando acerca del trabajo.**


Tell him/her that I can be reached at _____.

**Dígale que me puede llamar al número _____.**


Thanks a lot, and good-bye.

**Muchas gracias, y adiós.**


JUST A SUGGESTION


Set up a schedule using the following guide words as examples. They can be useful no matter what the job is:


| | |
|---|---|
| You start ___ | **Empieza ___** |
| You finish ___ | **Termina ___** |
| From ___ | **De ___** |
| Until ___ | **Hasta ___** |


| | |
|---|---|
| Go to lunch at _____. | **Vaya a almorzar a _____.** |
| We don't work on _____. | **No trabajamos los _____.** |
| We'll see you on _____. | **Nos vemos el _____.** |

And here are other ways to express the same instructions:

| | |
|---|---|
| Be here at _____. | **Esté aquí a _____.** |
| Quit at _____. | **Para a _____.** |
| You may leave at _____. | **Se puede ir a _____.** |
| Take a break at _____. | **Tome un descanso a _____.** |
| Come at _____. | **Venga a _____.** |
| You will work at _____. | **Va a trabajar a _____.** |
| You re off at _____. | **Sale a _____.** |

TRY SOME

Read through this common conversation between a contractor and his employees on a typical job site. Then, highlight the words, phrases, or sentences that you will use the most:

English Speaker:

Hey, you guys, we need to get started right away.

**Oigan ustedes, tenemos que comenzar ahora mismo.**

Spanish Speaker:

What do we do first?

**¿Qué hacemos primero?**

English Speaker:

Let's finish the wall. Use the bricks over there. Is the mixer set up?

**Vamos a acabar con el muro. Usen los ladrillos que están allí. ¿Está lista la mezcladora?**


Spanish Speaker:

Everything's ready. But are there enough bricks?

**Todo está listo. ¿Pero hay suficientes ladrillos?**


English Speaker:

I have more in the truck. Bring the wheelbarrow!

**Tengo más en el camión. ¡Traiga la carretilla!**


Spanish Speaker:

And what about the sand?

**¿Y qué pasa con la arena?**


English Speaker:

Don't worry, there's plenty. Now help me stack these bricks.

We have a lot to do.

**No se preocupe, hay bastante. Ahora, ayúdeme a amontonar estos ladrillos. Tenemos mucho que hacer.**

# EMERGENCY AND SAFETY

To check if someone's feeling OK, use these expressions:

| | |
|---|---|
| Do you need help? | **¿Necesita ayuda?** |
| What's the matter? | **¿Qué pasó?** |
| Where does it hurt? | **¿Dónde le duele?** |

| | |
|---|---|
| Calm down | **Cálmese** |
| Lie down | **Acuéstese** |
| Don't worry | **No se preocupe** |

| | |
|---|---|
| Are you…? | **¿Está…?** |

| | |
|---|---|
| hurt | **herido** |
| sick | **enfermo** |
| dizzy | **mareado** |
| exhausted | **agotado** |
| faint | **desmayado** |
| sore | **dolorido** |
| feeling ill | **mal** |

As long as we're talking about poor health, don't hesitate to learn the following words:

| He's got (a)… | Tiene… |
|---|---|
| broken bone | **el hueso quebrado** |
| bruise | **la contusión** |
| burn | **la quemadura** |
| cold | **el resfriado** |
| cut | **la cortada** |
| fever | **la fiebre** |
| flu | **la influenza** |
| sprain | **la torcedura** |

The word "pain" is "**dolor**" in Spanish. Check out the pattern:

| I have (a)… | Tengo… |
|---|---|
| headache | **el dolor de cabeza** |
| sore throat | **el dolor de garganta** |
| stomach ache | **el dolor de estómago** |

To be on the safe side, get acquainted with these expressions:

He/She is bleeding.
**Está sangrando.**

He/She is vomiting.
**Está vomitando.**

He/She is unconscious.

**Está inconsciente.**


Tell me about (the) ...       **Hábleme acerca de...**


accident                      **el accidente**

bad fall                      **la mala caída**

fatigue                       **la fatiga**

seizure                       **el ataque**

sunstroke                     **la insolación**

electric shock                **el choque eléctrico**


You never know what can happen, so keep on pronouncing everything you read:


He's suffering from...

**Sufre de...**


dehydration

**la deshidratación**


shock

**la prostración nerviosa**


frostbite

**el congelamiento**

heat stroke

**la postración**

poisoning

**el envenamiento**

insect bite

**la picadura de insecto**

| Bring (the)… | **Traiga…** |
|---|---|
| aspirin | **la aspirina** |
| Band-Aid® | **la curita** |
| bandage | **el bendaje** |
| crutches | **las muletas** |
| disinfectant | **el desinfectante** |
| medicine | **la medicina** |
| First Aid kit | **el botiquín de primeros auxilios** |
| extinguisher | **el extintor** |

| He needs… | **Necesita…** |
|---|---|
| CPR | **la respiración artificial** |
| medical attention | **ayuda médica** |
| an interpreter | **un intérprete** |

Stay with command words and phrases. Memorize a few at a time:

Call (the) ... **Llame a ...**

| | |
|---|---|
| 911 | **nueve-uno-uno** |
| ambulance | **la ambulancia** |
| clinic | **la clínica** |
| doctor | **el doctor** |
| office | **la oficina** |
| hospital | **el hospital** |
| neighbor | **el vecino** |
| operator | **la operadora** |
| paramedic | **el paramédico** |
| police | **la policía** |
| relative | **el pariente** |
| tow truck | **la grúa** |
| home | **la casa** |
| fire department | **el departamento de bomberos** |

SAFETY

**La seguridad**

Have you reviewed all potentially dangerous items that with everyone? If not, do so immediately:

Be careful with (the)...!
**¡Tenga cuidado con...!**

| | |
|---|---|
| tool | **la herramienta** |
| ladder | **la escalera** |
| vehicle | **el vehículo** |
| scaffolding | **el andamio** |
| machine | **la máquina** |
| electricity | **la electricidad** |
| fire | **el fuego** |
| gas | **el gas** |
| oil | **el aceite** |
| paint | **la pintura** |
| dust | **el polvo** |
| exhaust | **el escape** |
| fumes | **el vapor** |
| glass | **el vidrio** |
| pressure | **la presión** |
| blade | **la hoja** |
| hole | **el hoyo** |
| edge | **el borde** |
| point | **la punta** |
| rebar | **la varilla** |

Keep going, but now refer to more than one item:

| | |
|---|---|
| Avoid (the)… | **Evita…** |
| | |
| toxic materials | **los materiales tóxicos** |
| waste | **los perdicios** |

| | |
|---|---|
| wires | **los alambres** |
| flames | **las llamas** |
| sewage | **las aguas sucias** |
| cables | **los cables** |
| chemicals | **los productos químicos** |

| | |
|---|---|
| There is/are... | **Hay...** |

| | |
|---|---|
| vibration | **vibración** |
| sparks | **chispas** |
| noise | **ruído** |
| smoke | **humo** |
| smell | **olor** |
| malfunction | **malfuncionamiento** |
| explosion | **explosión** |

| | |
|---|---|
| It's too… | **Es muy…** |

| | |
|---|---|
| heavy | **pesado** |
| high | **alto** |
| dangerous | **peligroso** |
| windy | **ventoso** |
| dark | **oscuro** |
| wet | **mojado** |
| loud | **ruidoso** |
| hot | **caliente** |

Some Spanish words are easier to remember than others:

| It's... | Es... |
|---|---|
| flammable | **inflamable** |
| combustible | **combustible** |
| explosive | **explosivo** |

JUST A SUGGESTION

Folks who speak Spanish may call out for help with one of these:

| Help! | **¡Socorro!** |
|---|---|
| | **¡Ayúdeme!** |
| | **¡Auxilio!** |

Make sure everyone is doing all he can to avoid problems on the job:

| Put on (the)… | **Póngase…** |
|---|---|
| hat | **el sombrero** |
| sunscreen | **la protección para el sol** |
| knee pads | **las rodilleras** |
| shin guards | **las espinilladeras** |
| boots | **las botas** |
| apron | **el mandil** |
| gloves | **los guantes** |

| | |
|---|---|
| hard hat | **el casco duro** |
| harness | **el correaje** |
| belt | **el cinturón** |
| mask | **la máscara** |
| respirator | **el respirador** |
| ear plugs | **los tapones del oído** |
| safety glasses | **los lentes de protección** |
| vest | **el chaleco** |
| safety line | **la cuerda de seguridad** |
| fall equipment | **la protección de la caída** |
| reflectors | **los reflectores** |
| long sleeves | **la camisa de manga larga** |

| Use (the)… | **Use…** |
|---|---|
| guardrails | **las barrandas** |
| safety rope | **la soga de seguridad** |
| scaffolding | **el andamio** |

Shout out these one-liners when danger is near:

| | |
|---|---|
| Danger! | **¡Peligro!** |
| Watch it! | **¡Ojo!** |
| Pay attention! | **¡Preste atención!** |
| Don't move! | **¡No se mueva!** |
| Stay put! | **¡Quédese ahí!** |

| Don't…it! | ¡No lo…! |
|---|---|
| touch | **toque** |
| move | **mueva** |
| do | **haga** |
| use | **use** |
| remove | **saque** |

| Get out of here! | **¡Sálgase de aquí!** |
|---|---|
| Stay off. | **¡No la monte!** |
| Everyone back! | **¡Todos hacia atrás!** |
| It's unsafe! | **¡No está seguro!** |
| Go get help! | **¡Ande a buscar ayuda!** |

Be sure you follow up on every medical emergency:

Tell me what the doctor says.

**Dígame lo que dice el médico.**

Bring me the forms.

**Tráigame los formularios.**

Show me the report when you finish.

**Enséñame el reporte cuando termine.**

Be creative as you form phrases that suit you best. Also remember that some safety one-liners can be posted at the job site as reminders:

Watch your step!

**¡Cuidado al pisar!**


Trabaje con cuidado.

**Work with care.**


Protect yourself.

**Protéjase!**


Keep going:


Ask someone to help you.

**Pida que alguien le ayude.**


Are you wearing all your safety equipment?

**¿Está usando todo el equipo de seguridad?**


Report all accidents to me.

**Entregue cualquier caso de emergencia a mí.**


JUST A SUGGESTION


Depending upon the job, you may also add a bit more detail:


Stay out of the trenches.

**Manténgase fuera de las zanjas.**

You need to change that blade.

**Necesita cambiar esa hoja.**

Don't stand under the beams.

**No se pare debajo de las vigas.**

TRY SOME

Name three places to call when there's an emergency:

_____   _____   _____

Name three things in construction that are very flammable:

_____   _____   _____

Name three items found in most First Aid kits:

_____   _____   _____

Give three commands that can be used on the job when someone gets physically injured.

_____   _____   _____

# DEMOLITION AND CLEAN-UP

Begin with a few demo command phrases:

| | |
|---|---|
| Knock it down | **Túmbela** |
| Tear it out | **Sáquela** |
| Break it up | **Rómpala.** |

| | |
|---|---|
| Put it on the pile | **Póngala en la pila** |
| Stack them here | **Amóntelas aquí** |
| Haul it away | **Llévala** |

| | |
|---|---|
| Throw it outside | **Tírela hacia afuera** |
| Fill it up | **Llénela** |
| Load it in | **Cárguela** |

| | |
|---|---|
| Pull (the)… | **Jale…** |

| | |
|---|---|
| chain | **la cadena** |
| rope | **la soga** |
| cable | **el cable** |

This time, refer to equipment you might find at a demolition job:

| | |
|---|---|
| Use (the)… | **Use…** |

| | |
|---|---|
| bulldozer | **el tractor oruga** |

| | |
|---|---|
| driller | **la perforadora** |
| wrecking ball | **la bola de demolición** |
| loader | **la cargadora** |
| dump truck | **el camión volquete** |
| trailer | **el remolque** |

| | |
|---|---|
| Bring (the)… | **Traiga…** |

| | |
|---|---|
| wheelbarrow | **la carretilla** |
| chainsaw | **la motosierra** |
| sledge | **la almádena** |
| mallet | **el mazo** |
| hammer | **el martillo** |
| scraper | **el raspador** |
| chisel | **el cincel** |
| prybar | **la palanca** |
| saw | **la sierra** |
| pick | **el pico** |
| hook | **el gancho** |
| ax | **el hacha** |

## JUST A SUGGESTION

Put other words together to form short instructive one-liners:

| | |
|---|---|
| This part | **Esta parte** |
| All of it | **Todo** |

| Not that | **Ese no** |
|---|---|

These are primarily used for cleaning:

| Carry (the)… | **Lleve…** |
|---|---|
| blower | **la sopladora** |
| brush | **el cepillo** |
| bucket | **el balde** |
| dustpan | **la pala de recoger basura** |
| mop | **el trapeador** |
| rag | **el trapo** |
| sponge | **la esponja** |
| towel | **la toalla** |
| shovel | **la pala** |
| broom | **la escoba** |
| rake | **el rastrillo** |
| vacuum | **la aspiradora** |
| pump | **la bomba** |

| We need (the)… | **Necesitamos…** |
|---|---|
| trash bag | **la bolsa de basura** |
| dumpster | **el basurero grande** |
| trashcan | **el bote de basura** |

Stay with the clean-up project:

| | |
|---|---|
| Clean (the)… | **Limpie…** |
| area | **el área** |
| room | **el cuarto** |
| place | **el lugar** |
| worksite | **la zona de trabajo** |
| pathway | **el camino** |
| equipment | **el equipo** |
| Remove (the)… | **Quite…** |
| puddles | **los charcos** |
| cobwebs | **la telarañas** |
| mud | **el lodo** |
| dirt | **la suciedad** |
| dust | **el polvo** |
| sawdust | **el serrín** |
| Pick up (the)… | **Recoja…** |
| debris | **los escombros** |
| rest | **los restos** |
| waste | **el desecho** |
| scrap | **los desperdicios** |
| trash | **la basura** |

| | |
|---|---|
| spillage | **el derrame** |
| rubble | **la rocalla** |

| | |
|---|---|
| I don't need (the) extra ____ | **No necesito ____ extra.** |

| | |
|---|---|
| material | **el material** |
| sand | **la arena** |
| rock | **la piedra** |
| gravel | **la grava** |
| wood | **la madera** |
| metal | **el metal** |

| | |
|---|---|
| Put (the) extra ____ here. | **Ponga ____ extra aquí.** |

| | |
|---|---|
| aluminum | **el aluminio** |
| cardboard | **el cartón** |
| copper | **el cobre** |
| fiberglass | **la fibra de vidrio** |
| foam | **la espuma** |
| glass | **el vidrio** |
| iron | **el hierro** |
| liquid | **el líquido** |
| lumber | **las tablas** |
| mesh | **la malla** |
| plaster | **el yeso** |
| plastic | **el plástico** |
| plywood | **la madera contrachapada** |

| | |
|---|---|
| rubber | **la goma** |
| steel | **el acero** |
| wall tile | **el azulejo** |
| floor tile | **la loseta** |

The bulk of demo and clean-up involves commands, so keep memorizing those words that go with your vocabulary:

| | |
|---|---|
| Give me (the)… | **Deme…** |
| Look for (the)… | **Busque…** |
| Count (the)… | **Cuente…** |

Some commands are useful word strings and a little harder to pronounce:

| | |
|---|---|
| Shake it out | **Sacúdalo** |
| Roll it up | **Enróllelo** |
| Throw it way | **Bótelo** |

The words "this" (**este**) and "that" (**ese**) do wonders in demolition and clean-up work:

| | |
|---|---|
| Save this | **Guarde esto** |
| Cover this | **Cubre esto** |
| Recycle this | **Recicle esto** |
| Empty this | **Vacíe esto** |
| Pick up this | **Recoge esto** |

| | |
|---|---|
| Remove that | **Saque eso** |
| Sweep that | **Barre eso** |
| Clean that | **Limpie eso** |
| Wash that | **Lave eso** |
| Polish that | **Lustra eso** |

Continue to develop your own job-specific list of Spanish verbs:

| You're going… | **Va a…** |
|---|---|
| to wipe | **pasar un trapo** |
| to chip | **mellar** |
| to chisel | **cincelar** |
| to take apart | **desarmar** |
| to break | **romper** |

## JUST A SUGGESTION

Descriptive words are also popular in clean-up work, so practice vocabulary pairs with opposite meanings:

| It's… | **Está…** |
|---|---|
| clean | **limpio** |
| dirty | **sucio** |
| full | **lleno** |

| | |
|---|---|
| empty | **vacío** |
| neat | **ordenado** |
| sloppy | **chapucero** |
| new | **nuevo** |
| old | **viejo** |
| heavy | **pesado** |
| light | **ligero** |

## TRY SOME

Connect the words that best relate to one another:

| | |
|---|---|
| **llenar** | **desecho** |
| **trapeador** | **cincelar** |
| **piedra** | **vaciar** |
| **basura** | **mazo** |
| **martillo** | **grava** |
| **mellar** | **escoba** |

# CONSTRUCTION COMMANDS

One incredible way to plant basic verbs into the memory is through the use of commands.

The "command" form of verbs can be practiced all day in construction, since all you're doing is telling others what to do. (Respectfully, of course!)

To simplify things, all commands in this book are considered "formal". If you are interested in learning about "informal" communication, you may need to consult a Spanish book or take a course in Spanish grammar.

"Commands" are actually unique forms of Spanish verb infinitives: See the pattern for regular "**ar**" verbs? The ending is "**e**":

| | | | |
|---|---|---|---|
| to speak | **hablar** | to walk | **caminar** |
| Speak! | **¡Hable!** | Walk! | **¡Camine!** |

Now observe what happens to most "**er**" and "**ir**" verbs. Conversely, they end in "**a**":

| | | | |
|---|---|---|---|
| to write | **escribir** | to open | **abrir** |
| Write! | **¡Escriba!** | Open! | **¡Abra!** |

| | | | |
|---|---|---|---|
| to run | **correr** | to read | **leer** |
| Run! | **¡Corra!** | Read! | **¡Lea!** |

Try some:

| | | | |
|---|---|---|---|
| to paint | **pintar** | Paint! | _____ |
| to eat | **comer** | Eat! | _____ |
| to nail | **clavar** | Nail! | _____ |

Obviously, any "irregular verb" forms would have to be learned separately. Read, practice, and memorize the following basic commands in Spanish. In construction, many of them can be used all by themselves:

| | |
|---|---|
| Bring | **Traiga** |
| Buy | **Compre** |
| Call | **Llame** |
| Carry | **Lleve** |
| Change | **Cambie** |
| Clean | **Limpie** |
| Come | **Venga** |
| Continue | **Siga** |
| Drive | **Maneje** |
| Fix | **Arregle** |
| Give | **Dé** |
| Go up | **Suba** |
| Look for | **Busque** |
| Pick up | **Recoja** |
| Put inside | **Meta** |
| Put | **Ponga** |
| Read | **Lea** |

| | |
|---|---|
| Remove | **Saque** |
| Set up | **Prepare** |
| Take | **Tome** |
| Talk | **Hable** |
| Throw out | **Tire** |
| Use | **Use** |

This time, give an order with some authority:

| | |
|---|---|
| Go! | **¡Vaya!** |
| Help! | **¡Ayude!** |
| Listen! | **¡Escuche!** |
| Look! | **¡Mire!** |
| Move! | **¡Mueva!** |
| Run! | **¡Corra!** |
| Sign! | **¡Firme!** |
| Start! | **¡Comience!** |
| Rest! | **¡Descanse!** |
| Walk! | **¡Camine!** |
| Work! | **¡Trabaje!** |
| Write! | **¡Escriba!** |

Accelerate the learning process by grouping commands in pairs with opposite meanings:

| | |
|---|---|
| Plug in | **Enchufe** |
| Unplug | **Desenchufe** |

| | |
|---|---|
| Turn on | **Prenda** |
| Turn off | **Apague** |
| Empty | **Vacíe** |
| Fill | **Llene** |
| Load | **Cargue** |
| Unload | **Descargue** |
| Close | **Cierre** |
| Open | **Abra** |
| Raise | **Levante** |
| Lower | **Baje** |
| Start | **Empiece** |
| Finish | **Termine** |

You can also add a word or two to create a complete sentence:

| | |
|---|---|
| Take | **Tome** |
| Take the tool. | **Tome la herramienta.** |
| | |
| Sign | **Firme** |
| Sign here. | **Firme aquí.** |
| | |
| Call | **Llame** |
| Call the painter. | **Llame al pintor.** |
| | |
| Listen | **Escuche** |
| Listen to the question. | **Escuche a la pregunta.** |

| Speak | **Hable** |
|---|---|
| Speak more slowly. | **Hable más despacio.** |

| Write | **Escriba** |
|---|---|
| Write the information. | **Escriba la información.** |

| Bring | **Traiga** |
|---|---|
| Bring the truck. | **Traiga el camión.** |

| Read | **Lea** |
|---|---|
| Read the warning. | **Lea la advertencia.** |

| Return | **Regrese** |
|---|---|
| Return tomorrow. | **Regrese mañana.** |

| Answer | **Conteste** |
|---|---|
| Answer in English. | **Conteste en inglés.** |

Some one-word commands are a little tougher to pronounce. Notice the accent mark on these commands ending in "**se**":

| Wait! | **¡Espérese!** |
|---|---|
| Hurry up! | **¡Apúrese!** |
| Sit down! | **¡Siéntese!** |
| Stand up! | **¡Levántese!** |
| Stay! | **¡Quédese!** |

Bear in mind that to give commands to more than one person in Spanish, you generally add an "**n**" to the basic command word:

Hurry up, you guys!          ¡**Apúre<u>n</u>se!**

Run, you guys!              ¡**Corra<u>n</u>!**

Some of the most common commands in construction Spanish end with the little word "**me**":

| | |
|---|---|
| Listen to me | **Escúcheme** |
| Explain to me | **Explíqueme** |
| Tell me | **Dígame** |
| Call me | **Llámeme** |
| Give me | **Deme** |
| Send me | **Mándeme** |
| Answer me | **Contésteme** |
| Bring me | **Tráigame** |

Obviously, commands can be as specific as you like:

| | |
|---|---|
| Connect… | **Conecte…** |
| Install… | **Instale…** |
| Drill… | **Taladre…** |

Negative commands are easy. Just say "**No**":

Come!          Don't come!              ¡**Venga!**    ¡**No venga!**

Read, you guys!    Don't write, you guys!    **¡Lean!**    **¡No lean!**

Take any item from your lists of vocabulary and place it after one of the commands below:

| | |
|---|---|
| Bring… | **Traiga…** |
| Check… | **Revise…** |
| Carry… | **Lleve…** |
| Change… | **Cambie…** |
| Clean… | **Limpie…** |
| Close… | **Cierre…** |
| Connect… | **Conecte…** |
| Empty… | **Vacíe…** |
| Fill… | **Llene…** |
| Fix… | **Arregle…** |
| Give… | **Dé…** |
| Load… | **Cargue…** |
| Look for… | **Busque…** |
| Lower… | **Baje…** |
| Move… | **Mueva…** |
| Open… | **Abra…** |
| Park… | **Estacione…** |
| Pick up… | **Recoja…** |
| Put inside… | **Meta…** |
| Put… | **Ponga…** |
| Raise… | **Levante…** |
| Remove… | **Saque…** |
| Set up… | **Prepare…** |
| Take… | **Tome…** |
| Throw out… | **Tire…** |
| Unload… | **Descargue…** |
| Look at… | **Mire…** |
| See… | **Vea…** |
| Use… | **Use…** |

Add more command words to the list above if you like. For example, did you give instructions to the flagmen?

| | |
|---|---|
| Put on the vest. | **Póngase el chaleco.** |
| Turn on the walkie-talkie. | **Prenda el walki-talki.** |
| Go to the entrance/exit. | **Vaya a la entrada/salida.** |

| Watch the traffic. | **Dirija el tráfico.** |
| Use the flags and signs. | **Use las banderitas y los letreros.** |
| Move the cones. | **Mueve los pivotes.** |
| Stay in this area. | **Quédese en esta área.** |

## JUST A SUGGESTION

Look what happens when you add verb infinitives to "**Favor de...**", which implies, "Would you please...":

| Please... | **Favor de...** |

| write the number | **escribir el número** |
| go to the roof | **ir al techo** |
| speak in English | **hablar en inglés** |

By adding the word "**no**" in front of the verb, you communicate the command "don't":

| Please don't use that saw. | **Favor de <u>no</u> usar esa sierra.** |

## TRY SOME

To improve communication, take a few Spanish verbs and change them into command forms. See if you can notice any pattern:

| to clean (**limpiar**) | **Limpie** | <u>**Limpie aquí, por favor.**</u> |

| | | |
|---|---|---|
| to dig **(excavar)** | **Excave** | _____ |
| to carry **(llevar)** | **Lleve** | _____ |
| to throw away **(tirar)** | **Tire** | |
| to fill **(llenar)** | **Llene** | |
| to push **(empujar)** | **Empuje** | |
| to use **(usar)** | **Use** | |

# FORM-A-PHRASE VERB CHART

Here's an easy way to master Spanish action words. Simply open up with a "catch phrase" and then add on the verb of your choice. On any construction site, these are the first words you should say:

| | |
|---|---|
| Please ... | **Favor de ...** |
| Please arrive on time. | **Favor de llegar a tiempo.** |

| | |
|---|---|
| Don't ... | **No ...** |
| Don't arrive late. | **No llegar tarde.** |

Here are more "catch phrases". Add any verb of your choice:

| | | |
|---|---|---|
| You have to ... | **Tiene que ...** | *terminar* |
| It's best to… | **Hay que…** | *excavar* |
| You should ... | **Debe ...** | *revisar* |
| You need to… | **Necesita…** | *trabajar* |
| You can … | **Puede …** | *salir* |

| | | |
|---|---|---|
| It's important to… | **Es importante…** | *pintar* |
| It's necessary to… | **Es necesario…** | *clavar* |
| It'd be a good idea to… | **Sería buena idea…** | *llamar* |

| | | |
|---|---|---|
| I'm going to… | **Voy a…** | *soldar* |
| I just finished … | **Acabo de …** | *descargar* |
| I want to ... | **Quiero ...** | *subir* |

## JUST A SUGGESTION

Some phrases can be turned into questions. Heres one that's easy to say:

Do you know?                             **¿Sabe?**

Do you know how to drive a truck?        **¿Sabe manejar un camión?**


## TRY SOME

Form a simple phrase using the verbs below:

| English | Spanish | Phrase |
|---------|---------|--------|
| clean | **limpiar** | **Favor de limpiar.** |
| pick up | **recoger** | **Tiene que recoger la basura.** |
| move | **mover** | _____ |
| lower | **bajar** | |
| dig | **excavar** | |
| spray | **rociar** | |
| carry | **llevar** | |
| throw away | **tirar** | |
| arrange | **arreglar** | |
| fill | **llenar** | |
| pull | **jalar** | |
| push | **empujar** | |
| use | **usar** | |

# PRONUNCIATION GUIDE

Spanish is pronounced the way it's spelled, and vice-versa. So pronounce each sound the same way every time the corresponding letter appears. Spanish sounds are usually made toward the front of the mouth instead of back - with little or no air coming out. And, short, choppy sounds are better than long stretched-out ones. Accented (´) parts of words should always be pronounced LOUDER and with more emphasis (**olé**). If there's no accent mark, say the last of the work LOUDER and with more emphasis (**español**). For words ending in a vowel, or in **n** or **s**, the next to the last part of the word is stressed (**importante**).

Made in the USA
Las Vegas, NV
24 November 2022

60235348R10240